STARTING A BUSINESS

WHEN YOU'RE AFRAID TO

MICHAELA CAVALLARO

CENTENNIAL BOOKS

STARTING A BUSINESS

WHEN YOU'RE AFRAID TO

CENTENNIAL BOOKS

Table of Contents

172

CHAPTER 02

BUSINESS SUCCESSES

46 Low Investment, High
Probability of Success
50 Success Stories From
the Trenches
54 Big Names,
Humble Beginnings

CHAPTER 03

FRANCHISING VS. BUYING

62 Different Types
of Franchises
66 Understanding Your
Role as a Franchisee
70 Growing a Franchise
72 The Advantages and
Disadvantages of Buying
an Existing Business

INTRODUCTION

6 Want to Open Your Own
Business? Start With
Some Careful Planning

CHAPTER 01

GETTING STARTED

10 Reasons to Start
Your Own Business
16 Entrepreneurship
by the Numbers

20 What Makes a Good
Business Concept?
22 Doing Market Research
for Your Business Plan
26 Timing Is Everything
30 The Noticeable Perks
of Running Your
Own Home-Based
Business
34 Naming Your Business
36 Smart Business
Strategies
40 Deciding on a
Business Location

20

46

CHAPTER 04
ORGANIZING FINANCES

76 Financing Your Business
79 Choosing a Business Structure
82 Bookkeeping Basics
85 Licenses and Regulations
88 Protecting Your Business With the Right Insurance
91 Paying Taxes as a Small Business
94 Understanding Profitability
96 Saving for Retirement When You're an Entrepreneur

CHAPTER 05
MANAGING EMPLOYEES

100 When to Hire More Staff
102 Recruiting and Hiring
104 Management and Retention
107 Employee Benefits

CHAPTER 06
OPTIMIZING OPERATIONS

112 Setting Clear Goals
114 Managing Cash Flow and Creating a Budget
118 Working With Vendors
121 Real Estate: Should You Lease or Buy?
124 Legal Steps When Starting a Business

128 Create a Disaster Strategy for Your Small Business
132 Buying vs. Leasing Goods
134 Managing Inventory
137 Deciding How Much to Charge

CHAPTER 07
MARKETING

142 Building Your Business' Identity
146 Effective Advertising, Social Media and More
150 Sizing Up the Competition
154 Understanding Your Customer

CHAPTER 08
LOOKING AHEAD

160 Work-Life Balance for Entrepreneurs

163 Change Is the Only Constant
166 Expanding or Acquiring Another Business
169 Exit Strategies and Succession Plans
172 Diversifying Your Wealth

CHAPTER 09
WORKSHEETS

176 Business Plan Prep
177 Brand Development
178 Market Research
179 Business Structures at a Glance
180 Cash Flow
181 Staying on Top of Your Budget
182 Profit and Loss
183 Small-Business Resources
184 Your Retirement Options at a Glance
185 Disaster Resources

Your New Business Starts Here
Whether It's a Brand-New Idea or a Lifelong Goal, You Can Create Your Own Company

Owning your own business may be a longstanding dream. If so, you wouldn't be alone. In fact, there are more than 30 million small businesses in the United States. These companies have a big impact: They form the beating heart of the American economy, employing nearly 60 million people, or about half of the nation's working population.

Every business owner starts somewhere. Perhaps you've identified a problem that needs solving, or an underserved demographic whose needs you want to fulfill. Maybe you've decided to buy an existing business that aligns with your interests and the work you want to do.

In any case, owning your own business can have big benefits. First—and most significantly—owning a business allows you to follow your passion. As the owner, you'll make big decisions that will determine your business' pursuits, policies, culture and staff—the people who'll work side-by-side with you. What's more, becoming your own boss allows you to decide where, when and how you do your work. You get to set your own schedule and decide whether to work in an office or from home in your pajamas.

This book will serve as your guide to everything you need to know about starting a business, from identifying a good business concept to doing market research to putting together a proper business plan.

A successful business requires careful planning and organization. We'll guide you through the nitty-gritty of funding your business, choosing the right business structure and tracking your finances. We'll dive into optimization strategies to keep your business running smoothly, and teach you how to build your brand and market to the right consumers.

As with many small businesses, you may be your sole employee. But eventually, you may find you

The most important skill to have when it comes to starting a business is your own enthusiasm.

need extra help. We'll offer tips on how to hire top employees and, just as importantly, how to get them to stick around.

Finally, entrepreneurs must keep an eye on the future. We live in uncertain times, and the coronavirus pandemic has shown how vulnerable businesses can be. This book will teach you how to prepare your business for disaster and where to turn for help if the unthinkable happens.

We'll also help you consider whether and how you want to expand in the future, how to address changes in the market and what your wishes are for exiting your business when that time comes.

A profitable, well-run business can become a big source of pride. It should, of course, help you build a steady source of income, but you may find it also builds your sense of self-worth and satisfaction. So let's get started! —*Michaela Cavallaro*

7

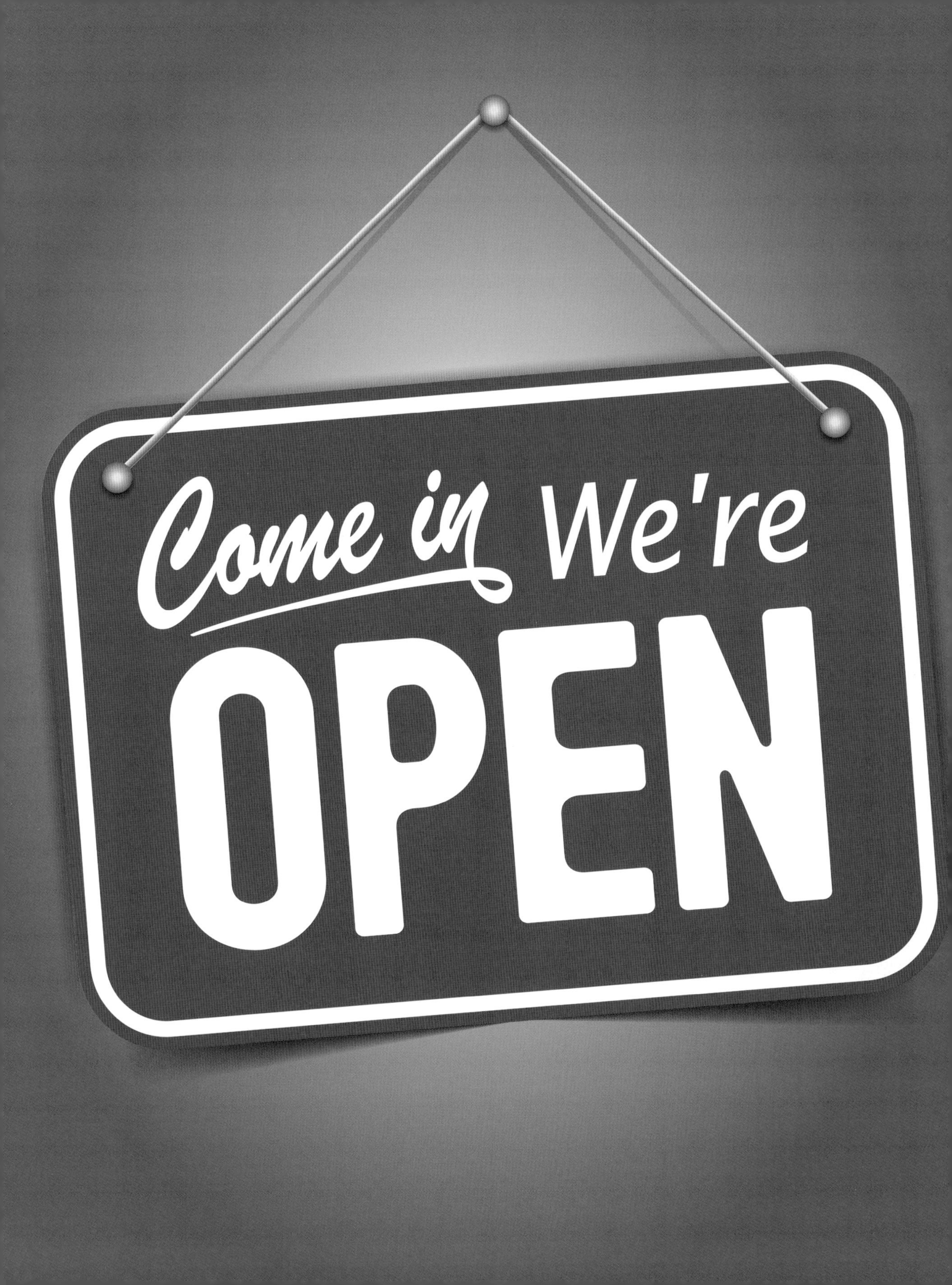
Come in We're
OPEN

Getting Started

Here's everything you need to know
to get your business off the ground

Reasons to Start Your Own Business
Following Your Passion and Becoming Your Own Boss Has Many Rewards—But Also Risks

For many people, starting a business is a cornerstone of the American dream. It's a path that promises independence and the ability to build something from the ground up, all while doing something you love. There are millions of small businesses across the country, and many new ones spring up every year.

Recently, the coronavirus pandemic dealt a serious blow to small businesses. Even those with loyal customer bases and great track records weren't immune to the mandatory shutdowns and phased reopenings that brought things to a halt in much of the country. And despite promises of government support through the CARES Act, many business owners even today remain uncertain about the future.

The economic landscape today may look less than ideal for taking a chance on your own. After all, if entrepreneurs who have been at it for years are being forced to close their doors, what chance does someone who is just starting out have to survive?

On the other hand, there are a lot of reasons someone might choose a down market to start a business. For example, some costs involved in running a business—from online ads to commercial rents—have dropped due to the pandemic crisis, lowering the barrier to entry. What's more, many workers have now seen first-hand the precariousness of their job positions. These individuals may look to entrepreneurship as a way to create meaningful and potentially stable work for themselves in the long term.

Though the coronavirus pandemic has changed American life, these shifts have created openings where new businesses developed with this "new normal" in mind can thrive. Entrepreneurs are often innovators and problem-solvers by nature, and those who are able to provide solutions in this moment may see their businesses take off in powerful ways.

In order to succeed, you'll need a strong and detailed business plan.

Becoming your own boss gives you the freedom to create your own schedule.

Working in a field you're passionate about can be more rewarding than a traditional career.

If you're wondering whether opening a business is right for you, take some time to consider why you're drawn to entrepreneurship, as well as its challenges and rewards.

What Do You Hope to Achieve?

There are many reasons people decide to start their own venture. As an entrepreneur, you'll want to identify your "why." In other words, what's motivating you to make your enterprise a success? Once you understand what's most important to you, you can create a business plan that reflects those priorities. Here are some of the most common reasons people strike out on their own:

▪ **Being Your Own Boss** If you're tired of someone else calling the shots, you may feel like it's time to start working for yourself. Instead of climbing your way up the ladder, you'll start (and generally, stay) at the top. You'll determine your business' policies and culture, and whom to hire. You'll also get to decide when and where you work, which can mean great flexibility and freedom from the typical 9-to-5.

▪ **Following Your Passion** Starting a business in a field you care about can be immensely rewarding. Whether it's a mission-driven organization or a retail shop that caters to a niche market, your venture is an opportunity to express yourself and invest time in something you feel strongly about. For people particularly drawn to service, starting a mission-driven endeavor or nonprofit can be a powerful way to turn personal beliefs into a fulfilling career.

▪ **Greater Earning (or Doing) Potential** Not all (or even most) small-business owners get rich. Still, if you feel stuck working for a low hourly wage or performing tasks that you're overqualified for, running your own enterprise can open

Spotting a niche in the market and having a plan to fill it can put you on the path to small-business success.

the door to greater earnings or a more engaging career—particularly if your current job doesn't offer meaningful paths for advancement. For many business owners, the correlation between their ventures' success and their own earnings can be a powerful driver to work hard.

▪ **Solving a Problem** Frequently, startups come about when someone has a "light bulb moment"—a spark of inspiration that they're ready to turn into reality. If you've identified a problem and are ready to offer a solution, you may have the makings of a successful enterprise. Of course, there's more to building a business than having a good idea, but the ability to identify and fill a need is a key component of the entrepreneurial spirit.

Understanding the Challenges

Once you know why you want to launch your own business, it's important to prepare for the hard work and challenges that come along with entrepreneurship. Before you quit your day job, carefully consider some of the risks and realities that are sure to await you.

▪ **Get Ready to Work Hard** When you're the boss, the buck stops with you. If one of your employees calls out sick, you may be stuck filling in for them. When a supplier fails to deliver your materials on time, it's up to you to create a new plan to maintain production. Even though running your own business can offer a certain degree of flexibility, it also comes with plenty of responsibility. Get ready to wear a number of different hats and to work more hours than you might have expected.

▪ **Every New Work Venture Is a Risk** Most startups, even if they're ultimately successful, will face challenges. Employee turnover can cause costly disruptions, commercial rents can rise over time, and (as the coronavirus pandemic showed) the economic landscape can shift dramatically without warning. But the inherent risk in starting a small business doesn't have to be a deterrent. Instead, focus on ways you can plan for potential lulls or disruptions. Strategies can include maintaining a healthy personal savings account for emergencies or crowdfunding startup capital to help cover costs until your business becomes profitable.

▪ **Planning Is Key** The swagger of some entrepreneurs might lead you to think that running a small business is all about taking great risks and shooting from the hip. However, the reality is usually quite the opposite. In order to succeed, you'll need a strong and detailed business plan that helps you figure out exactly what your costs will be, what you'll need in order to accomplish your goals, and how you'll attract customers and turn a profit.

If you're ready to take on the risks and do the hard work, starting a business may be right for you. With the right combination of ingenuity, perseverance and planning, you may be on track to reap the benefits that entrepreneurship has to offer. ▪

PRO TIP

Looking for an idea for your new business? It can help to start by identifying a problem that you hope to solve and offering a solution.

Being in charge means added pressure—but also additional rewards.

Entrepreneurship by the Numbers
You May Be Surprised at What a Large Economic Impact Small Businesses Have

Hundreds of thousands of small businesses open every year in the U.S., bringing diversity and jobs to the American economy. Here's a look at some of the statistics on entrepreneurship today:

Size Matters

The U.S. Small Business Administration (SBA) defines a "small business" as having up to 499 employees. However, most are significantly smaller than that. In fact, the majority don't have any paid employees besides the owner.

Still, small enterprises make up an admirably significant chunk of America's economy and job market. Consider these statistics:

- 99.9% of all firms in the U.S. are small businesses.

- 47.3% of all private-sector employees in the U.S. work for a small business.

- Between 2000 and 2018, small businesses created 9.6 million new jobs. During the same period, large companies created only 5.2 million.

- Small businesses are responsible for 40.7% of the private sector payroll in the U.S.

Types of Small Businesses

Small businesses operate in every sector of the economy, and can take many different forms, including sole proprietorships, franchises and even nonprofit organizations. There's no one model for what a small business looks like or what it can accomplish—some are startups requiring little more than a home office, while others employ hundreds of people working from multiple locations.

- The average business in the U.S.—including companies of all sizes—employs 11 people.

- Small enterprises provide the majority of jobs in the fields of food service, small hotels

Be sure to know who
your customers are,
what they need and
how to reach them.

and other accommodations, construction, real estate, agriculture and recreation.

▪ 5.3% of small-business employers are franchises—they're independently owned, but they maintain an ongoing contractual relationship with a larger corporation that often boasts a well-known name.

Taking the First Steps

A startup doesn't have to require huge amounts of financing or investment capital. In fact, many business owners begin with the resources they already have. Even if you dream of eventually running a large enterprise, it's often wise to start small. Consider that:

▪ 81% of small businesses have no paid employees—they are simply individuals working for themselves.

▪ Half of all small businesses are home-based, which helps keep overhead low.

▪ 19% of small businesses are family-owned and operated.

▪ Personal and family savings are the most common sources of financing for small-business expansion—used by 21.9% of small businesses.

PRO TIP

Opting for a home-based business can keep startup costs low—you won't need to worry about expenses like leasing space or extra utilities.

Measuring Success

It's true that starting a new venture is always a risk. But it's also true that year after year, many small firms manage to survive and thrive:

▪ 80% of small businesses survive their first year.

▪ About half of small enterprises survive for at least five years.

▪ One-third of small businesses survive for at least 10 years.

▪ In 2017, the median income for the owner of an incorporated company was $51,419.

▪ The median income for an unincorporated self-employed person in 2017 was $25,240.

Talk to an accountant about the tax implications of going into business with your spouse.

While sales receipts and net income are typical ways to measure the success of any business, it's also important to remember that many business owners find a deeply satisfying sense of personal fulfillment in running their own venture. The desire to succeed can be a helpful motivator to work hard, but for many, owning a business is about more than that. The reward of getting to wake up each day to work on something they're passionate about can be the most important marker of success. ■

Four out of five small businesses are still going strong one year after they've opened. Keeping operating expenses low can help.

What Makes a Good Business Concept? To Achieve Lasting Success, You'll Need More Than Just a Bright Idea

No single formula can determine whether a business will succeed or fail. As the coronavirus pandemic has illustrated, some factors are simply beyond our control. Natural disasters, major political shifts and other events can derail previously sound business plans. However, there are some things that you can do to increase your chances of success regardless of the environment around you. Before you decide to open shop, ask yourself the following questions:

What Problem Are You Solving?

Conventional wisdom among entrepreneurs says that any successful venture begins by identifying a problem and then figuring out how to solve it. For example, in 2007, a pair of roommates in San Francisco identified a problem when they realized that a large design conference was coming to town but there weren't enough local hotel rooms available for all of the attendees. Their solution? A service that allowed visitors to pay to stay the night in a local home—a platform that would become known as Airbnb.

But not every new business has to completely revolutionize an industry. For example, maybe the only coffee shop in your town doesn't open until 9 a.m., leaving early birds with nowhere to grab their java before work. A new coffee shop or truck that opens at 6 or 7 each morning could solve that problem, simply by offering different hours than the existing café.

Is There a Market for It?

Before you decide to invest time and money in starting a business, make sure that you know who your potential customers will be and how you'll reach them. The U.S. Small Business Administration recommends clearly defining the demographics of the customers you want to reach. In other

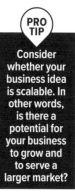

PRO TIP

Consider whether your business idea is scalable. In other words, is there a potential for your business to grow and to serve a larger market?

Base your business on something you'll care about so you'll stay motivated.

words, what is your target customer's age group, education level and income level? Where do they live? And will you have access to enough of those people to make your business profitable?

A good first step toward understanding future customers is looking at the online reviews of your potential business competitors. Reviews on websites like Yelp and Google Reviews can provide important insights about who a business' customers are and what's important to them.

If you can't find a competitor that's comparable to your business idea, interview family, friends and even some strangers to find out what they think of your concept, and whether they could be potential customers. Remember: Just because you would buy your product doesn't mean that everyone else will.

Are You Passionate About the Concept?

Starting a business can be a big commitment. To be successful, you'll need to devote time, energy and—most likely—money toward making your dream a reality. Before you go all in, make sure that your concept is one you can commit to for the long haul. After all, if you're going to be your own boss, shouldn't it be at a job you love?

Science even backs up the idea that your venture should be based on something you care about. A study by scientists at Duke University showed that when people find a task interesting and enjoyable, their chances of success actually improve. In other words, making sure your business concept is something you care about isn't just about finding satisfaction day to day—it's a fundamental part of a strong business plan. ∎

21

Market Research for Your Business Plan
Get to Know Your Customers
and What They Really Want

No matter how great an idea you have for a business, you need customers to buy what you're selling. To ensure your idea is worth the time and resources you're about to invest in it, you need market research: an overview of the potential clients you'll serve, one that's backed by data. To conduct your research, here's a look at the types of questions you need to ask and where to find the data to answer them.

Know What You Need to Know

The goal of market research is to get a good sense of your customer base to help you figure out how to bring a product or service to market. Start by answering the following:

- What types of similar products or services are already available?

- How many competitors already exist in your marketplace?

- How successful are your competitors?

- Are consumers satisfied with their current options, or are they compromising?

- How old are your customers?

- How much disposable income are they willing to spend on your products and services?

- Where do they prefer to shop?

- What kinds of jobs or hobbies do they have?

- Where do they live, and how hard will it be to reach them?

Finding Sources for Your Answers

Start by looking at information that's already been published about your market. Reports from government agencies such as the U.S. Census Bureau and the U.S. Bureau of Labor

Find out how
your product
compares to
existing goods
and services.

23

The goal of market research is to get a good sense of your customer base.

Combing through the data is key when creating a business plan.

Statistics can be good starting points for scoping out customer demographics. Trade publications and networking organizations may produce market studies that you can use to understand trends specific to your industry or region. It's also worth combing through competitors' information, including blogs, ads and press releases, to get a sense of how they approach the market.

Once you're satisfied that the market generally exists, dive a little deeper by contacting potential customers directly to get their opinion on key pieces of information. You can find out what they're willing to pay for goods and services, whether they prefer to make purchases in person or online, or what might improve the chances of getting them to choose you over a competitor. For example, customers interested in higher-quality products than they can currently get may be willing to pay more for them. Conversely, customers looking for more value might abandon competitors for a lower-priced item of similar quality.

You can gather this information through online surveys, focus groups or interviews in person or by phone. The process can be labor-intensive, and it's important to speak with a diverse group of people to ensure your information accurately represents your customer base. You could also hire a consultant to do this type of work for you.

PRO TIP

Trade associations are a rich resource, offering market statistics and access to members you can contact if you have questions.

When you finish your research, you should have detailed information on which customers to target, how many prospective customers you have and how much they're likely to spend. This will create a solid foundation for your business plan, such as refining your offerings, targeting your marketing efforts and figuring out the right price to charge. ■

Banks may have tightened lending standards, but there are opportunities to be had.

Timing Is Everything
There Are Risks and Opportunities Involved in Starting a Business Right Now

If you're wondering whether it's a good idea to start a new business on the heels of a global coronavirus pandemic and financial downturn, you're not alone: According to the Census Bureau, the rate of new business applications slowed down in the first quarter of 2020 as the global financial and health crises began that February.

But if past recessions are any indication, this downturn will also pass, and businesses that are started now could go on to achieve great things. Consider this: Disney was incorporated in 1929, just as the Great Depression began. Uber, Square and Venmo were among the startups that grew out of the Great Recession of 2008 and 2009.

That said, starting a business involves risk in the best of times. According to the U.S. Bureau of Labor Statistics, even in March 2019, in the 11th year of the longest bull market in history, 20% of new businesses failed within their first year; nearly half failed within their first five years.

Don't be shy about asking for rent discounts.

Any business that starts now will face a very real set of challenges, such as weak consumer spending. What's more, banks have tightened lending standards on business loans to levels comparable to those seen during the Great Recession, which can limit easy access to cash. Also, uncertainty continues surrounding how businesses will even be allowed to operate if the coronavirus outbreak worsens in the future or there is other financial uncertainty.

Weigh challenges like these carefully before deciding to open a business. If you decide to proceed, take heart: The current environment may actually be good news for the right type of startup. Here are three reasons why:

Access to Capital

Efforts to save flagging small businesses have meant lower interest rates for loans. The closure of many small businesses also can bring opportunities for entrepreneurs in the form of used equipment for sale at a discount, or opportunities to lease newly vacated space at advantageous rates.

Increased Resiliency

Businesses that launch now will certainly undergo a stress test due to the weakened economy. Assuming the economy eventually bounces back, a business built to survive in lean times could have more upside potential built into it—and may wind up better positioned to survive future economic shocks.

Preadaptation to the New Normal

Business operations and consumer behavior changed rapidly during the pandemic—and some changes are unlikely to disappear even as the pandemic fades. For new enterprises, this

We are in a "new normal," which means having to quickly adapt to market changes.

new reality will already be ingrained in their business plans and daily operations, while existing ventures will need to continue to adapt.

For example, shocks to global supply chains may create long-term changes in an effort to prevent similar issues from occurring in the future. Established companies may be left scrambling to reconfigure their supply chain and vendors, while new businesses can build these new realities into their plans from the get-go.

Consumer behaviors have also shifted, as more people have been forced to rely on cashless transactions and contactless delivery through the pandemic. These options are safe and convenient, and will likely remain popular as the pandemic fades.

Additionally, the widespread ability for companies to function with fewer physical offices could increase the number of people working from home full time.

While the current environment certainly presents difficulties for startups, it also presents unique opportunities. With a solid business plan, relatively inexpensive loan rates and a flexible, entrepreneurial approach, now may be the time to launch an innovative idea. ∎

PRO TIP

In hard economic times, you may be able to find good deals on office space or new and used supplies, which can help you save money on startup costs.

Despite some current risks, the timing may be right for certain well-planned startups.

29

Your co-workers
may look a little
different when
you work at home!

The Noticeable Perks of Running Your Own Home-Based Business Some People Find That Their Residence Also Makes an Ideal Office

If you're thinking your kitchen table could double as a work desk, you're in really good company. Amazon, Disney and Nike are just a few of the global giants whose beginnings can be traced to an entrepreneur's humble home office.

A home-based business is any business that shares an address with where you live. Whether you're selling handcrafted goods or offering bookkeeping services, if your home and business operate out of the same location, yours qualifies as a home-based business.

For some small-business owners, running their company from home is enticingly convenient, cost-effective and fun. But for others, there may be too many rules or hazards that make working from home difficult or even impossible. Before you launch a company from your breakfast nook, let's take a closer look at the benefits and challenges you may face.

Pros

Many traditional 9-to-5ers consider working from home a dream, and there are some big advantages that make running a home-based business appealing.

- **Gain More Comfort and Time** Instead of spending your days beneath the fluorescent lights of a traditional office, you get to work from the comfort of home and in the ways that best suit you, whether seated at a desk, outside on your patio or lying on the couch. You also eliminate a daily commute, which leaves more time for other priorities.

- **Fewer Costs** Working at home may help keep your overhead low, ensuring you don't have to lease or buy a commercial space to open your venture.

PRO TIP

Work-life balance is important. Set office hours with a clear start and finish time to help keep you from feeling like you're always on the clock.

31

Keeping family close
can be an appealing
perk of working at home.

Without a separate place of business, you may be able to avoid buying new furniture, setting up a separate account for utilities and outfitting it with other necessities you already have at home.

▪ **Flexible Location and Hours** You may reap some rewards from not having to show up at a brick-and-mortar business every day. You can work remotely from home or a café. Or you may be able to travel more easily and run your business while you're on the road. And you may find it easier to set your own schedule and fit in non-work activities during traditional work hours.

Cons

In some cases, home may not be conducive to running a business. You may find that what appeals to some—family and pets nearby, for example—interrupts your workflow, making it hard to accomplish necessary tasks.

▪ **Lack of Work-Life Balance** Without a distinct line between your work and home, business matters may bleed into your off time and interfere with your personal life. On the other hand, you may find that friends and relatives don't respect your office hours at home and expect you to be available to take their calls or run errands when you really need to be working.

▪ **Having Too Much Alone Time** If you're used to seeing co-workers every day—taking coffee breaks, collaborating on projects, building professional relationships that become meaningful friendships—it can be jarring to work in complete solitude. The isolation you may experience working from home may make it difficult to stay productive and happy. ▪

PRO TIP

If you are using part of your home for business purposes, you may be eligible for a home office deduction when you file your taxes.

VILLAGE BAKESHOP

105

open

When cooking up your business' name, go for something that will be easy to remember.

Naming Your Business
Following These Tips Can Help You Decide on What to Call Your Venture

The first step in building a brand for your business is choosing a name. The word or phrase you come up with will appear on all your promotional materials, products, storefront (if you have one), website and anything else attached to your organization. So it's worth taking the time to choose a name that represents your business well. Here are a few tips about how to proceed:

▪ **Make It Meaningful** It's easy to think of successful companies with names that say little or nothing about their products or services—think Apple, Google, Nike or Amazon. But these names are exceptions to the rule. Especially for small, locally rooted businesses, something that has some connection to their offerings can save a lot of unnecessary explaining. So start by thinking of names that tell potential customers what your venture is about. Also consider the tone of your name and whether it matches the values of your business.

▪ **Make It Catchy** Word of mouth will likely be an important part of growing your business, especially at first, so you want a name that will be easy to remember and has a nice ring to it. When in doubt, keep it short and simple. Say it out loud to see how it sounds, and think about how it will look with a logo. Once you've brainstormed a list of potential names, test them out with your friends and family.

▪ **Make Sure It's Available** Run an internet search to be sure another business in your area hasn't claimed it already. Consider what domain names are available as well. When you've chosen a name you like, search the U.S. Patent and Trademark Office at uspto.gov to find out if it's been trademarked, which provides federal protection for usage. If it has, using the same name could open you up to litigation. If it's not, consider trademarking the name yourself. Your state may require you to register an entity name, which provides legal protection on the state level. ▪

35

Smart Business Strategies Develop a Plan That Positions Your Venture for Success

Almost every business needs a written plan. It's essential if you're seeking financing, and well-advised even if you're not trying to attract banks or outside investors. That's because formulating a strategy will force you to think clearly about your business, identifying opportunities and risks so you will be prepared for those inevitable surprises—both good and bad—as your venture grows.

How long should a business plan be? One page might suffice for a lean startup plan in which you briefly describe your company's product or service, how you'll reach customers and how soon you expect to make a profit. The goal of this type of plan is to attract early investors with a brief "elevator pitch." But eventually, you'll need a more comprehensive plan—one that may be five to 20 pages long.

You can find hundreds of business-plan templates online, and the federal government's Small Business Administration (SBA) has guidelines on its own website at sba.gov. That said, there is no single format or structure—indeed, areas you will want to include will vary depending on your business. However, every business plan should address four major topics:

- **Company Description** How is the company organized, and who are the key employees?

- **Opportunity** What are you selling and to whom, and how does your product or service set you apart from your competitors?

- **Execution** Where will you buy raw materials, and how will you reach customers?

- **A Financial Plan** How much money will the company earn, and when?

In addition, most plans have an executive summary at the beginning, and an appendix at the end. Let's break down these key components of a good business plan.

A business plan forces you to think carefully about opportunities and risks.

37

■ **Executive Summary** This introductory section is often just a few paragraphs. Here, you engage readers by telling the compelling high-level story of your business—what sets it apart and why it will succeed. Although this section comes at the top of the plan, consider writing it last, after you have a clear sense of what the rest of your business plan is going to say.

■ **Company Description** Your company description will state your corporate legal status (S corporation, LLC, etc.), physical location and number of current employees. It should also include the history of the company (if you bought an existing firm, for example); any intellectual property, such as software, you have patented; and most importantly, a summary of your management team.

If you have experienced employees in key positions—if you already have a proven, seasoned manager, for example—name them and cite their qualifications. If you still have open positions to fill, describe the skills you're looking for. If you're running things all by yourself, describe your own experience and skills.

Opportunity

This is the heart of your business plan. Here you will address three main topics:

■ **The Need** Start by identifying a gap or problem in the market. For example: "The only Italian restaurant on the east side of my town is a takeout pizza joint; no one is serving sit-down homemade pasta dishes." Then describe your solution: "I plan to open a friendly neighborhood trattoria on the east side of town."

■ **The Target Market** Who are your customers? Not everyone is looking for pasta carbonara like your grandma used to make. So be specific: "There's an Italian restaurant on the west side of town that's packed every night with millennials; my restaurant will attract young professionals throughout the east side."

■ **The Competition** Every business has its competitors. That Italian place on the other side of town might be a long drive, but it's not in Siberia. Say there's an established French restaurant right on your block. What are you offering that they don't? It could be that their service is poor, or they overcharge for wine, or you're offering a more sophisticated experience. Write a passionate description about what will set you apart.

Execution

If the opportunity section explains *why* you want to start your own business, the execution section answers *how*. Here you will present two key parts of your plan:

■ **Marketing and Sales** How will customers find your product or service? Maybe you'll have a storefront or an online store; maybe you plan to sell to larger retailers. If your business provides a service, you might write a blog that attracts customers. Describe your promotional plan—it could include social media posts and advertising, or hiring a PR agent to get stories in the press.

■ **Operations** What vendors will supply you with raw materials or other supplies? If you're selling a product, how will you distribute it? Do your research and make realistic distribution plans.

Financial Plan

This needs to show projections of how your sales will (hopefully) increase, when you'll start making a profit and how you'll pay your bills in the meantime. Your financial plan should also

Revisit your business plan often to make sure it's keeping up with changes in the market.

include metrics, such as the percentage of your costs that you expect will go to raw materials and payroll.

Key parts of the financial plan include:

▪ **Income Statement** Sometimes called a profit and loss statement (P&L), this should show your sales minus all of your costs (such as equipment and materials, rent, payroll, advertising) to determine your profit. Your P&L will include a projection for the next three years.

▪ **Balance Sheet** Your balance sheet is a snapshot of your business assets (such as inventory and cash) and liabilities (what you owe) at a specific point in time. Your balance sheet is not a projection. Rather, it shows what your business is worth now.

▪ **Cash Flow Statement** A cash flow statement details how you are going to pay your bills every month, even if your revenue is low. For example, the money could come from a bank line of credit, your personal savings or simply from accumulated revenue.

▪ **Appendix** The appendix is a catchall for information that didn't quite fit into the other sections of your business plan, such as photographs and descriptions of your products, screenshots of your website, and so on.

Finally, your business plan should be a living document, not a static one. Taking time to revisit and update it on a regular basis can help show potential investors that you're on top of the market—and that you know what it takes to be successful. ▪

Deciding on a Business Location Consider These Nine Important Things Before Signing Your Lease

Make sure your customers will be able to get to your door.

Choosing the right location for your business requires careful consideration. Having enough space to carry out your business operations and being in the right place to attract customers are both crucial for your success. There is a lot to consider—and it's not easy to change your mind once you've committed. This checklist can help in your search.

Budget

Your first consideration is how much money you have in your budget to devote to space alone. Remember, you have to pay the rent or mortgage each month and still have enough money left over to cover other necessary expenses, such as utilities and insurance payments. How much can you afford to spend making additional changes to the space? Do you need to make any interior or exterior renovations, or will you have to add any furnishings, such as display shelves or storage?

Retail businesses can benefit from being in areas with high foot traffic to attract passersby.

Demographics

Consider who your customers and employees are, and find a location that will bring you close to both. Consider their habits as well. For example, younger adults are buying fewer cars; if they're your target market, will your business be convenient to public transportation? It's also worth considering the cost of labor, which varies between states and also within metropolitan areas.

Foot Traffic

Not every business needs it, but if you are opening a retail shop or restaurant, random passersby can generate a lot of revenue. While there are so-called "destination" businesses—such as famous restaurants that people will travel miles to reach—don't count on becoming one immediately with a new venture.

Accessibility

How easy is it for customers looking for you to actually find you? Is there convenient parking? Can people who use wheelchairs get in and out of your space easily? If you rely heavily on shipping, are you close to major roads or interstates? Is there space to receive shipments?

Competition

Your instinct might be to avoid competitors, and that's often wise. But businesses that rely on window-shopping can thrive amid competition. Consider how high-end fashion retailers are often located in the same district or even same street. Such clusters can also drive search-engine results when people are looking for you online.

Zoning

Cities large and small regulate the location of commercial activities. Even if your chosen spot is zoned for business, there could be limits on business types or hours that affect you. Consider local rules about signage, which is a basic form of advertising. And don't assume a residential area is off-limits: Some businesses with limited foot traffic, like consultancies or insurance agencies, are welcome in residential neighborhoods. Check with your local planning agency or a lawyer familiar with small businesses in your area.

Infrastructure

It is rare for commercial space to be in move-in condition. Before making a decision, consider the changes you may need to make—and how much they will likely cost you. Some could be basic, like updating heating systems or replacing dingy fixtures. More complicated renovations—like moving walls or replacing a roof—can be pricey, so get estimates to make sure you can afford them before committing to a particular location.

Location History

If similar businesses have tried and failed in your location, that's a red flag. It can be hard to say why certain spots never seem to work. Even if you're convinced your enterprise will be different, customers may have preconceived notions about an area that may hinder success.

Room to Grow

Consider front-end floor space, like restaurant seating or store aisles, and back-room space, like offices or a warehouse. You don't want to pay for more than you need, but some breathing room may be good. Avoid signing a long lease if you think you'll need a bigger location after a few years. ∎

PRO TIP

The tax landscape can vary by state, county and city. Research and consider which locations offer the most business-friendly tax environments.

Keep demographics in mind when picking locations.

Business Successes

Understand the special sauce that has
helped some small ventures to thrive

Creating a social media management business doesn't require a lot of overhead expenses.

Low Investment, High Probability of Success
Here Are 10 Options for Starting Up a Business Without Much Capital

You don't need a boatload of money to start a business. Sure, some business ideas require a lot of overhead expenses before they can get off the ground—you can't open a restaurant without buying or leasing commercial space, for example. But many other enterprises don't require much capital at all, allowing you to get started without the risk of a huge financial loss.

This list will give you a taste of the possibilities for starting a low-investment business. Get inspired and use your unique skills to start a venture you're passionate about, with little cash up front.

Landscaper

Some service-based businesses will never go out of style. Landscaping is a perfect example: As long as people own homes and lack the time or energy to maintain their lawns and gardens, these services will stay in demand. It may require a small investment in basic equipment if you don't already own it, but you don't need to spend a lot to get started. This venture is perfect for people who like working outdoors and enjoy creating beautiful spaces. Once you start establishing a reputation and have a roster of clientele, you can consider investing in more and better equipment, and maybe even a team of employees.

Bookkeeper

Bookkeepers are always in demand, since many small businesses prefer to outsource their accounting. If you're organized, detail-oriented and good with numbers, getting started is relatively easy and inexpensive. Technically, all you really need is a computer, an internet connection and good bookkeeping software—but it may also be worthwhile to invest in a brief training program, and to get certified from a reputable authority like the American Institute of Professional Bookkeepers.

47

Photographer/Videographer

It may be easier than ever to use your phone to take photos and shoot videos, but few people have the knowledge and skill to create professional-quality images—which is why there's still a market for photographers and videographers. Start by offering to cover events for friends and family at little or no cost. Once you've built a portfolio, share it on a website and start finding clients through referrals and social media. You can even rent high-quality equipment on a project-by-project basis as you get started. Then, when you make enough money, you can invest in your own gear.

Medical Transcriber

This opportunity involves transferring dictations from doctors into documents that become part of patients' official records. It's a job you can do from home, either working directly with medical institutions or with companies that provide medical-transcription services. To break into the business, it helps to take an online training course and obtain a national certification. This will familiarize you with speech-recognition software, electronic health-record systems, medical terminology, anatomy and pharmacology.

Social Media Manager

PRO TIP

Service-based businesses are a great option if you don't have much capital to start out with. Examples include landscaping or bookkeeping.

One idea for a startup is to help other small businesses with tasks they don't have the time or ability to accomplish in-house. Most small businesses have a social media presence, but not all do the best job translating that presence into more visibility and customers. As a social media manager, you can help them deploy marketing strategies on Facebook, Instagram, Twitter, Snapchat, etc., and engage with their customers and partners.

Caterer

If you love to cook, consider transferring your passion into a catering business that serves events in your community. Focus on making the kind of food you know best, whether that's regional fare or a particular kind of dessert. Be aware of your state's rules about where food can be made and the licenses you need to make it for public consumption. Some states allow at-home cooking, while others may require you to rent space in a professional kitchen, which can add to your startup costs.

Start small by catering for modestly sized dinners and parties, then gradually expand to take on larger events as you gain experience, equipment and personnel. You might also consider supplying some of your products to local coffee shops and restaurants.

Life Coach

This is a relatively new profession, but it has become mainstream in recent years, with more people turning to paid experts for help with taking stock of, and planning, their professional or personal lives. If helping people is something that you enjoy and you're good at solving problems, this could be the career path for you. Before jumping in though, consider taking a coach certification course from a respected organization like the International Coach Federation. This will make you more credible to potential clients.

Woodworker

Turning a hobby into a small business can be a great way to ensure you are passionate about your work. For example, even as inexpensive,

Turn a love for woodworking into a business by selling your creations online.

assemble-it-yourself furniture floods the marketplace, there is still high demand for unique, custom-made furniture and home goods. If you're an enthusiastic woodworker, you can try to make a living at it by selling your creations on sites like Etsy and Craigslist, as well as on your own website. Start by offering a few custom products that you can easily reproduce.

Marketing Consultant

Marketing consultants help businesses build their brands. It's an ideal profession for someone with strong communication skills, a lot of creativity and the ability to develop and follow through on long-term strategies. Many people in this field have marketing degrees and experience—but you don't necessarily need either to do this well. If you didn't study marketing in school, consider taking an online course to brush up on topics like web development and video creation. Then build a portfolio by partnering with local businesses on specific marketing campaigns at a low cost.

Professional Organizer

As more people try to minimize disorder in their homes and rid themselves of unnecessary possessions, professional organizers have become all the rage. If you're highly organized, can create a repeatable method for getting living spaces in order and want to help clients feel better about their home environments, organizing other people's chaos could be a good option. You can start by offering your services at a very low rate—or even for free—so you can document your successes and collect testimonials on a website. You can also include an online portfolio to display before-and-after photos of organizing work you've done for clients, all for little to no upfront cost.

These are just a handful of businesses that don't require a lot of money to get going. If you don't see something that appeals to you here, get creative with what you're passionate about. While there's no guarantee your new business will prove to be a success, it can be easier to take the first step when you know it won't cost you an arm and a leg. ∎

Success Stories From the Trenches Meet Three Entrepreneurs Who Found Their Space in Crowded Markets

Small businesses often begin when passionate people identify and fill a gap in the market. Here's a look at how three entrepreneurs got their start and built businesses that work.

Lukafit

New York City

Mbali Ndlovu wanted to start exercising more—so she organized a group of 10 friends in New York who could give one another a sense of community and accountability. The collective eventually grew to more than 1,000 members, and the group became a source of unintentional market research. Ndlovu and her peers agreed: Activewear brands were not catering to black women or curvy body types. Their leggings didn't fit at the waist, and activewear companies rarely included black women in their advertising and branding campaigns. Ndlovu and her friends wanted to feel confident about their bodies and see themselves represented in the fitness world.

It was obvious that the women in Ndlovu's collective represented a large but overlooked consumer market, so she started Lukafit to address black women's activewear needs. After years of development, Lukafit's first product, "squat-proof" leggings designed with a high waist and in vibrant prints, sold out of their first three production runs in 2017. Ndlovu describes her customers as "obsessed," and she largely credits word-of-mouth with building brand awareness.

Community Impact Newspaper

Pflugerville, Texas

John and Jennifer Garrett took a gamble. They started Community Impact Newspaper from their home in Pflugerville in 2005, around the

PRO TIP

One part of small-business success is identifying and focusing on an underserved niche and solving problems for your customers.

Whimsical, relatable graphics are part of Lukafit's allure.

Lukafit

51

same time newspaper revenues across the country began a steep decline.

The enterprise began simply enough. John, a former ad director for the Austin Business Journal, wasn't satisfied with the level of local community news in his area. So with $40,000 from a credit card, he and his wife, Jennifer, decided to start their own newspaper.

PRO TIP

Consider a business model that saves time for customers by cutting down on choices. This can also help your customers feel less overwhelmed.

The couple says they avoided the "refrigerator journalism" typical of community newspapers—think profiles of student athletes for proud parents to hang on the fridge. Instead, they offered in-depth journalism and breaking news coverage on their website at the hyperlocal level.

Rather than use traditional distribution models like rack sales, they opted to mail their monthly newspaper to every residence in targeted ZIP codes, a model advertisers have since come to appreciate.

The Garretts' gamble has certainly paid off well in Pflugerville—and beyond. While print media has shrunk, the Garretts' chain of free, local newspapers has grown to encompass editions delivered to 2.7 million homes and businesses in 35 communities and counting. Their company employs 220 people in communities from Arizona to Tennessee and generates $27 million in annual revenue.

Farmgirl Flowers

San Francisco

Christina Stembel founded her flower-delivery service, Farmgirl Flowers, in 2010. She carved out space in a market dominated by larger competitors by offering something radically different: While other florists boast an infinitely customizable range of bouquets, Farmgirl Flowers offers only one bouquet design per day, created with ethically sourced flowers.

While having only one option may seem counterintuitive, it actually saves customers' time and cuts down on waste. Stembel has also established

Offering quality over quantity is what helped propel Farmgirl Flowers to success.

an aesthetic that consumers have grown to trust. They can order blindly, knowing they won't end up with something generic, like a dozen deep-red roses and a sprig of baby's breath (the company received national attention in 2016 for eliminating red roses from its Valentine's Day offerings).

When she started, Stembel's unlikely business model was new in the florist industry, but she knew in her heart that there was a demand for sustainable floral products. Her timing was right: That demand expanded beyond the Bay Area and has reached all across the country. Today, Farmgirl Flowers is among the most successful bouquet-delivery companies in the U.S., employing about 90 designers, shipping all over the country and hitting $30 million in revenue in 2019. ∎

Big Names, Humble Beginnings
Three of America's Most Recognizable Brands Started Small Before They Got Off the Ground

Many of the brands that now dominate the consumer marketplace had surprisingly simple beginnings. Here are three large companies that watched their good idea blossom into something a whole lot bigger.

Microsoft

Albuquerque, New Mexico

When Paul Allen and Bill Gates read a *Popular Electronics* feature on the Altair 8800 back in 1975, they had an idea. Known today as the first personal computer, the Altair 8800's (relatively) small size brought computing to a wider public and, as Allen and Gates predicted, boosted demand for software. The old high school friends decided they would be the ones to write that software. They contacted MITS, which produced the Altair 8800, and told the company

they had software that interpreted the BASIC programming language for the new computer. But the truth was that the pair hadn't actually written those programs yet. So when MITS agreed to license and distribute the software, Allen and Gates hurried to develop it, and Microsoft was born.

The Albuquerque-based business generated $1 million in software sales during its first four years. But becoming the behemoth that Microsoft eventually turned into required the company to get in early on several more seismic shifts in the tech world, such as the rise of the internet and the evolution of the video-game market. In its first 10 years of existence, Microsoft would release several major software products, including MS-DOS, Microsoft Word and the Windows operating system. Each time, the company was able to stake out new territory early enough to gain dominance.

Microsoft started out as a small business in Albuquerque.

Now a huge brand, Burt's Bees began with two friends selling wax candles.

For his ability to recognize important trends early, Gates largely credits his habit of constantly reevaluating his assumptions. When something doesn't turn out the way he initially expected, he doesn't get angry or defensive. Instead, he says, he gets curious: What was wrong about his view of the world? What could he study to improve it?

From its humble beginnings, Microsoft has become one of the largest companies in the world, worth nearly $1.5 trillion.

Burt's Bees

Dover-Foxcroft, Maine

Burt's Bees began with a pair of friends selling candles in Maine. Beekeeper Burt Shavitz had been stockpiling beeswax from his honey operation, unsure about what he would eventually do with it. Artist Roxanne Quimby, who had met Shavitz while hitchhiking, found a candle-making recipe, and in 1984, their candles debuted at a local craft fair, where they made about $200 in sales.

The two decided to continue their enterprise, which made about $20,000 in its first year of business. But their big break came in 1989, when the company began supplying candles to Zona, a trendy New York City boutique.

This partnership led to a flurry of new sales, necessitated several new hires, and positioned the company for success in a new venture: lip balm. In 1991, Quimby began to produce a beeswax lip balm from a recipe that she found in an old *Farmers' Almanac*. Beauty care was just beginning to take off at the same time that consumers were gaining an interest in natural products. The company's rustic image became an asset among customers looking for natural beauty care products.

Burt's Bees' product line has grown from beeswax lip balm to a vast array of goods, including skin care, makeup and toothpaste.

The company continued to expand over the next decade and a half, launching new products from soaps to toothpaste. In 2004, a private equity firm acquired 80% of Burt's Bees for $173 million—and three years later, Clorox acquired the brand for $925 million.

Trader Joe's

Pasadena, California

Joe Coulombe knew his way around the grocery business. Since 1958, he owned Pronto Markets, a small chain of Los Angeles–area convenience stores. But by the end of the 1960s, he noticed that the new generation's tastes were changing: Young shoppers wanted more natural and organic foods, as well as exciting foods, like exotic cheeses, that would tempt their increasingly adventurous palates.

So in 1967, Coulombe abandoned Pronto Markets and opened the first Trader Joe's in Pasadena, California, to serve this demographic. The first store (which is still operating in the same spot) capitalized on the mid-century tiki craze, with a nautical theme and a name that referenced the famed tiki bar chain Trader Vic's.

Coulombe offered his customers a kitschy atmosphere and a unique selection of foods and beverages at reasonable prices. For instance, when it opened, the store had an unmatched selection of California wines. In 1972, Trader Joe's introduced a granola as its first private-label product. It would build its identity using this model, focusing on offering inexpensive, in-house foods and dry goods.

In 1979, Coulombe sold Trader Joe's to German entrepreneur Theo Albrecht—whose family also owns the German supermarket giant Aldi Nord—for an undisclosed sum and stayed on

Trader Joe's draws shoppers for its unique offerings and ability to capitalize on culinary trends—at budget-friendly prices.

as CEO until 1988. Like any successful business founder, Coulombe got ahead of a market trend: growing interest in natural, organic and gourmet food items. But he also bucked trends to maintain Trader Joe's identity, winning customers with a smaller selection than most grocery stores offered and fewer brand-name items, which gave customers unique choices. That nonconformity continues to define the chain, which—unlike many other grocers—has no loyalty program and no self-checkout lanes, for example.

Trader Joe's expanded into northern California in the late 1980s and became a nationwide chain in the 1990s. It has only continued to grow since then, taking in $13.3 billion in revenue in 2017. ∎

The top-selling item at Trader Joe's: Everything But the Bagel Sesame Seasoning Blend.

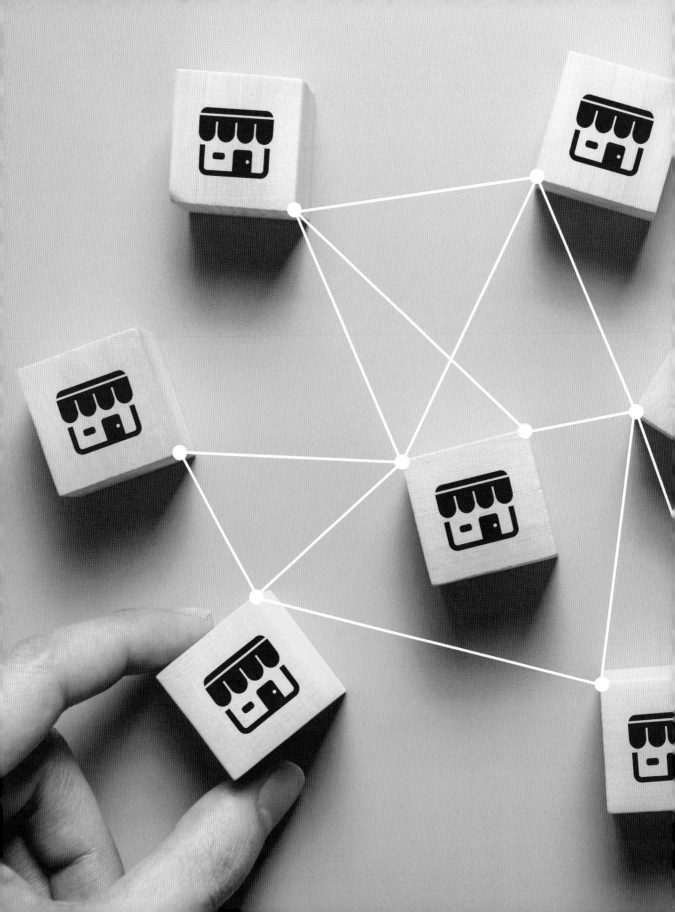

Franchising vs. Buying

It's important to understand these options
when starting or expanding your business

There are more than
750,000 franchise
establishments
operating in the U.S.

Different Types of Franchises
Licensing Offers a Streamlined
Way to Start Your Own Business

Launching a business on your own can be daunting. It often takes lots of upfront investment, with no guarantee that you'll make it back. But opening a franchise can let you be your own boss while relying on a proven model or product. Most companies that offer franchises have already established themselves as national brands, so they often come with a built-in customer base. Instead of you having to sway potential customers through advertising or online reviews, you'll have an immediately recognizable business name or products, and people will know what to expect.

Before you get into the nuts and bolts of how franchising works, it's important to understand a few key terms:

▪ **Franchiser** The franchiser is the company whose business model you'll be replicating, or whose products you'll be selling or manufacturing. For example, if you open up your own McDonald's franchise, the McDonald's corporation would be the franchiser.

▪ **Franchisee** The franchisee is the small-business owner who has agreed to the franchiser's terms to operate his or her own small business. If you've opened up your own McDonald's location, you are the franchisee.

▪ **Licensing** Licensing describes the legal right for the franchisee to use the franchiser's brand and trademarked products. Every relationship between a franchisee and franchiser will include an extensive legal document called the franchise disclosure document, which outlines the extent and limits of the franchise license.

There are a few different franchise models offered. Each

PRO TIP

Opening a franchise can help you get your feet wet in the business world without having to come up with a new product or attract a customer base.

one presents a different relationship between franchiser and franchisee.

Business Format Franchise

The business format franchise is the most recognizable type of franchise. Fast-food chains such as McDonald's or Subway are examples of business format franchises: Each individual franchise replicates the franchiser's concept. Things like employee uniforms, menus, décor and signage are consistent from one location to another. While this model means the franchisee loses certain freedoms—for example, choosing what types of products to offer, or how they want to decorate their location—they also receive thorough and ongoing support from the franchiser to help start and grow their business.

Product Franchise

Also known as a distribution franchise, this type is one in which the franchisee agrees to sell the franchiser's products on an exclusive or semiexclusive basis. This type of franchise offers the franchisee more freedom to determine how they want to run various aspects of their business.

Exxon is a prominent example of this kind of franchise. For instance, a franchisee can open an Exxon-branded gas station, giving them access to Exxon's line of fuel products as well as the license to use Exxon's trademark, signage and advertising tools. However, not all Exxon-branded gas stations look alike, and each gas station can sell a different variety of products such as snacks, beverages and even prepared foods.

Manufacturing Franchise

A manufacturing franchise provides the franchisee with the right to manufacture (and generally, distribute) the franchiser's products. Coca-Cola products operate under this type of franchise agreement. The Coca-Cola Company sells its concentrated syrups to its manufacturing franchisees, which in turn mix the syrup with water and sweeteners, bottle the beverages and sell and deliver them to retailers. This type of franchise saves the franchiser from having to manufacture, store and deliver enormous amounts of product. Instead, franchisees each take responsibility for producing and distributing the product for their own area or set of clients.

Fast-food chains frequently provide franchise opportunities.

Job Franchise

A job franchise can be the simplest and least expensive kind to open, requiring relatively little in the way of initial investment and franchise fees. Job franchises are generally service-oriented, rather than product-oriented. For example, fitness enthusiasts can become Jazzercise franchisees, allowing them to lead Jazzercise workouts. Similarly, Dream Vacations offers franchisees the opportunity to start their own travel agency—a business that requires very little in infrastructure or startup costs, because it's a service and can be run from the franchisee's home.

No Guarantees

It's important to remember that even with a nationally known brand, no business venture comes without its own inherent risks. The same rules for success apply to a franchise as they do to any other business. You'll have to put in plenty of time and hard work, and to think like an entrepreneur—all while remaining accountable to the franchiser. If you decide that owning a franchise is right for you, be sure to shop around for the franchise model and franchiser that will best suit your interests and skills. ∎

03 | **BEING A FRANCHISEE**   01 | 02 | 03 | 04

Understanding Your Role as a Franchisee
Yes, You'll Be Your Own Boss—
But There's More to It Than That

To understand your role as a franchisee, it helps to understand the franchiser-franchisee relationship. According to the Federal Trade Commission, a business must meet three specific criteria to be defined as a franchise:

▪ The franchiser provides the franchisee with a trademark or other symbol of its brand for commercial use.

▪ The franchiser maintains the right to significantly control—or provide significant assistance to the operation of—the franchisee's business.

▪ The franchisee is required to pay the franchiser at least $615 during the first six months of their business operation.

Before you purchase or open a franchise, the franchiser is legally required to provide you with a franchise disclosure document (FDD). An FDD contains 23 points of information that describe your responsibilities as a franchisee and explain what you can expect from the franchiser. Here are some of the things an FDD covers:

Costs

The first thing you'll need as a franchisee is capital to cover startup costs. Generally, you'll be expected to cover typical business startup costs, such as obtaining and building a location and procuring equipment. However, your FDD will also specify the amount you'll pay to the franchiser as an initial franchise fee—essentially a licensing fee that gives you the right to use the franchiser's brand, products and, in some circumstances, their business format. Franchise fees vary widely, and can run anywhere from several hundred dollars to tens of thousands of dollars.

PRO TIP

Read your franchise disclosure document carefully to make sure you fully understand what your franchiser will expect of you.

You can expect some aspects of training to come from the franchiser.

Franchisees are usually responsible for tracking and replenishing their inventory.

Once your business is open, you'll generally also pay ongoing royalty fees to the franchiser for as long as you remain in business. These royalties are often a percentage of your total sales. By paying back into the franchiser's business, you are helping fund things like national advertising campaigns and product development.

Ongoing Responsibilities

As a franchisee, you're responsible for the daily operations of your business, including costs and obligations such as:

■ **Hiring and Managing Your Employees** As the owner of your business, you'll be responsible for assembling and overseeing your team of employees. You'll also set their wages and schedules. In many cases, franchisers will provide guidance and training materials to help you along the way.

■ **Ordering and Maintaining Product** Whether you're running your own fast-food franchise location or bottling and selling soft drinks, you will be the one in charge of ordering all of the products you need from your supplier (in many cases, the franchiser or its affiliates).

■ **Updating and Adapting** Many FDDs give the franchiser the power to change their products and their requirements of franchisees over time. For example, if your franchiser starts offering a new line of blended drinks, you may be required to buy the equipment necessary for your franchise to make those drinks.

PRO TIP

Communicate regularly with your franchiser to take advantage of their insights on how to manage employees and grow your business.

■ **Communicating With the Franchiser** Your relationship with the franchiser doesn't end once you sign the FDD. Most franchisers expect their franchisees to communicate regularly to report on factors like sales, business trends and challenges. You may also be required to participate in training sessions.

The Franchiser's Role

The franchisee isn't the only party with ongoing responsibilities, though. Your franchise agreement should also stipulate what is required from your franchiser. Their responsibilities usually include the following:

■ **National and International Marketing and Advertising** A nice aspect of being a franchisee is that you're not responsible for your own advertising. The money you pay in royalties (and sometimes in a separate advertising fee) helps fund widespread advertising campaigns that benefit all of the brand's franchisees.

■ **Training and Advice** Part of the franchiser-franchisee relationship is that the franchiser is able to offer advice to franchisees on how to attract customers, manage employees and grow a business. Established franchisers are often happy to provide insight to help you run your business, since your growth is their growth.

■ **Ongoing Evaluation** To make sure that franchisees are maintaining the franchiser's standards, franchisers often have representatives monitor and evaluate franchise locations. These representatives can provide guidance on how the franchisee can improve their business practices and align themselves more closely to the brand.

There are many different structures for franchising. The one you choose will have a lot to do with what your responsibilities are as a franchisee. If you're unsure about what will be expected of you, ask your franchiser to clarify any items in the FDD that you're unclear about. ■

03 | **GROWING A FRANCHISE** | 01 | 02 | 03 | 04

Growing a Franchise
Maximize Brand Recognition and Develop Relationships to Increase Your Success

Becoming a franchise owner allows you to acquire a proven business model and market-tested products or services. As a franchisee, you may also have the opportunity to expand your business by opening multiple locations. In fact, more than half of all franchises are operated by multiple unit owners. But before you decide to open a second location, there are some important considerations you need to take into account.

Does Your Franchise Agreement Allow It?
Check your franchise agreement closely to make sure multiple-unit development is allowed. Some companies prefer that their franchisees develop their businesses one at a time, while others will grant rights to multiple locations.

Can the Market Bear It?
When you opened your first franchise, you likely had to do a lot of market research to determine

the right location. You'll need to do the same for all subsequent units. Find out the answer to questions like where your potential customers live and work, what their consumption patterns are and who your competitors in the area are.

Are You Ready to Up Your Management Game?
The more units you open, the more staff you will need, including managerial staff. Single-unit operators may be used to taking a very hands-on approach to running a business. Multiple-unit owners, however, must be prepared to train staff and delegate tasks.

How Will You Finance Your Growth?
If you don't have enough capital to cover the costs of expanding, you can try for a bank loan. Many franchisers also offer funding tied to opening new franchise locations. As a franchisee, you have the benefit of a system of support that can serve as a foundation for growing your business. ■

Managing employees is a major component of running a successful franchise.

The Advantages and Disadvantages of Buying an Existing Business
Going This Route Can Save Time and Money—But Beware the Risks

Becoming your own boss doesn't necessarily mean building a brand-new company from the ground up. You can also buy an established enterprise and make it your own. Buying an existing business comes with several advantages and can save you time and money on startup costs, but there are some disadvantages, too. For example, you might inherit dated technology or find it harder to put your unique spin on the venture. Consider these other pros and cons to buying an existing business.

Advantages

▪ **Acquiring a Proven Business Model and Structure** Buying an existing firm can significantly reduce your startup time and costs. Building a business from scratch means purchasing initial inventory, hiring and training employees, and finding suppliers. When you purchase an existing firm, those systems and relationships may already exist. You'll also acquire a product or service that has been market-tested and a customer base that's familiar with your product, so you can devote fewer resources to marketing.

▪ **Easier Financing** Securing funding for a new enterprise is challenging. Lenders and banks may prefer lending to an established venture with a track record of generating revenue. What's more, some small-business loans require collateral, such as real estate assets or equipment. If you're starting your own business, you may not have the collateral necessary to secure one of these loans. However, when you buy a business, lenders are able to view a record of financial performance and may perceive that as less of a risk to them than financing a startup.

PRO TIP

Lenders and banks may be more willing to extend a loan to an established business that can demonstrate its ability to earn revenues.

You'll hope to inherit a skilled and experienced team if you buy an established enterprise.

■ **An Established Supply Chain** Buying an existing enterprise means you'll also obtain an established supply chain. Building relationships and networks with vendors and suppliers takes time, and buying an existing company means these systems are already in place.

Disadvantages

■ **Purchasing Costs** While financing may be easier when buying an existing company, there are higher upfront costs. When you buy an existing business, you're not just purchasing space or supplies: You're buying a proven concept, its intellectual property, an established customer base and assets—all of which will increase the price.

■ **It Takes Time to Learn the Ropes** The supply chains, structures and systems of an existing business can reduce your operating costs, but they also could mean a learning curve. It can take a fair amount of time to get accustomed to internal processes and familiarize yourself with aspects of the company's financials and relationships with vendors.

■ **You Might Acquire Hidden Problems** It's important to do your research on any existing business you're considering purchasing. Carefully review the company's financial documents, including balance sheets and tax returns. Even with a healthy amount of due diligence you may inherit problems you weren't able to anticipate, like a poor brand image, disgruntled employees or damaged equipment.

Before buying an existing business, consider the direction in which you'd like to take it and if your skills are a good match. While you likely won't find a company without any potential disadvantages, given the right preparation, buying an existing business could be the key to your success. ∎

73

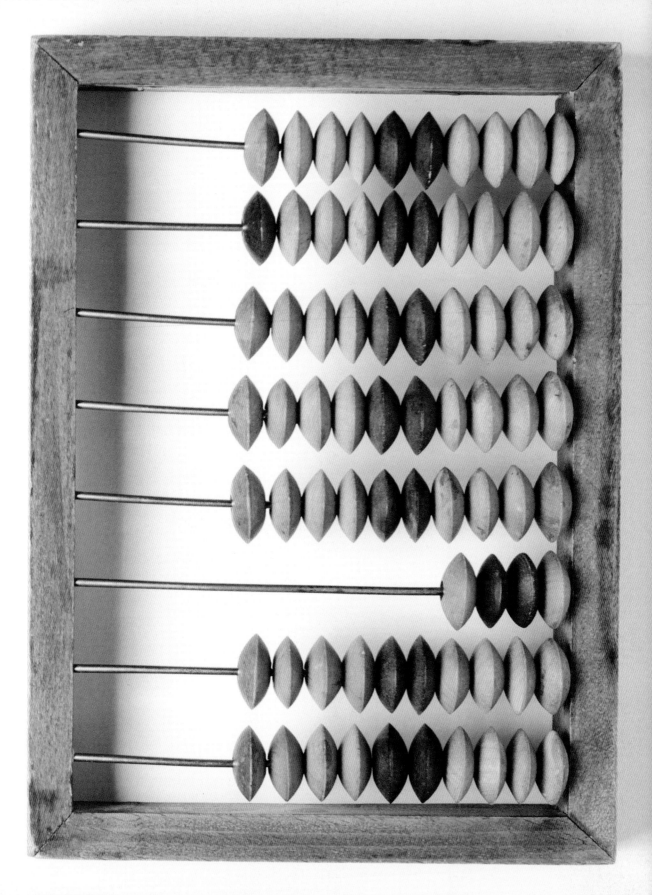

Organizing Finances

What to know about funding a business, choosing a structure and keeping expenses in check

04 | **BUSINESS FINANCING**　　　　　　　　01 | 02 | 03 | 04 | 05 | 06 | 07 | 08

Financing Your Business
Here's Where to Find the Money to Help Get Things Off the Ground

You've surely heard that old saying: "It takes money to make money." Whatever type of venture you envision, you'll need cash to keep it going until your revenues outpace your expenses. Fortunately, there are lots of ways to finance a small business—some of which you might not have considered.

Financing falls under two broad categories: debt and equity. Debt financing is when money is borrowed to start a business; like a mortgage, you pay it back over time, with interest. Equity financing is when someone invests in your business in return for an ownership share; rather than earn interest, they take a piece of your profits. Many businesses finance with a mix of debt and equity. Here's a look at some of the options available to help you start your small business.

PRO TIP

Crowdfunding is a relatively new way to tap the internet as a resource, while promoting a new product or service and building a customer base.

Personal Savings
Using your own source of cash to pay for your business startup means that you won't owe interest or monthly payments. Of course, this option is not always possible, even for the most diligent of savers. And there are opportunity costs, meaning if you use your savings for your business, that money can't be used for any other investments, like the stock market. Some new business owners are tempted to tap cash in their retirement accounts, but doing so can mean stiff early-withdrawal penalties—and potentially leave you with inadequate funds in old age.

Family and Friends
One step up from using your own savings is sourcing cash from people you know via a loan or an equity stake. Consider what might happen

Have a solid business plan ready when you apply for a bank loan to fund your venture.

to those relationships if your business fails. Be sure your supporters understand the risk.

Credit Cards

Maxing out your credit cards to start a business is risky. If you're taking cash advances from the card, you'll pay high interest rates. On the other hand, you won't face the scrutiny required for a bank loan. Many business owners use personal credit cards to buy inventory, then pay off the bill as revenue comes in. While this approach may be convenient—and helps rack up reward points!—it's risky if your revenue falls short.

Bank Loans

Banks have whole departments geared to loans for small businesses. You'll need a solid plan to convince them that your enterprise is viable.

Using your personal savings is an interest-free way to cover startup costs.

Another bank product used by many small businesses is a line of credit. You can draw on a line of credit slowly over time to buy inventory, make renovations, pay bills and make payroll during slow periods. You can then pay back the loan as revenue comes in. Most banks will want to see your business firmly established before they will agree to a line of credit, however.

PRO TIP

Before you qualify for a business line of credit, you'll likely need to have been open at least six months and have at least $25,000 in revenue.

SBA Loans
The Small Business Administration (SBA) underwrites loans issued through participating banks. The SBA guarantees a portion of the loan —meaning if your business fails, the bank still gets most of its money back from the SBA.

That provision makes banks more likely to lend to you, and at a better interest rate than you'd receive otherwise. The SBA microloan program provides up to $50,000 for small businesses and can be used for everything from inventory to equipment and working capital.

Angel Investors
Angel investors are wealthy individuals who invest in small businesses that they think have a good plan. Their goal is to make money when the business takes off, but they also get satisfaction from helping a startup get off its feet and hopefully succeed. Keep in mind that if your business underperforms, that angel investor could get noisy—and demand changes. Always have the details of such partnerships spelled out in a contract, written by a lawyer who handles commercial agreements. ∎

Choosing a Business Structure
The Entity You Select Has Both Financial and Legal Implications

When starting your own business, you must choose what type of business entity it will be in the eyes of the law. Choosing the right structure can have major implications, affecting factors including your tax burden, your legal liability and even how much paperwork you'll have to file. That's why it's important to consider your options carefully, and to choose the structure that best fits your unique vision.

Sole Proprietorship

A sole proprietorship is the easiest kind of business to form. In fact, if you perform business activities but don't register as a business, your business is automatically considered a sole proprietorship. You must register with your state if you're planning to sell taxable products or services, however. And if you plan to hire employees, you'll need to obtain an employer identification number (EIN) from the IRS.

The federal government doesn't separate the business assets and liabilities of sole proprietors from their personal assets and liabilities. As a result, your business income will be taxed as personal income, and you are personally responsible for debts and legal obligations arising from your business activity. Moreover, you're required to pay a self-employment tax— 15.3% on the first $137,700 worth of net income for 2020. (Visit irs.gov for updated numbers.)

The bottom line: Consider a sole proprietorship if you're looking for an easy setup and your business is relatively low-risk.

Partnership

If you're going into business with at least one other person, you might want to consider registering your business

PRO TIP

If you're not sure what business structure to use, the SBA offers free business counselors. Or contact an attorney or accountant.

Here's the buzz: The structure you choose will determine how your business is treated legally.

as a partnership. There are two main types of partnerships: limited partnerships (LPs) and limited liability partnerships (LLPs).

Limited partnerships consist of at least one "general partner" and at least one "limited partner." Limited partners have limited liability for legal obligations, while general partners have unlimited liability, often in exchange for more control within the company. Both general partners and limited partners must pay personal taxes on business profits, and general partners must pay self-employment taxes.

Limited liability partnerships do away with general partners. No partner in a limited liability partnership can be personally liable for the actions of other partners, and for the most part, partners' personal assets are protected from legal action. However, assets within the partnership may be targeted, and individuals may be liable for their own actions.

A partnership can be a great choice for some small groups of professionals—such as lawyers, accountants or architects—looking to share the cost of doing business.

LLCs are popular business structures for high- or medium-risk businesses. They may also be appropriate for owners who have significant personal assets they want to protect. Be aware that an LLC may have to be dissolved if any member chooses to leave.

Corporation

The corporation is the business structure that offers the most separation between an organization and its owners. Unlike with other types of business, corporations pay income tax on their profits. As with LLCs, legal liabilities fall to the company, rather than the individuals who own it.

Corporations require much more paperwork to set up and to maintain than other types of businesses, and they cost more to form. On the other hand, they have an advantage when it comes to raising capital, since corporations can sell shares of its stock in exchange for a share of their profits.

There are two types of corporations (corps): C corps and S corps. C corps are allowed to have an unlimited number of global shareholders, but they often face taxes on both their profits and dividends. S corps are limited to 100 shareholders, all of whom must be U.S. citizens. Unlike with C corps, the money that S corps make is not subject to corporate tax. Instead, S corps allow profits to pass through directly to owners' personal incomes.

Take your time as you decide on a structure for your business, paying special attention to your tax and liability situation. While it is possible to switch from one structure to another, it's not always easy and could result in extra taxes and legal fees. ■

Limited Liability Company (LLC)

Unlike sole proprietorships and partnerships, limited liability companies are considered to be separate entities from the people who run them. In most cases, your personal assets will not be affected by any potential legal action your company faces.

The business is not subject to corporate taxes, and you can pass profits through to your personal income. Note that all members of an LLC owe self-employment taxes, and many states require high filing fees.

04 | **BOOKKEEPING** | 01 | 02 | 03 | 04 | 05 | 06 | 07 | 08

Bookkeeping Basics
Tracking the Numbers Is
Essential to Running Your Business

For many small-business owners, dealing with the numbers side of operations can be downright intimidating. But keeping careful, organized financial records from the start of your business is critical to keeping things on the right track and avoiding future headaches. Here's a look at the basics of keeping your books in order.

Bookkeeping 101

The term bookkeeping refers to maintaining a record of all of your company's business transactions and managing its accounts. The information you record through the bookkeeping process allows you to calculate your profitability, plan for the future, make sound financial decisions, identify any potential problems and avoid errors. Your books also help you track key figures you'll need for filing your taxes, applying for loans and preparing financial statements for investors.

What to Track

Whether you manage your books yourself or you get help and hire a bookkeeper, these are the accounts you'll need to keep up to date:

- **Revenue** The income from a sale.

- **Expenses** Business costs such as wages, rent, utilities and office supplies. You can subtract expenses from revenue to determine your company's profit.

- **Assets** The resources and items your company owns, including inventory, cash and real estate.

- **Liabilities** Not to be confused with expenses, these are debts such as bank loans, credit card debt or money owed to suppliers.

- **Equity** The overall value of your business. Subtract total liabilities from total business assets to determine equity.

If your finances are relatively simple, you may be able to keep track of them yourself.

Every company, regardless of its size, needs to keep track of revenue, expenses and other key data.

Stay up to date on your bookkeeping to avoid potential errors.

Managing Your Accounts

To maintain accurate numbers, you'll want to record transactions for each account promptly. Schedule a regular time to document and categorize your transactions—at least weekly—and organize them by date.

Aside from keeping an eye on your accounts, it's also important to maintain organized files for receipts, invoices, bank statements, payroll documents and other records in case you ever need to verify numbers—in the event of a tax audit or payment dispute, for example. These records can also help clear up any discrepancies or errors in your bookkeeping.

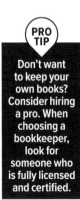

PRO TIP

Don't want to keep your own books? Consider hiring a pro. When choosing a bookkeeper, look for someone who is fully licensed and certified.

Helpful Tools

If you're a sole proprietor or your business is very simple, you may be able to stay on top of your books yourself. In that case, you'll likely want to use a digital spreadsheet or accounting software such as QuickBooks to record your data. Accounting software can often link to your company bank account, which can make the numbers even easier to track.

However, if you have multiple employees and a lot of transactions to track, bookkeeping can quickly become complicated and you may find you need some help. Many small-business owners hire a bookkeeper or work with a certified public accountant to reduce their workload and ensure their financial records are in order.

One big reason to work with a professional: They're trained to catch errors. If you're tracking everything on your own, it's hard to check your own work, and you may miss some mistakes. Bookkeeping professionals are experienced in this area. They can help ensure your data is complete and accurate, and they'll likely spot any mistakes you may have missed on your own.

Managing financials is a critical part of owning a business. Whether you tackle the job yourself or you enlist a professional, knowing the basics can help you get started on the right foot. ∎

Licenses and Regulations
Get Familiar With the Government Requirements for Running Your Business

Applying for permits and studying business law isn't exactly what inspires people to start businesses. But they're necessary steps to get your venture off to a good start and save yourself headaches down the line.

Ensure a smooth opening by getting to know the different kinds of licenses and regulations you'll need to deal with.

Federal, State and Local Licenses

If your business activities are regulated by a federal agency—such as the U.S. Department of Agriculture—you'll need a federal license to operate. Consider the type of business you're starting and contact the relevant federal agency to find out what licenses you'll need, how much they cost and how to apply.

Your state, county and city also issue necessary licenses to do business in your area. Visit the

Getting a seal of approval is critical for many new businesses.

websites of your state and local governments to find exactly what you need locally. If you operate out of your home or conduct your business primarily online, you still need to apply for the relevant permits. And remember that many licenses need to be renewed regularly.

Some of the most common business licenses include the following:

▪ **Basic Business Operation License** You'll need a basic license from the city or county to operate.

▪ **Employer Identification Number (EIN)** EINs are necessary for all corporations, partnerships and limited liability companies. The number is assigned by the Internal Revenue Service. Even if your business is organized as a sole proprietorship, you'll need an EIN if you want to hire employees, open a solo 401(k) or file for bankruptcy.

▪ **Zoning Permits** Zoning is a tool cities use to govern how buildings are used. Contact your city or town's planning department to make sure your business conforms to local zoning requirements. Some, but not all, home-based businesses can operate in residential neighborhoods, so be sure to check if you're working out of your house.

It can feel like a hassle to go through the hoops of obtaining necessary licenses, but it's often an essential part of doing business.

▪ **"Doing Business As" (DBA) Permit** You'll need to register a DBA with the state if you'll be conducting business by a name other than your state-registered entity name (or, in the case of a sole proprietorship, your own legal name).

▪ **Health Department Permits** If your business serves food, you'll need a permit from the state or local health department, which will require a health inspection.

▪ **Sales Tax License** If your business sells goods or services to retail customers, you'll need to get a sales tax license for, and pay taxes in, each state in which you do business.

▪ **Fire Department Permits** Many places of business, especially those such as bars and restaurants that host groups of people, need a permit from the local fire department, dependent upon their inspection.

▪ **Special State-Issued Licenses** You'll need a state-issued license if your business sells alcohol, lottery tickets, gasoline or firearms, or offers services in state-regulated fields, such as medicine or auto repair.

▪ **Special Federal Licenses** You'll likely need a special license issued by a federal agency if your business involves investment advice, drug manufacturing, meat products, broadcasting, trucking, air transportation, alcohol, tobacco or firearms.

PRO TIP Federal licensing requirements and fees will vary by business activity and issuing agency. Check with agencies for details.

Business Regulations

Operating a business usually requires more than just permits. Legal compliance often includes following state, federal and local regulations.

Your state, county and city may each require you to file for a business license.

These regulations may involve record-keeping, paperwork and taxes.

Record-keeping requirements depend on your business structure. Corporations are expected to hold annual meetings, record minutes, maintain bylaws and track stock transfers. Limited liability companies (LLCs) enjoy less cumbersome record-keeping requirements but must hold on to important documents and maintain a members list. Partnerships and sole proprietorships have few, if any, such requirements.

Filing requirements vary state to state, but businesses may have to submit an annual or biennial statement along with a filing fee, franchise tax and notification of changes, such as address, name or membership. Federal filing requirements are typically limited to federal taxes and, for businesses with 50 or more employees, reporting health coverage information to the IRS. ∎

04 BUSINESS INSURANCE   01 | 02 | 03 | 04 | 05 | 06 | 07 | 08

Protecting Your Business With the Right Insurance
A Solid Plan Minimizes Threats to Your Financial Security

Your business is vulnerable to unforeseen costs. An accident, lawsuit or weather disaster can be enough to make an otherwise successful operation suddenly unsustainable. A good business-insurance plan shields your company from unexpected financial loss.

The risks you face can vary depending on your particular line of business. To choose the right insurance plan, you'll first need to familiarize yourself with the different types of insurance and what they cover.

PRO TIP

If you've expanded your operations or purchased new equipment, talk to your insurance agent to make sure you still have proper coverage.

Legally Required Insurance

Each state sets its own business insurance requirements. Your state's department of insurance or your city offices will be able to tell you exactly what kinds of coverage you need to launch your business. Most commonly, states require at least these three types of insurance:

- **Workers' Compensation Insurance** has two components. It replaces lost income for employees injured at work and provides temporary and permanent disability awards. It can also protect employers against lawsuits.

- **Unemployment Insurance** pays cash benefits to some jobless workers to help tide them over while they look for other work. It's funded by payroll taxes paid to both the state and the federal governments. Companies with larger payrolls or businesses that lay off more workers pay more into the state unemployment trust fund.

- **Workplace Disability Insurance** replaces lost income for employees who can't work due to non-work-related illness, injury or disability, or pregnancy. Policies can provide short-term

Proper insurance can protect your business from losses due to unforeseen events.

The risks you face can vary depending on your line of business.

Workers' comp protects employees injured on the job by replacing part of their income.

- **Product Liability Insurance** is aimed at businesses that are involved in the manufacturing, wholesale, distribution and retail sale of physical goods. It protects your business in the event of a lawsuit over a defective product.

- **Professional Liability Insurance** protects service businesses against financial loss from things like malpractice, error and negligence.

- **Commercial Property Insurance** is useful if your business owns a lot of property, whether it's real estate or physical assets. These policies cover loss of or damage to property from events such as a fire, smoke, hail storms, wind storms, protests and vandalism.

- **Home-Based Business Insurance** is a rider you add to a homeowner's insurance policy to insure equipment and cover third-party injuries for your home-based business.

- **Business Owner's Policies** bundle multiple coverage types into one plan to simplify the buying process and potentially save you money. These policies typically protect against all major property and liability risks.

or long-term coverage. California, Hawaii, New Jersey, New York, Rhode Island and Puerto Rico are the only jurisdictions that require businesses to have short-term disability insurance.

Other Common Types of Insurance

Depending on your business, you may benefit from one of the following types of insurance:

- **General Liability Insurance** covers events, relevant to any business, you may be found legally responsible for, including injuries, property damage, medical expenses, libel, slander, defending lawsuits, settlements and judgments. Some clients may require that you carry general liability insurance before you can work with them.

How to Buy a Policy

Once you've determined the kind of insurance you need to protect your business, look for a reputable licensed insurance agent who understands your industry. For recommendations, consult business colleagues or a trade organization like the National Federation of Independent Business (NFIB).

Once you have an agent, compare the costs and coverage of several plans to find one that suits your business. Once a year, review your plan with your agent and see whether it's still the most appropriate one for your needs. ∎

Paying Taxes as a Small Business
Learn at the Outset How Much Your Company Will Owe to Avoid Surprises Down the Road

I f you've been an employee but never an employer, the ins and outs of business taxation may be a total mystery. Understanding the taxes your company will owe can help you decide how to structure your business. And the more you learn early on, the better prepared you'll be when it comes time to pay. Here's an overview of the taxes you'll pay as a small-business owner.

PRO TIP

Carefully consider taxes when choosing a business structure for your company. The entity you choose will have an impact on how you are taxed.

Federal Income Tax

With few exceptions, small businesses are subject to federal income taxes. The specific tax rate that applies to small businesses varies depending on how they are set up. Some small businesses are established as C corporations, which are taxed at a flat corporate rate of 21%.

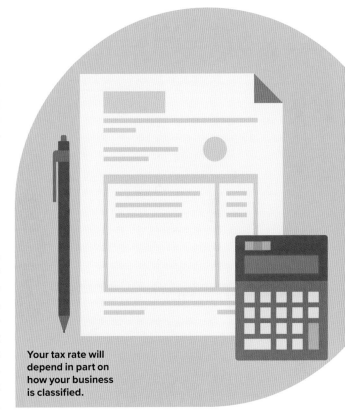

Your tax rate will depend in part on how your business is classified.

Using an experienced tax expert can help you avoid penalties, audits and headaches.

But many small businesses aren't structured as C corps. Instead, they're "pass-through entities," such as a sole proprietorship, a limited liability company (LLC) or an S corporation. And their tax rate is based on the owner's federal income tax bracket. (See "Federal Income Tax Rates" below for 2020 brackets; visit irs.gov for updated information.) So if your business is considered a pass-through entity, the company's federal income tax rate will be the same as your own federal income tax rate.

Employment Tax

If your business is not structured as a corporation, you'll pay self-employment taxes. These taxes help fund your Social Security and Medicare benefits.

If your business is a corporation, the salary you draw will be subject to employment tax. And if you have any employees, you'll also have to pay employment taxes on their salaries or wages. Employment taxes cover Social Security, Medicare, federal unemployment tax and federal income tax withholdings.

FEDERAL INCOME TAX RATES

Tax Rate	Single Filers With Income Over...	Couples Filing Jointly With Income Over...
37%	$518,400	$622,050
35%	$207,350	$414,700
32%	$163,300	$326,600
24%	$85,525	$171,050
22%	$40,125	$80,250
12%	$9,875	$19,750
10%	$0	$0

State and Local Taxes

Aside from federal taxes, your business may also need to pay state and local taxes, which can vary by state, county and city. This category often includes sales tax, commercial property taxes and state income taxes.

PRO TIP

Tax law is known to be complex, so it can help greatly to hire a tax professional who can make sure you're not over- or under-paying taxes.

Estimated Quarterly Payments

While many taxpayers are used to filing a tax return and—if they owe anything—paying a tax bill just once a year, it's important to note that businesses are required to pay taxes throughout the year.

Any small business that expects to owe $1,000 or more in taxes for the year has to make estimated quarterly payments to the IRS. This requirement also applies to freelancers and independent contractors. Failure to pay—or paying too little—can result in penalties. The quarterly due dates are typically April 15, June 15, Sept. 15 and Jan. 15.

Lean on the Experts

Tax law is notoriously complex, but you don't have to navigate the rules on your own. Working with a tax professional can give you the confidence that you're paying the correct amounts on time and adhering to all applicable laws, which can help you avoid a big unexpected tax bill, potential penalties and even an audit. An expert can also advise you on ways to make sure you're not paying more than you should. Look for someone who is either an enrolled agent (EA), a certified public accountant (CPA) or a tax attorney—all of whom have special training in preparing and managing taxes.■

Understanding Profitability
Keep an Eye on the Bottom
Line to Gauge Your Success

Big sales numbers don't necessarily always mean big profits. To grow your business effectively, it's important to understand the difference between revenues and actual profits, or earnings.

Calculating Earnings

Revenues are any funds that you earn through your business, such as sales, subscriptions or rental income. Revenues are also called "top-line" numbers, because they appear at the top of your profit-and-loss statement. This standard business document records your income, expenses and earnings for a specific period of time.

To learn how to calculate your earnings, let's look at an example. Say you've started a gelato-delivery business, and every time you sell some gelato, your business makes $8 in revenue. The more pints you sell, the more revenue you make. But revenue only tells half of your earnings story. Unfortunately, making gelato isn't free. To figure out your profit, you need to subtract your expenses—such as equipment, ingredients and the cost of labor—from your revenue. Whatever you have left is profit.

In general, your expenses will include everyday costs for office supplies, rent or payroll for any staff. They could also include costs directly related to making a product, such as ingredients or parts. Sales, payroll and business income taxes may also be part of the equation, depending on your specific business. The key is to account for all the money that flows out of the business, so that you know how much of your revenue actually sticks with you as a profit.

The Margin Multiplier

Your profit is also known as net earnings or the bottom line, because it's the money your business actually generates (or loses, if your expenses are higher than your revenues). This bottom-line figure is an important gauge of business success, because while your revenues

Determining your profit margin can help you grow a healthy business.

Your net income is calculated as your total revenue earned minus your total expenses or operating costs.

could look very impressive, your net earnings could be low, or even negative, if your expenses are too high.

The relationship between revenues and earnings is known as your profit margin. The higher your margin, the more revenue you retain as earnings. Margins are usually expressed as a percentage, calculated by dividing your earnings by your revenue. Say you have $50,000 in revenues and $40,000 in expenses. Your profit margin is 20% ($10,000 divided by $50,000).

You have two basic levers to increase your margin: raise your revenues or decrease your expenses. Of course, these decisions can have other effects on your business. Customers may be less likely to buy your products at a higher price point, for example. Likewise, cutting expenses could affect the quality of your products.

As you make these decisions, keep an eye on ways to bring more of your top-line revenue through to your bottom-line earnings. Doing so will help you build your business, ensuring you get the most benefit from future revenue increases. ∎

Saving for Retirement When You're an Entrepreneur
Here's How to Choose the Right Plan for You and Your Employees

It's crucial to consider retirement funds when you are running your business.

Starting a small business requires many sacrifices, but saving for retirement shouldn't be one of them. The good news: As an employer, it's up to you to choose the type of retirement plan to use for your business. The best one for you will depend on two key factors: how many employees you plan to have and how aggressively you want to help them save. You'll also need to decide whether contributions will come from your business, employees themselves or both.

Traditional and Roth IRAs

Consider a traditional or Roth IRA if you're flying solo, don't expect to save much and want to keep things simple. A traditional individual retirement account (IRA) allows individuals to contribute earnings up to an annual limit ($6,000 for those under 50 and $7,000 for those 50 and older, in 2020; visit irs.gov for current numbers). Contributions are made with pretax earnings, grow tax-deferred and are taxed as income when you make withdrawals after age 59½. Roth contributions are made with after-tax earnings and the account grows tax-free. Roths are not subject to income tax when you make withdrawals after age 59½, as long as you've had the account for at least five years.

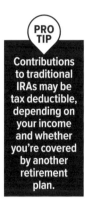

PRO TIP

Contributions to traditional IRAs may be tax deductible, depending on your income and whether you're covered by another retirement plan.

SEP IRAs

A simplified employee pension (SEP) plan is a tax-deferred plan for anyone who owns a business, is self-employed, has employees or is a freelancer. Employers and employees can make contributions to the accounts. These plans work for businesses of all sizes, so they can be a good fit for a business that could grow from one employee to many.

Here's how they work: Employees over the age of 21 who made more than $600 in the previous tax year and have worked for the employer in three of the past five years must be included in the plan. Employers can contribute up to 25% of an employee's compensation or $57,000, whichever figure is less. If you're making self-employed contributions, the same limits apply.

SEP plans are relatively easy to set up and administer. If you earn a lot of money from your business, you can put a lot of money into retirement savings. Remember that the percentage of compensation you decide to contribute applies to all qualified employees—including yourself.

SIMPLE IRAs

Tax-deferred SIMPLE IRA plans allow both employer and employee contributions. Employee contributions were capped at $13,500 in 2020 (go to irs.gov for current numbers). Employers must match contributions in one of the following two ways:

- They must match employee contributions on a dollar-for-dollar basis up to 3% of the employee's annual compensation. Or...

- They must contribute 2% of the employee's compensation up to an annual limit of $285,000 in 2020 (go to irs.gov for current numbers).

Businesses with 100 employees or fewer generally qualify for these plans. A SIMPLE IRA offers more flexibility than SEP plans, but if you are your only employee, the SIMPLE route is probably more complicated than necessary.

Individual 401(k)

For sole proprietors, an individual 401(k) is also an option. These tax-deferred plans are subject to the same overall contribution limits as an SEP IRA, but they also allow both employer and employee contributions. As a result, you may be able to contribute more to an individual 401(k) than you could to a SEP IRA. ∎

> As an employer, it's up to you to choose the type of retirement plan that you want to use for your business.

Managing Employees

Hire, train and retain the right talent

Don't be afraid to bring on employees if you get stretched too thin.

When to Hire More Staff
Consider These Things Before Hanging Up the "Help Wanted" Sign

Bringing on new employees is a big decision. It means extra management time, and it can be expensive. According to the Small Business Administration, the true cost of a new hire can be anywhere from 1.25 to 1.4 times his or her actual salary when you account for unemployment taxes, workers' compensation, recruitment and training. That said, the monetary and other costs of hiring staff are part of the delicate balance between staying profitable and having the capacity to meet customer demand.

Here are some signs that it's time to start taking employment applications:

■ **You Do Too Much Work Yourself** Most small-business owners expect to roll up their sleeves and wear many hats. But if you find yourself stretched thin or bringing work home all the time, it may be a sign that you need more staff. Spending too much of your day performing tasks that another employee could do can take away from your ability to manage the business as a whole and undermine your results.

■ **You Ask Too Much of Existing Employees** The people who work for you want to feel needed, but if you're continually asking them to put in more hours than they've agreed to, or to perform tasks outside of their job description, you probably need more people power. Overtaxing your employees can lead to turnover, which can be costly and disruptive when you have to bring on and train all new staff.

■ **You're Scaling Up** If your sales have been consistently growing over time, you may be ready to do some hiring. A larger staff can help you maintain quality even as the demands on your business grow. Look at your books to determine whether you can realistically afford a new employee. If the potential costs of bringing on someone full time seem prohibitive, consider bringing on a hire part time, or outsourcing certain tasks to freelancers who can work on an as-needed basis. ■

Recruiting and Hiring
Follow This Advice to Help Attract the Most Talented Hires You Can

Small businesses face a unique set of challenges when it comes to recruiting and hiring employees. They lack the visibility and resources of larger companies, particularly when they're just getting started. And finding the right candidate to join your team becomes especially important when it consists of relatively few people.

That's why small businesses should pay special attention to recruiting and hiring. From attracting desirable applicants to identifying the ones who best fit your long-term vision, taking the right steps to find the right employees now could save you a lot of headaches down the line.

Nail the Job Description

A well-thought-out job description can make a huge difference in attracting qualified candidates. Make sure your description is clear, professional and succinct. Job seekers often sift through dozens of descriptions every day, so sloppy wording or extraneous information could keep your listing from attracting attention.

Be as specific as possible when talking about what the job entails and what you expect from applicants. Clear expectations will help attract qualified workers and screen out candidates who don't fit the bill.

Take Advantage of Referrals

People in your extended network can be an excellent resource for recruiting. Now that you've defined the job clearly, ask friends and family if they know anyone who might be a good fit. Fellow business owners can also be a great source of referrals. Connect with them through your local chamber of commerce or networking events.

Referrals can't guarantee perfect hires, however, so it's important to put referred candidates through the same interview and screening process that you'd use for anyone else you're

Finding trusted employees can give your business a boost.

considering for the position. But making use of the connections of people in your community can be an efficient, inexpensive and effective way of finding new employees—especially for new business owners.

Use Online Job Postings Effectively

These days, most job searches are done online. Familiarize yourself with the many job-posting websites that are out there so you can decide which ones best suit your needs and find job seekers where they are posting their skills.

The biggest and most successful job-posting sites—including Monster, Indeed, LinkedIn and CareerBuilder—are a good place to start. For new businesses, however, it can be hard to stand out on sites like these. Niche job sites that target specific kinds of workers—whether industry-specific or a particular demographic, like recent college graduates—can help you focus your search.

Harness Social Media

Social media can help you spread the word that you're looking for people to join your team. LinkedIn, Twitter, Facebook and other platforms play a crucial role in the job-search ecosystem. Postings on these sites can help you find active job seekers, and reach people who are searching passively or whose friends or acquaintances are looking for jobs. Plus, social media platforms are great places to build your brand and establish a presence in your community.

As you get your business off the ground, establishing a positive reputation will become a powerful recruitment tool, helping you find passionate employees who share your values and are eager to help contribute to the success of your business. Before long, job seekers may even come to you before you go looking for them! ∎

PRO TIP

The more clearly you define what you're looking for in an applicant, the easier it will be to attract the right person for that particular opportunity.

Management and Retention
Learn How to Hang on to
Top-Performing Employees

Now that you've hired a team of workers, it's key that you also make sure they stick around. Employee turnover can be costly—replacing someone can be one-half to two times that employee's annual salary—and can lead to low morale or instability in the workplace. One of the best ways to retain employees is to keep them productive and engaged. Effective management benefits your business by maintaining morale, boosting performance and lowering the turnover rate. It also saves you the time and money you would otherwise spend constantly searching for new hires.

Here are five tips for successfully managing your existing team of employees so you can keep your retention rate high.

Communicate Well—and Often

Clear communication between employees and managers keeps everyone on the same page.

This effort starts with articulating your business' mission. What purpose do you see your venture serving in your community and in the world at large? Communicate this purpose regularly to your employees, so they understand how their day-to-day tasks are contributing to the organization's bigger goals.

It's also crucial to clearly convey your expectations to employees. Many small businesses ask their workers to perform a wide range of tasks, and it's not always clear which responsibilities fall to which employee. Confusion on this point can lead to frustration, which lowers morale and can hurt productivity over time.

Finally, try to create an environment in which all of the members of your team feel comfortable asking questions and sharing their ideas. Consider establishing an ongoing daily or weekly meeting in which you discuss your short-term goals and ask your employees for their input on your plans.

To keep employees engaged, offer them opportunities for career development.

A fun work atmosphere can help keep employee morale high.

are a chance for you to convey expectations and make sure your employees are on track. But they're also a chance for you to listen to feedback about what's working and what's not for your employees. Constructive criticism is less likely to get buried beneath everyday routines when you've created a formal space in which to share it.

Offer Financial Rewards

Money is a big motivator. Consider offering stock options, profit sharing or other financial rewards for your star employees. Annual bonuses and significant raises also go a long way toward keeping employees around. And if an employee comes to you and asks for a raise, do your best to meet their demand (assuming they're contributing to the business on a high level).

Provide Competitive Benefits and Perks

A competitive benefits package can be the difference between an employee sticking around or leaving. Many employees expect to have access to health insurance, retirement plans, paid time off and other benefits. Companies that want to get ahead of expectations might offer less-common perks like tuition reimbursement, parental leave and flexible scheduling. Smaller perks—like gym memberships and a well-supplied office refrigerator—can also keep employees happy.

Focus on Employee Development

No one wants to feel like they're stuck in their jobs. Give employees a chance to learn, perform new tasks and advance to higher positions within your business.

Employee development can take many forms. Train workers to learn a new skill, ask managers to coach new employees, or reimburse employees who further their education by taking classes related to their job. And when you're looking to fill a high-level position, give current employees the first chance. If you've taken time to help them learn, they'll likely be the most qualified anyway.

Conduct Regular Performance Reviews

Hold yourself and your employees accountable by conducting regular performance reviews—one every few months is standard. These meetings

People often switch jobs for reasons that have little or nothing to do with company culture, and no policy can ensure that your employees will work for you for as long as you'd like. But strategies like these can help you retain the employees who are the heart and soul of your business. ■

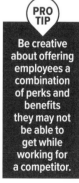

PRO TIP

Be creative about offering employees a combination of perks and benefits they may not be able to get while working for a competitor.

Employee Benefits
Here's What You Must Offer Your Employees, and What Is Optional

Attracting and retaining great employees can be crucial to business success. Offering employee benefits can be a way to make sure top talent is excited to work with you and will stick around. You'll have to offer some employee benefits as required by federal law, but you also can consider offering other optional benefits at your discretion.

Required Employee Benefits

Federal laws require all business owners to offer certain benefits to their employees.

▪ **Workers' Compensation** If an employee is injured on the job, workers' compensation pays their medical and rehabilitation bills, as well as disability or death benefits (meaning continued salary to the employee or survivors). In almost every state, workers' compensation policies are written by private companies—so you can shop around, just as you would for car insurance.

▪ **Unemployment Benefits** You're required to fund both federal and state unemployment coffers through payroll contributions. Currently, the federal rate is 6% of the first $7,000 each employee earns; state contributions are in addition to that, and can vary widely.

Optional Employee Benefits

These may be one of your best tools to differentiate yourself from competitors and attract the best talent.

▪ **Vacation Time** About three-quarters of private industry workers receive some form of paid vacation, and offering this benefit can help you stay competitive and boost morale. Decide which holidays your employees will have off and how many extra days a year are available to them for

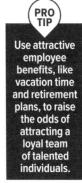

PRO TIP

Use attractive employee benefits, like vacation time and retirement plans, to raise the odds of attracting a loyal team of talented individuals.

Offering paid vacation time can be a good way to reward long-term employees.

vacation. Many companies will increase the number of vacation days that they offer the longer an employee works for them, as an incentive to keep the employee with the company over the long term.

▪ **Paid Time Off (PTO)** combines vacation time, sick time and personal days into one pool of time employees can draw on at their discretion.

▪ **Flexible Scheduling and Work-From-Home**
Flexible scheduling allows employees to vary the times they start or finish work to accommodate things like child care or a spouse's work schedule. Whether you can offer flexible scheduling will largely depend on employees' responsibilities and how dependent other workers or customers are on their presence. For example, customer-facing positions may present fewer

times and give them more control over their scheduling. Employees may also be more productive and less likely to leave their jobs for something that might be closer to their home. Employers can benefit, too: They can save on office space and can consider looking outside of their geographical region when hiring workers.

▪ **Health Insurance** With health insurance costs (as well as the related cost of long-term disability insurance) skyrocketing, many small businesses have decided they just can't afford to offer it. Still, it's worth consulting with a local insurance agent about some affordable options. Generally, the monthly premium is split between you and the employee—in both cases tax-free—and the rate will be based on your location, the deductible, the provider network and the size of your staff. You can split the monthly premium however you like. You could pay the whole amount, or none, or any combination in between. Keep in mind that whichever option you choose will also apply to your own health insurance, if you elect to receive it through your business.

One key caveat: If you offer health insurance, an employee who chooses to opt out and instead sign up for insurance under the Affordable Care Act will probably not qualify for the federal health care subsidy. In many cases it makes more sense to let employees get government subsidized insurance. While you can't directly pay for an employee's premium in this case, you can certainly increase their (taxable) salary to offset some of the cost.

options for flexible scheduling than positions that require office workers to spend much of their day at a computer.

Some employees may not need to come into the office every day, or at all, as many businesses learned pretty quickly during the coronavirus pandemic. Offering work-from-home options can help employees cut back on their commute

▪ **Retirement Savings Plans** The retirement plans that are available to small businesses include SIMPLE and SEP IRAs, both of which let workers stash pretax savings into investment accounts, with some or all of the contributions coming from you. ▪

CHAPTER 06

Optimizing Operations

Learn what you need to know to
keep your business running smoothly

06 | **SETTING GOALS** | 01 | 02 | 03 | 04 | 05 | 06 | 07 | 08 | 09

Setting Clear Goals
Ensure Your Startup's Success by Using the SMART Method

Clear objectives are an important part of optimizing your small-business operations. They keep you moving forward and give your business focus and direction.

One strategy for goal-setting goes by the acronym SMART, which stands for:

Specific
Measurable
Achievable
Relevant
Time-based

Run through the SMART checklist as you set your business objectives to determine whether a particular goal is clearly defined and fits your business model.

Here's how to use the SMART method to set and evaluate goals for your small business.

■ **Set Clear-Cut Targets** If you're struggling to set goals, try working backward. Think about the big picture, and then get specific about the detailed steps you'll need to take to get there. For example, say you want to improve your business' digital presence. That statement alone is too vague to be useful. To reach your goal, you'll need to go a step further and identify specifically what you mean—perhaps creating a Facebook page for your business, or updating your website.

■ **Measure Your Progress** Setting a measurable goal includes making a plan with milestones, so you can see if you're moving in the right direction. For example: If you want to build your customer base, identify exactly how many new clients you'd like to gain over the next two months. At the end of this period, compare your goal with your actual results.

■ **Make Them Achievable** There's little sense in setting a goal that you know you won't be able

Having a specific action plan to help you reach your goals will keep you on track for success.

to meet—or one that isn't connected to your business' purpose. Choose actions that you can accomplish given your particular constraints, whether they're time, skills and/or resources. Or even better, identify which of those gaps you can fill to help you work toward your objective more efficiently.

▪ **Focus on Relevance** This means they should align with your broader values and other business goals. If you're thinking about implementing a program or service and it doesn't contribute to your long-term objectives, you may want to rethink your plan.

▪ **Create a Time Frame** Open-ended goals leave you with no sense of urgency. Developing a time frame for each step helps you prioritize, making it easier to see exactly what you need to do, and when. Each desired result should be accompanied by an action and a set date. Regularly check in on your goals and time-frame plan to see what you've accomplished and determine what steps you need to take next.

▪ **Celebrate Your Successes** Marking milestones in a fun way can encourage you to stay on track even when you hit some of those inevitable bumps in the road. ▪

Managing Cash Flow and Creating a Budget They're Both Essential to Keeping Your Business Running Smoothly

No matter your product or service, running a small business costs money. And to keep operating—and ultimately survive—your company needs cash.

Keeping a close eye on your cash flow is critical to success: Research has found that cash-flow problems are the leading cause of failure in small businesses that fold within their first five years.

Understanding cash flow and carefully managing it can help you steer clear of the financial challenges that have often proved ruinous for some small businesses. Once you have a clear picture of your cash flow, you'll be better able to determine your budget, including what you can afford and where you need to cut back.

Positive vs. Negative Cash Flow

Cash flow refers to the money flowing in and out of your business. The cash coming in likely stems from sales and accounts receivable. And the cash your business spends may be going to pay your vendors and employees, and to cover ongoing overhead expenses like rent, utilities and supplies.

Cash flow can be either positive or negative. You have positive cash flow when the funds that are coming in are greater than the cash going out. Negative cash flow occurs when the cash leaving the business amounts to more than what's coming in.

It's important to note that profit and cash flow are different, so tracking only your profit-and-loss statements won't be enough to keep you in a positive cash flow. While your profit-and-loss statement accounts for revenue minus expenses, that figure doesn't necessarily reflect the cash you actually have on hand. So, while you may have billed for products or services sold, if you haven't collected the money, your cash flow could still be negative.

Cash coming into your business usually comes from sales and accounts receivable.

115

Tracking Cash-Flow Statements

A cash-flow statement is a tally of cash collected and spent during a particular period of time. For example, if you create a monthly cash-flow statement, it will show a total of the money coming in, and another total for the cash outflow during the month you're tracking. Subtract expenditures from inflows to calculate your net cash flow, which may be positive or negative.

You can track your company's cash flow by regularly taking a careful look at your cash-flow statements. These give you a snapshot of your business' cash accounts. Reviewing them periodically helps you see where you may run into potential problems. For instance, you might notice clients who pay late, an increase in expenses or seasonal decreases in revenue.

It's a good idea to make a quarterly and annual review of cash-flow statements at a minimum, but you may also want to take a look on a weekly or monthly basis. These more frequent reviews may alert you to some immediate issues, while the quarterly and yearly check-ins allow you to see the big picture and look for patterns that you can plan for in the future. For example, you may find that January and February are slower months for sales. That knowledge allows you to better prepare for next year, building up your cash reserves to last through those lighter months.

PRO TIP

Use your cash-flow statement as the foundation for your budget to keep your expenses from growing larger than your business can afford.

Building a Budget

Once you start tracking your cash flow, you'll have a solid understanding of how much it actually costs to run your business and how much revenue you can expect to generate. You can use that data to build an annual budget.

A variety of cash-flow management tools can help you keep track of your finances.

A budget is an essential tool that will keep your company's spending on track and prevent overspending that would hurt your cash flow and put your business at risk.

When you create a budget, start with an annual goal for revenue and profits. Looking at cash-flow statements from the previous year or several months can help you develop these targets. Then, determine your operating costs: List all of your known expenses, including salaries and wages, rent, utilities, insurance, materials, supplies, marketing and travel. If you don't have a year's worth of data to draw from, you can make your best estimate for these figures and readjust throughout the year.

After you have an itemized list of your projected revenues and expenses, create a monthly budget that accounts for your fixed expenses as well as seasonal fluctuations and variable expenses. For example, perhaps you know your spending will increase in March, when you're gearing up for the summer rush, and you know revenues will be up during that season, when you're moving lots of product.

Next, compare your expenses to revenues, and look at your cash-flow projections to see whether you need to make changes. If your expenses outweigh your revenues or leave profit margins too narrow, you may need to reevaluate your spending and look for ways to make cuts. For example, you might put off upgrading your

Take regular snapshots of your cash accounts to head off potential issues.

office equipment, or shop around for lower-cost vendors to bring down your spending.

Analyzing Your Budget

Setting a budget is a useful exercise that helps you see exactly how much money your business needs to bring in and the spending limits you need to maintain to keep hitting your target revenue and profits. Returning to that document routinely and doing a budget analysis is key to staying on track—and making necessary changes as your business grows.

You can perform a budget analysis by comparing your cash-flow statements to your budget on a regular basis. Look for areas where your business is overspending and consider where you can cut back, or whether you need to increase your budget for a particular expense.

You may find that you're maintaining a positive cash flow and profits are growing. In that case, there may be room in your budget to reinvest in your business and help it grow—perhaps you can afford to travel to an industry conference, or you could add another employee to your payroll to help increase sales.

Understanding cash flow can help you develop a budget that keeps your revenue and profit goals on track. Revisit these numbers often to stay on top of your company's finances, and address issues before they become serious problems. ∎

06 | **WORKING WITH VENDORS** | 01 | 02 | 03 | 04 | 05 | 06 | 07 | 08 | 09

Working With Vendors
Cultivate Good Relationships
With Your Suppliers

Vendors are companies and individuals from whom you buy the things you need to run your business. If you're a retailer, your vendors would include the wholesalers that make or distribute the products you sell. They also include companies that provide your office supplies, and services like bookkeeping and trash collection. All businesses must interact with vendors, and your relationships with them will be a key factor in your success.

Finding Vendors

If you're buying an existing business, the seller probably has vendor relationships they can pass along. Make it a part of your purchase agreement that the seller will provide their vendor contacts—and write letters of introduction.

Finding new vendors requires some research. To source local service providers, start by asking other businesses in your area for references. But don't assume the best bookkeeper lives in your neighborhood. A recent trend has been cloud-based payroll and accounting services, such as Gusto or Zenefits.

If you're a retailer, in most states you'll need to collect sales tax. The first stop should be your bookkeeper, who may recommend hiring a tax-collection service like Avalara or TaxJar.

For products you want to buy for resale or use in your office, search online for the distributor or manufacturer. Most companies selling to businesses will have a section of their website devoted to business-to-business accounts. On that page, you'll be walked through the steps necessary to set up an account.

Vetting Vendors

Before committing to a vendor, do some background research. Start by checking them

Some vendors literally provide the ingredients you need to run your business.

For retailers, vendor relationships are the key to timely restocking.

■ Contacts for several current vendors who can confirm that you pay your bills on time.

■ Your employer identification number (EIN).

■ Your sales tax ID (if you're a retailer), so you don't pay tax on wholesale purchases.

■ The person at your business who pays the bills.

How to Pay Vendors

Most vendors will make new account holders without references prepay with a check or credit card. Once you're established, you should be able to get better terms. The most common arrangement is called net 30, which means you must pay the bill within 30 days of shipping (in the case of merchandise) or services rendered. Since retailers typically sell their products at twice what they've paid wholesale (so-called keystone pricing), they aim to sell half the merchandise they've purchased within 30 days—that way, the wholesale bill is paid for when it comes due. Most vendors accept payment by check, ACH (automated clearing house) or bank wire, but some take credit cards.

out on the Better Business Bureau website at bbb.org, which can help you see complaints that have been filed against them and verify their licenses and insurance policies. Ask for references from your top-choice vendors whom you can call and interview about their experience. When you can, take your vendor for a test drive: Ask if a trial period is possible before making any long-term commitments.

Establishing Vendor Accounts

Vendors typically vet the businesses they work with. They'll ask for a credit reference sheet, which should generally list:

■ Your bank account information and a name and contact at your bank.

Don't Forget Shipping Costs

Many businesses overlook the cost of inbound freight, which is what you pay to have vendors deliver products to you. However, since you are paying the bill, vendors have little incentive to shop around on postal rates. Ask if they'll ship using your own delivery service accounts, which you can monitor for the best price. Remember: Distance makes a difference, in price and time. ■

PRO TIP

Once you've established a relationship with your vendors, ask about making an arrangement so you don't have to pay up front.

Real Estate: Should You Lease or Buy? Both Arrangements Have Advantages

The decision to buy or lease comes down to the specific needs of your business and what spaces are available. Here are some things to consider when weighing the choices.

Comparing Available Spaces

You can't decide whether to lease or buy without weighing both the strengths of the specific properties you're considering and your finances. If you'd prefer to own but can't find a space for sale in your ideal location, leasing may end up being the wiser choice. Likewise, if your hunt for a property for lease has only turned up spaces with unsuitable layouts, you might want to consider expanding your search to include properties for sale as well.

You may find that high real estate prices make buying infeasible. But in some real estate markets, the cost of ownership may be much less than monthly rent, especially if there is ongoing financial uncertainty.

Calculate what option works best for your business.

Advantages of Buying

▪ **No Landlord** When you buy, you'll never be surprised by a rent hike, and you won't risk leasing from a negligent landlord or one whose interests don't quite align with yours.

121

Buying real estate means you'll be in charge of renovations and repairs.

- **Stability** If you need to permanently install machinery or make major modifications to the space, you don't want to be forced to relocate and uproot your setup when a lease expires or the building changes hands.

- **Equity** As you pay off your mortgage, you'll build your own equity. Later, you can use that as collateral for a loan, and eventually, you can sell the property if you like. It may even have grown in value in the interim.

- **A Second Income Stream** If your business occupies only part of the building, you may be able to lease out the rest of it.

Advantages of Leasing

- **Flexibility** If you outgrow your space, leasing offers you the freedom to leave your current location for another place that fits your needs better.

- **Protection** If property values drop, leasing can keep you from ending up underwater on a mortgage. And if an economic downturn forces you to close your business, you won't need to find a buyer during a recession.

- **Fewer Responsibilities** When you lease, you don't deal directly with things like property taxes, maintenance and certain insurance requirements. That frees up more time to focus on your business.

Like many business decisions, figuring out whether to buy or lease is about weighing trade-offs. You can only know what's right for you if you understand your business needs and compare specific spaces and terms. ∎

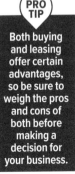

PRO TIP

Both buying and leasing offer certain advantages, so be sure to weigh the pros and cons of both before making a decision for your business.

For small-business owners, dealing with legal issues is a fact of life.

Even a few hours spent with an experienced lawyer can prevent costly problems.

Legal Steps When Starting a Business
Knowing How to Navigate Contracts, Trademarks and Other Documents Is Key

For many of us, hiring a lawyer means gearing up for a legal fight. But for small-business owners, dealing with legal issues is a fact of life. The good news is that these issues are typically pretty minor—like deciding how to incorporate the business or creating employment contracts.

As you launch your venture, find a lawyer who specializes in working with entrepreneurs and small businesses. And if you're focused on a specific industry niche, look for lawyers with experience serving businesses like yours. Fortunately, just about every community has lawyers experienced in those tasks. A few hours of their time helping you dot your i's and cross your t's can save you a lot of hassle and help prevent potentially costly problems down the road.

Contracts and Hiring Agreements
Contracts are legally binding documents that spell out an employee's job title, responsibilities, benefits, salary and bonuses, and other important details of employment.

Contracts tend to be more comprehensive than hiring agreements. They might specify how much work a person is required to do, how they will be compensated and the length of the employment term—which means you could be obligated to continue paying that person even if you fire them. If you're just starting out with a few employees, you probably won't need detailed contracts.

Though a formal contract may not always be necessary, you'll definitely want all your employees to sign hiring agreements. These will state the employee's job title and salary, as well as the understanding that the person is an employee at-will, meaning

PRO TIP

Ask friends, colleagues and even vendors to recommend local small-business lawyers. This is one search for which Google isn't your best bet.

they can be fired for any reason—except for illegal reasons, like discrimination.

A lawyer can help you know for sure if you need contracts or hiring agreements, as well as help you write the actual terms.

Noncompete Clauses

Few things are more frustrating than watching a former employee you've trained and mentored open a copycat business—and steal your customers. A noncompete clause (NCC) can be included in a contract or hiring agreement, or drawn up separately to guard against this practice. But be careful: There are limits.

Laws vary by state but generally speaking, you can't prevent a wage earner—such as a shipping clerk or a waitress—from taking a similar job at a competitor. People generally have the right to job-hop in search of better pay. Some states have even stricter limits. In California, all noncompete clauses are illegal and unenforceable except for business partners, though the state does have laws protecting trade secrets.

You may well encounter an NCC if you sell your business and are thinking about opening a new, similar business. Say you own a beauty salon with a loyal customer base: The new owner of your business might reasonably prevent you from opening a salon within a 25-mile radius for a few years, while they get established.

Nondisclosure Agreements

Some of your employees might have sensitive information about your business. That could include detailed financial data (payroll, profits and losses) but also trade secrets like special recipes, or the code for software you invented. Any employee familiar with such proprietary information should be asked to sign a nondisclosure agreement (NDA).

You also may be asked to sign an NDA by a client or partner who wants to protect sensitive financial or operational information. Consider running these agreements by your lawyer before you sign them, to make sure they're not overly broad or otherwise problematic.

Trademarks

You don't need to be told that the name of your business is important; it's how customers will find you. The same is true of the names of any products you might be creating and selling. To prevent other companies from stealing your intellectual property, you need to trademark those names and ideas, which means registering them (and any logos) with the United States Patent and Trademark Office.

Many lawyers specialize in trademark registration. For instance, they'll search through databases and determine if other companies in your field have already registered your name. This step is important to prevent you from getting slapped with a trademark infringement suit. Don't assume that just because you have a small business you can get away with using a well-known name. Even if your actual name is Nordstrom, you can't legally open a clothing store called Nordstrom.

PRO TIP

A professional human resources consultant can often help write up your policies and procedures as well as your employee handbook.

Employee Handbooks

If you have more than two or three workers, this is essential. A typical one spells out company policies related to workplace safety, absenteeism, sick days and even

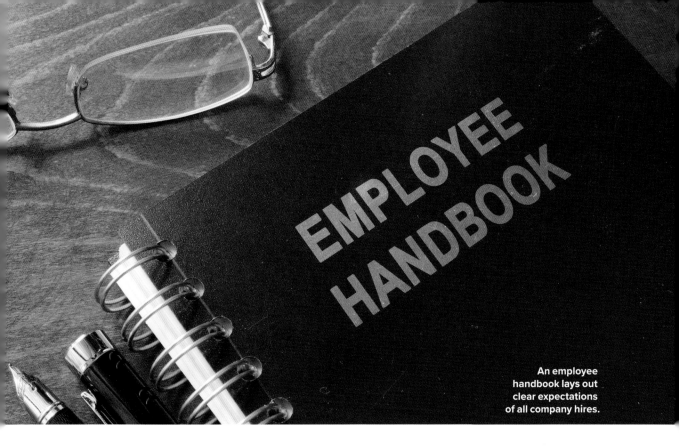

An employee handbook lays out clear expectations of all company hires.

dress code. It should lay out the process for disciplinary actions and performance reviews. If employees work online, you may want to create policies around personal computer use on the job, such as scrolling through Facebook. If workers can't come in due to bad weather, are they expected to work from home? On-the-job harassment—including sexual, physical and verbal—should be clearly forbidden in writing.

A good handbook is also the place to introduce new employees to your company's history, culture and values, which will help them feel like part of a dedicated team. It should also list your responsibilities, including federal and state nondiscrimination laws, and the federal law that forbids retaliating against whistleblowers.

It might seem overly cautious, but having all your policies in writing can protect you from lawsuits. You may not have to hire a lawyer to draw up your handbook—often, you can outsource

Though a formal contract may not be necessary for everyone, you'll definitely want all of your employees to sign hiring agreements.

that job inexpensively to a professional human resources consultant who specializes in guiding small businesses through the development of workplace policies and procedures.

By working with a lawyer and making sure you have the right documents in place from the beginning, you can be sure that you're getting your business off on the right foot and giving yourself as much legal protection as possible. ∎

127

It's important to know how you'll respond to a disaster before it strikes.

Create a Disaster Strategy for Your Small Business
Smart Planning Can Decrease Your Risk and Mitigate Damage

Natural disasters, global pandemics or even malicious computer viruses can have dire and costly effects on your daily business. However, by maintaining proper preparation and smart policies, you can minimize the potential impact of these disasters on your operations.

Here are tips to prepare your business for the unexpected—and what to do if disaster strikes.

Conduct a Risk Assessment

Prioritize protection efforts by zeroing in on the risks most relevant to your business. Identify and analyze specific hazards you are most at risk for. For example, coastal businesses may be particularly vulnerable to flooding from hurricanes, while a jewelry store's biggest concern may be theft.

As you identify your biggest risks, look for vulnerabilities that could make your business more susceptible to damage. If cyberfraud is a concern, check when your company's cybersecurity measures were last updated. And if your business is located in an earthquake-prone area, have your building inspected to check for any construction issues that should be fixed.

The Small Business Administration (SBA) provides preparedness checklists on—and safety tips for—specific hazards, such as fires, floods and earthquakes. You can find these on the SBA website at sba.gov.

Write an Action Plan

Once you've identified the biggest risks, write a detailed action plan for each one. For instance, say you're creating a plan in case of a fire: Start by planning evacuation routes to keep all of your

employees safe. Next, consider how to mitigate potential damage to property and buildings. For example, are there pieces of equipment or records that need to be moved when disaster threatens? Who is in charge of carrying out these tasks and when exactly should they do them?

Create a communications strategy for notifying employees in the case of an emergency. This should also include a plan for how to communicate with customers, including steps your business is taking to keep them updated and to address their needs. Maintain an updated list of emergency contact information for employees, vendors, suppliers and other key stakeholders, and identify who will be responsible for contacting these individuals before, during or after an emergency.

Be sure to back up your important records in the cloud or off-site.

Follow the Scout motto and "Be Prepared," as disasters can take on many different forms.

an off-site location so you'll always have access to them. The Internal Revenue Service (IRS) offers an online guide to protecting your information from a disaster at irs.gov/businesses.

Review Insurance Policies

You probably already have a commercial insurance policy that covers such things as damage to your business equipment or real estate. But you may want coverage that targets specific risks that may not be covered by your regular insurance. For example, flood coverage typically is not included in commercial property insurance policies. You might also consider business-interruption insurance, which covers lost income if your business is forced to shut down temporarily.

Identify Resources for Disaster Recovery

As part of your disaster action plan, identify resources that can provide aid and financial assistance if you need them after a disaster has occurred. The Federal Emergency Management Agency (FEMA) offers financial assistance to individuals who are affected by natural disasters, including money for housing and personal expenses like food, clothing and medicine. The SBA provides low-interest loans to businesses for damaged or destroyed assets and property.

A disaster plan is something you hopefully will never have to use—but you'll be glad to have it if the unthinkable happens. ■

Back Up Vital Records

Customer records, financial ledgers and bank statements are just some of the critical documents your company may rely on day in and day out. Make sure you have a plan to protect these records in case of a disaster. If you're reliant on paper documents, consider digitizing them. And if your records are digital, make sure they're backed up and stored in the cloud or at

Buying vs. Leasing Goods Weigh the Pros and Cons of Acquiring Business Equipment

From computers and cash registers to printers and sophisticated manufacturing tools, you probably need some type of equipment to run your business. And in many cases that equipment can be costly. For a new business with a small budget, finding the money to purchase critical equipment outright can be challenging. Leasing what you need can provide a more cost-effective alternative in some cases. But the final decision on whether to lease or buy can depend on these considerations:

Short-Term vs. Long-Term Costs

Leasing almost always costs less up front than buying. In many cases, you won't have to make any down payment at all—just start making lease payments and using the equipment. However, when you add up the cost of your lease payments over the entire term of the lease, you're likely to end up paying more than you would if you purchased the equipment outright. And at the

end of the lease, you still won't own the equipment, so you can't sell it to recoup some of the purchase price, as you could if you bought it.

With equipment that becomes obsolete relatively quickly, like computers, you may end up having to upgrade certain things regularly anyway. In that case, leasing could be a better bet, since you can simply move on to another lease when it's time to upgrade. On the other hand, you might be better off buying a piece of equipment with a long expected life span, since you'll likely be able to use it an extended period after you've paid it off.

Tax Breaks

Most of the time, lease payments for business equipment are deductible business expenses, so they provide a net reduction in your tax burden. You can also deduct the cost of equipment you purchase. And since the purchase price is usually much higher than a lease payment, the tax

In some cases, leasing business equipment can be a smart alternative to buying.

break is also larger. In 2020, a business could deduct up to $2.5 million of qualified business equipment in the first year of ownership. (Visit irs.gov for current numbers.)

How to Decide

To determine whether leasing or buying is right for your business, ask yourself these questions:

▪ Can I afford this purchase with cash on hand, or will I need a loan? If you decide to finance your purchase, compare the total cost of the loan, including interest payments, with the total cost of the lease.

▪ How long do I expect it to last? If you think you will need to upgrade your equipment relatively frequently, leasing might make more business sense. If, however, the equipment is very durable and will last several years, buying might be a better idea in the long run.

▪ What will I do when I'm done using the equipment? Owning equipment means you can potentially recoup some of its cost by selling it when you're done with it or want to upgrade. If you're leasing and finish using the equipment before the lease runs out, you may get stuck making continued payments on equipment you no longer need. ▪

Managing Inventory
Tracking Your Sales Can Help You Plan Ahead and Stay Efficient

You make money when your customers buy your products. In an ideal world, you'd have enough stock on hand to sell to every customer who comes through the door ready to buy. By the same token, you don't want to store a bunch of products your customers don't want to purchase. At best, unsold inventory wastes space you could be using to stock more popular items. At worst, it could become obsolete or unusable, generating losses for your business.

> **PRO TIP**
> Your inventory-management system doesn't just tell you what you have on hand. It also allows you to track sales trends and become more efficient.

An inventory-management system can help you figure out how to keep the right amount of products on your shelves at the right time. The better you manage your inventory, the less money you sink into unsold goods, and the larger your profits.

Inventory-Management Basics

It's almost impossible to manage your inventory through guesswork—you need data. At its most basic, an inventory-management system allows you to know:

- What goods you currently have on order or in production

- What goods you currently have in stock

- What products you've sold in the past

- How many units of each product you've sold

- When those sales took place—by week, month or even season

Tracking your sales information over time can help you identify and predict supply-and-demand trends. For example, you may find your customers buy certain items in higher quantity at certain times of the year. In that case, you'll

A well-kept inventory will make sure key supplies are replenished on time.

Hard data helps you stay on top of shifting supply trends.

Tracking Tools

While it's possible to manage inventory with a pencil and paper, most businesses opt for some form of software. Depending on your industry and the goods you sell, the best fit may range from a relatively simple system that provides real-time inventory and basic sales forecasting to a sophisticated system that tracks your manufacturing process from raw materials to finished goods.

Systems with more features likely cost more—but more isn't always better. Before you pay extra for sophisticated features, make sure they actually match your business needs. For example, if you run a single store, you probably won't need the ability to track inventory across multiple distribution centers and business locations.

Many inventory-management systems offer a free trial period. It can be a good idea to try out multiple software packages until you find one that integrates with your existing systems and that you find easy to access and use.

want to make sure you have more of those products on hand when customers want them.

Knowing what you have in stock at all times allows you to keep track of products that sell especially well, so you can be sure to replenish your supply before you run out. If you find some products don't sell well, you can reduce your inventory—perhaps by putting those items on sale, ordering fewer of them next time or discontinuing carrying them altogether.

You can also use your sales information to keep track of customer preferences over time. Keeping close tabs on inventory trends can warn you if items aren't moving quickly. The faster you respond, the more resources you'll have to put into building inventory of more popular items.

At a minimum, the software you choose should alert you when your product supply runs too low or too high. It should also provide reports that help you track and forecast demand. And as you build sales data over time, your inventory-management system should become more accurate, making your business more efficient. ∎

Before you pay extra for sophisticated features, make sure they actually match your business needs.

Deciding How Much to Charge
The Right Price Can Help Drive Both Sales and Profits

Once you've figured out what services you want to provide or what you want to sell, you need to decide how much to charge your customers. This decision is important because it largely determines how much money you'll make on each sale. It's also a complicated decision, because the price you charge affects how customers perceive the value of your product compared to the competition, as well as the quantity you're likely to sell.

Striking the Right Balance

The best price for your goods and services depends on a combination of factors: your cost to acquire or produce your goods or services, what your customers are willing to pay and how your product fits in the marketplace.

Getting your pricing right can be a delicate balancing act. If you set your price toward the low end of the market, you may be able to sell in greater volume. But if your prices are lower than that of your competitors who offer similar products or services, your customers may be somewhat suspicious of your pricing—or assume that your offering is inferior.

A price toward the high end of what customers are willing to pay will make the most profit per unit. But customers may be unwilling to pay a premium for your products, especially if they can get similar quality at a lower price from a competitor.

Surveying the Playing Field

Before you can decide on a strategy for pricing, it's important to do some market research. Take a look at what people are already willing to pay for similar products and

PRO TIP

Surveying potential customers can be an excellent way to discover the low and high limits of what you can charge for your goods or services.

services on the market. Also consider the type of customers that your competitors currently target. Decide whether you want to market to the same cohort and price your goods and services accordingly, or if you'd rather sell to a different group, perhaps one that is looking for additional value or quality at a higher price point. Consider surveying potential customers in advance of opening your doors to get a sense for the low and high limits of what you could charge, as well as how likely those customers might be to switch to your product at either a lower or higher price point.

Common Pricing Strategies

Once you understand the market and have an idea of where your products or services may fit in it, you can use that information to set prices for your business. Marketers have developed a variety of pricing strategies that can be useful for maximizing profits. Here are a few different approaches that have tended to work well for small businesses:

- **Penetration Pricing** If you feel confident that your offerings will outshine the competition, you might temporarily price your product toward the low end of the market to attract some initial attention. Then, once your customers understand the value and quality that you offer, you can gradually raise your prices back up.

- **Competitive Pricing** Choose a price for your product or service that is close to that of your competitors. Note that when you are using this strategy, you'll need to attract customers with other marketing efforts, such as advertising campaigns or promotions.

- **Skimming** If your product is unique in the marketplace, you can set your price toward

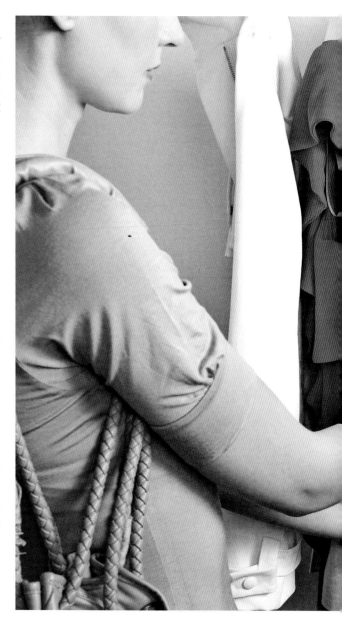

the high end of what you believe the market will bear. Just be prepared to lower your prices as your competitors catch up, or if your production costs fall in the future and you want to expand your customer base.

Charging too little for merchandise may backfire if customers assume it's poor quality.

■ **Cost-Plus Pricing** Take what it costs to produce your product and add your target profit on top of that. Just be careful not to set your price too high, or you're likely to have difficulty luring customers away from the competition.

■ **Bundled Pricing** Sometimes it's worth selling certain goods or services together at a discount. This can be a good way to introduce customers to the quality and value of your offerings without having to compete head-to-head on price. ■

139

Marketing

Develop your brand so you can
target your ideal customer

Maintaining a social media presence can be a powerful tool for marketing your business.

Building Your Business' Identity
Now That You Have an Idea for Your Startup, It's Time to Showcase What Sets It Apart

When you hear the word "brand," you probably picture recognizable companies and their trademarks—Nike's swoosh, Starbucks' mermaid or the golden arches of McDonald's, to name a few. But a brand goes beyond these tangible symbols to the heart of a company's identity—it's how we understand its values and know what to expect from it. Developing your brand involves figuring out how you'll convey what's special about your business to potential customers.

How to Get Started

Before you can start building your brand, you need to know what separates your business from the competition. That way, you can identify that to customers in the marketplace. There are many ways that your venture might distinguish itself. Here are some common ones:

▪ **Price Point** If you offer the exact same products as another business in your area, but at a much lower price point, emphasizing affordability can become part of your brand. On the other end of the spectrum, products at premium prices can be part of a luxury or artisan brand.

▪ **Scale** If your business is local and family-owned, but the competition is part of a large, faceless corporation, that distinction can help you appeal to customers who feel good about supporting local businesses and the personal relationships they can build with their owners. If your business is a franchise, your connection to a larger corporation is inherently part of your brand, and that lets your customers know exactly what they can expect.

▪ **Personality** Some businesses choose to distinguish themselves through their style or approach. For example, a mission-driven business that provides jobs to at-risk youth may want to project how that practice serves the community at large beyond the products it sells. A restaurant with flashy, unique décor can gain a reputation as much for its ambiance as for its food.

143

Know Your Customer

Ideally, when you created your business plan, you identified the kind of people you hope will frequent your business. Once you know who your customers will be, you can work toward figuring out how you'll appeal to them.

Some branding experts recommend coming up with a name for your potential customers and writing descriptions of them to help you visualize them as real people. For example, maybe you name your imaginary target customer Kendra. Her profile might be: Kendra is a busy mom who's trying to balance a full-time job with raising kids. She values quality time around the dinner table each night with her family.

While it might feel a little silly to write a description of an imaginary person, doing so can actually help you understand whom you're trying to reach and think about what might appeal to them.

In this case, Kendra might appreciate a product that's easy to order online during downtime at work. She may also prefer products that can be delivered to her house so she doesn't have to spend time driving across town. By emphasizing convenience and ease of ordering in your marketing materials, you can boost your chances of attracting customers like Kendra.

Create a Visual Identity

Once you're clear about how your business is unique and who you're trying to attract, it's time to create a visual identity for your company. Your visual identity will be reflected in the design of things, including the following:

▪ **Website** Your online presence is often the first thing potential customers will see.

▪ **Business Cards** Include your company logo.

Your brand is how you communicate your product or service to your customers.

▪ **Signage** Aim to keep these consistent in style.

▪ **Uniforms** These present a unified sense of identity when interacting with clients.

▪ **Packaging** If online sales are part of your plan, your logo and design can carry over here.

The primary elements of a visual identity are:

▪ Font

▪ Color palette

▪ Logo design

▪ Images, which may include illustrations and/or photographs

Choosing elements such as specific colors and fonts and using them consistently across your business creates a strong visual identity that your customers will learn to associate with your brand.

PRO TIP

Consistency is key to brand recognition. Use the same style and tone in your written materials, and keep imagery similar to make sure you stay on-brand.

Develop a Consistent Voice

You may never have noticed it consciously, but most businesses develop a "voice" that they use in written materials such as marketing, social media posts and sometimes even internal documents. Consider how these different sales messages sound:

- "This week only, we're pleased to invite you to an extraordinary sale."

- "Howdy pals! We sure do hope you'll mosey on down this week for our biggest sale yet!"

- "OMG. Huge sale. This week only. Don't miss it!"

All of these statements convey the exact same information: The business is having a big sale this week and wants its customers to know about it. However, each is written with a very different voice. Reading each one, you probably formed some ideas about the business and its target customers.

When crafting text for marketing materials, think about the kind of voice that will speak to your target customer. Once you've developed that voice, make sure to use it consistently across all written materials.

Social media is an easy way to reach your customer and help build your identity.

Utilizing Social Media

Today, more than 70% of Americans use some form of social media. These platforms can be powerful tools for marketing your business and helping to build brand awareness. If you're new to social media marketing, here are some tips to consider:

- **Choose Wisely** Rather than making sure you're on every available platform, choose a couple that make the most sense for what you do. For example, a craftsperson who sells artisan goods would be well-served by Instagram, which focuses on visuals and can serve as an online gallery. For an accountant or business consultant, LinkedIn might be a better fit, with its focus on building professional networks.

- **Post Consistently** Posting on a regular basis serves multiple purposes: It shows that your business is active, it reminds followers that you're there and it helps alert customers to any sales or news that you want to share.

- **Emphasize Quality, Not Quantity** While consistency is important, so is content. Don't prioritize posting frequently over creating content that followers will find useful. Stand-out posts are more likely to get shared and increase views.

Ultimately, your brand should be an extension of your business' values. View it as an opportunity to express what's special about your venture. If you find yourself struggling with delineating your brand, pros like graphic designers and marketing consultants may be able to help. ∎

Effective Advertising, Social Media and More When It Comes to Marketing, There Are More Options Than Ever

Getting your products or services in front of your target audience is an essential function of your business. You can choose to use traditional forms of advertising, or you may want to try and leverage social media to promote your company. Either way, a successful promotional campaign requires time, effort and careful planning.

Traditional and Digital Advertising

Most small businesses use some form of traditional advertising, such as print ads or television commercials. In 2019, 57% of small businesses reported using these outlets, which tend to be more expensive and less targeted than digital options. But they have advantages that make them attractive for some. For one, consumers see advertisements on traditional media as more trustworthy than those on the internet. And if your target demographic spends less time online, as older users tend to do, you may need to reach them through traditional channels.

Digital advertising, on the other hand, can be a cost-effective—and data-rich—way to get your products and services to your target audience. A digital-ad platform can place your ad in relevant search results, articles and social media feeds. And a pay-per-click arrangement means you will only pay for ads that prompt an interaction. Those interactions create useful marketing data, telling you about the effectiveness of your campaign and helping identify your target demographics.

Sometimes the algorithm that places your ad next to relevant content can associate your brand with unsavory news items or offensive videos. No matter what you're selling, it probably shouldn't be advertised alongside extremist conspiracy theories, for example. So before you launch a digital ad campaign,

Order Flowers Online

FLOWERS
DELIVERY

Fresh Flower Guarantee / 24/7 Customer Service

SHOP NOW

Digital advertising
can be a low-cost
way to reach your
target audience.

Choose a social media platform that's suited to your product and content needs.

be sure the platform has the tools in place to keep your brand safe.

Social Media

A social media presence can be a powerful tool to help new businesses reach customers. You can promote your business through low-cost organic content and build an audience of consumers you can reach directly.

While social media has become an essential promotional tool for many businesses, it has its pitfalls. So it's important to approach it with a deliberate plan. For example, consider if you want to offer another avenue for customer-service questions.

Choose a platform with a design that's well-suited to what you're selling. An Instagram feed can be a great place to showcase an architectural firm's growing portfolio or a bakery's expertly iced cupcakes. Any business that finds it easy to generate a stream of appealing, relevant images will fit in on the visually focused platform.

A plumbing and heating service, however, might do better with a Facebook page, where prospective customers can read reviews and find the website, hours and phone number. YouTube is a great place for media labels to host trailers, clips and full releases. Any business that wants to engage an audience with product demos and tutorials will find this platform useful.

Find where your target audience hangs out. Do your own research, and don't take the conventional wisdom at face value. For example, you may have heard that Facebook

PRO TIP

Build a rapport with your customers by responding to their posts on social media and addressing any questions or concerns they may have.

use is on the decline, especially among younger users. But the Pew Research Center found that 84% of millennials continue to use the site.

Building Your Social Media Brand

As you start a social media campaign, take your cues from the social media profiles of similar businesses. Learn what they do to successfully interact with their customers and find examples of effective content.

Review different sites' rules about how often you can post, decide on a posting schedule, and determine what types of content you will put up. Use a consistent voice, and be sure that every post reinforces your brand.

Other Promotions

You can spread the word about your business in ways beyond ads and social media. For example, work with a noncompeting business that targets the same audience you do.

Joint ventures can take various forms. For example, you can collaborate on an in-person event, or the business you partner with can offer discounted access to your products or services to their customers.

If you're very social media–savvy, you can try reaching out to influencers who can put your brand in front of large, targeted audiences quickly. For instance, a YouTuber who gives crafting tutorials could help give their viewers a unique promotional code for your online craft-supplies shop.

With a little research and planning, you can be sure to find an effective way to put information about your new venture in front of the right consumers. ∎

07 COMPETITION

01 | 02 | 03 | 04

Sizing Up the Competition
Identify, Analyze, Outsmart and Outsell Other Businesses

Every business has competition, and that's ultimately a good thing. It drives innovation and keeps prices in check—not only on what you sell, but also on the supplies you buy. That said, you might not feel so rosy about your competition when it comes to keeping your own customers. Savvy rivals pay close attention to your business, and you should keep an eye on theirs. After all, understanding your competition will only help to make your own business stand out from the rest. Here are three steps you can take to get to know your competition a little better:

Identify Rivals

Some will be obvious. Let's say you and another company both rent bicycles to tourists. You're in direct competition. But there's also indirect competition, which can be harder to spot. Consider a business that rents kayaks; they're angling for the same recreational customers as you are. Here's how to expertly spot whom you're up against:

▪ **Go Online** A web search for your products or services will turn up many competitors. Dive deep into those companies' websites to learn how much of their business is directly going up against yours, or if the overlap is small.

▪ **Attend Trade Fairs** Just about every business sector holds annual conventions or exhibitions, which essentially are about assembling your competition in one place. These meetings are great places to identify who's operating in your area.

▪ **Check the Chamber of Commerce** Your local chamber should keep a list of the businesses that are operating in your area—it's a great resource for information on similar ventures if you're focusing on the local market.

▪ **Search Patent Listings** The website of the United States

PRO TIP

Keep tabs on potential future competitors—firms that may not be in your market yet but may enter it one day, such as a growing company from abroad.

Visit competitors to take stock of their visual style, products and customer service.

151

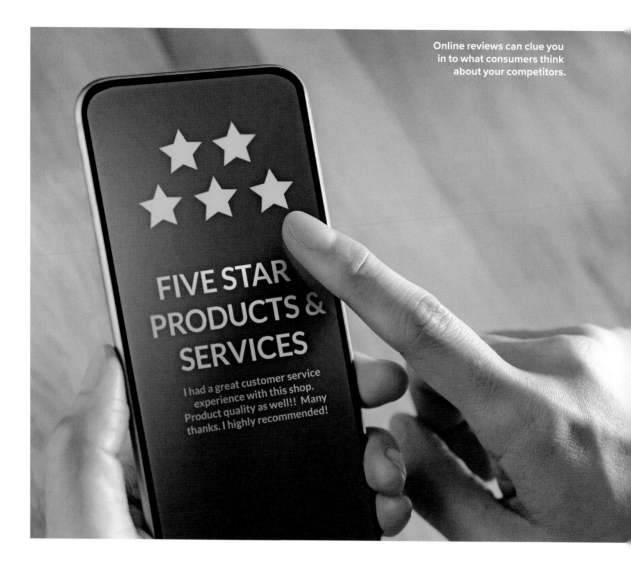

Online reviews can clue you in to what consumers think about your competitors.

Smart business owners are always following new developments from existing competitors to improve their own marketing efforts.

Patent and Trademark Office can help you find products that are similar to yours, so be sure to check out uspto.gov.

Analyze Competing Businesses

Once you've identified whom you're up against, the next step is making a critical assessment of their strengths and weaknesses. Take the following steps:

- **Become a Customer** You should consider buying something from them, then analyze the experience. Is the merchandise high quality? Is customer service attentive? Maybe the website is hard to navigate. Take it all in, right down to the packaging.

- **Read Social Media** Online reviews of competitors will tell you what customers think of them. Also consider searching the website of the Better Business Bureau at bbb.org for any complaints. Meanwhile, sites like LinkedIn and Monster can provide clues on the size and experience of their current staff.

- **Monitor Operations** Pay attention to where and how competitors advertise, and sign up for their email marketing messages. Where do they sell their products? Is the brand's overall packaging and website design up to date—or tired?

- **Talk to Your Customers** They might also buy from your competitors. What do they like about them? What don't they like?

- **Visit Your Planning Board** City planning boards deal with zoning variation requests from businesses. The minutes of their meetings can tip you off to local competitors that are hoping to expand or upgrade.

- **Pore Over Public Sources** Publicly traded companies must file public reports with the Securities and Exchange Commission at least once a year. These reports are packed with financial information and company news.

- **Attend Industry Events and Social Affairs** When you meet your competitors in these settings, be friendly. You're both in the same boat, after all. Do more listening than talking. If nothing else, you'll get a sense of their values and priorities.

Leverage Your Research

After analyzing your competition, put your knowledge to work.

- **Do Something Different** Are there gaps in a competitor's service or product lines that you may be able to fill? Maybe they have a nice brick-and-mortar retail shop but they don't take any online orders. Even direct rivals may offer different customer experiences; it's up to you to create your own.

- **Know Your Place** Many of your competitors likely also specialize in areas outside of your focus. For example, say you want to open a car-repair shop. You'll be in direct competition with the service department of a nearby new-car dealer. But the dealer's main business is selling a specific make of car and they probably only service that kind of car, as well. So you only overlap with part of their business, suggesting there is room for competition in town.

- **Price Wisely** Charging less than your competition is one way to stand out—but be careful. Price is only one factor in most buying decisions. If you set prices too low, some customers will assume you're cutting corners. You could wind up pricing yourself out of business.

Understanding the competition is a never-ending job. Smart business owners are always following new developments from their existing competitors. Among the many stories of businesses who were left in the dust with changing times is the classic example of buggy-whip makers, who went bust with the invention of the automobile. However, the Timken Company, which made wheel bearings for carriages in the 19th century, saw the changes coming and shifted its product line. The company is still in business, making advanced parts for all kinds of uses. ∎

07 | **CUSTOMERS** | 01 | 02 | 03 | 04

Understanding Your Customer
Build Your Venture by getting to Know Whom You're Selling to—and Anticipating Their Needs

Henry Ford's great innovation was inventing a car (the Model T) that ordinary people could afford. In 1921, he sold two-thirds of all cars in the U.S.—all of them black, and basically the same. Then along came Alfred Sloan of General Motors, who realized some customers wanted cheap cars while others wanted luxury models; some could pay cash, but some needed loans. Some even wanted a car that was red or silver. Just five years later, Ford had lost half his market share.

Ford bounced back with the popular Model A, but it was a tough lesson: Businesses that fail to understand their customers will lose business.

That's especially true today, when customers can view myriad purchase options with a simple swipe of their electronic device's screen—along with reviews and the ability to instantly compare prices.

Let's say you've already identified your potential customer base and are raking in sales. But now you want to know more about those customers. Maybe you're thinking of new products they might buy. Or maybe you just want to find more people like them. Here's how to grow your customer knowledge bank.

In Person
If you own a brick-and-mortar shop, use your customer encounters to collect intelligence. Even casual conversations can tell you what products they like or don't like, how much they're willing to spend, how often they buy

PRO TIP

Start a loyalty program to attract repeat business and perhaps open a continuous line of communication between you and your customers.

If you have a brick-and-mortar shop, pay attention to the customer experience.

Even casual conversations with customers can tell you about their needs.

155

Networking events allow you to stay more in touch with market demands.

products like yours and where else they like to shop. Lean in a little more and you can learn where they live, how often they come to your neighborhood and if they drive or walk.

Mailing Lists

A mailing list is essential for marketing, but it also helps you know more about customers. For example, if you do business online, you can track which customers clicked through to your website from a sales link in an email.

You can create email lists for free using Gmail, but paid services are more robust. Some will help you design a pop-up form on a Facebook ad that prompts the user to sign up. According to Mailchimp, a popular email-marketing platform and service, pop-up forms increase sign-ups by 50.8%. You can even run Facebook ad campaigns that target users who have similar profiles to your existing email list.

Events

Holding live events is a great way to learn more about your customers. Perhaps your business is on a street that holds an annual fair; maximize those public events with live music or special sales, then be sure to collect email addresses and talk to your customers.

You might also sponsor events like product demonstrations or guest speakers. Consider hiring an event planner to handle the details so you can work the room and meet customers. Promote events on Twitter and Instagram, using hashtags.

CRM Technology

If your head spins at the task of compiling data on customers, take heart—technology is on your side. Even small businesses have access to customer relationship management (CRM) software, which is basically a digital hub for all your customer data and insights, including orders, page views, in-store purchases, even age and location demographics. Combined with online ad buys and mailing list programs, CRM can even help you find new customers.

CRM software is powerful, but if you're a very small business it's best to keep it simple at first. Look for a program with an easy user interface that works with your mailing list software.

Social Media

Even the smallest companies maintain Facebook and Instagram accounts, which are great sources from which to gain intelligence on customers. When people like your page or picture, or leave a comment, it's easy to click back to their profile and learn more about who they are.

You can set up Google Alerts or use programs like Hootsuite to monitor online activity related to your business. And if you advertise online, tools like Google Analytics can tell you a lot about who's checking you out.

Reviews

It's true: Bad reviews can hurt your business—and your feelings. But if you think of reviews as customer intelligence, the few negative ones you're bound to get can be even more useful than praise. Pay attention to what people don't like about your product or service—and what they're looking for instead. And don't be afraid to reach out to reviewers who've panned you.

The ultimate goal in understanding your customers is anticipating their needs—even before they recognize them themselves. ∎

Looking Ahead

What to do now that your
business is up and running

Work-Life Balance for Entrepreneurs You Can Build Your Business and Have a Life (Yes, at the Same Time!)

Putting in the grunt work to start your own company can sometimes feel all-consuming. Establishing a good work-life balance might seem out of reach, but finding ways to take care of yourself is crucial for the long-term success of your business.

Entrepreneurs face unique challenges when it comes to finding balance. The freedom to create your own schedule can translate into never feeling like you're "off" and that you need to be working all hours of the day. While you may feel tempted to focus on nothing but work, research shows that putting in more hours doesn't necessarily translate into greater productivity.

Putting yourself last can take a toll on your mental and physical health and, in turn, harm your business. Here are four tips for avoiding burnout and creating a healthy work-life balance.

Prioritize Tasks

Take a look at how you're spending your hours by tracking what you do throughout the day. Then evaluate the list. What tasks are you spending time on that aren't adding value?

Using that information as a guide, decide which three or four tasks are most important to focus on each day. By zeroing in on what really matters, you can cut down on how many hours you work, and free up more time for other parts of your life, like spending time with friends or family.

Create a Schedule and Stick to It

As an entrepreneur, you may have a lot of freedom to use your time as you please—but this leeway may also mean that you don't have clear

> **PRO TIP**
>
> You might feel you are the only one who can handle certain parts of your business, but embracing delegation is one way to free up more of your time.

Engaging with younger employees in a relaxed environment can help balance the workweek.

161

Creating a schedule can help you juggle work and family as your business grows.

they know when you're available and, if applicable, whom to contact when you're not working. Knowing someone else is available when you're not can help you stick to your boundaries.

There may be periods when your workload is heavier and you need to adjust your availability. But setting clear boundaries from the beginning lays the groundwork for creating clear distinctions between work and the rest of your life.

Embrace Delegation

As a founder, it can be really tempting to believe you're the only one who should manage certain parts of your business. But as your business grows, it's important to bring on people you trust to uphold the mission and take over some of the company's operations. Not only does delegation help free up some of your time, but it also makes the business stronger and more sustainable: It means more than one person understands the ins and outs, and can keep things running smoothly.

What work-life balance looks like for you will likely change over time, as your personal and work lives ebb and flow. But establishing these habits and routines early will make your business more sustainable in the long run—and make your life more enjoyable, too. ∎

office hours. Develop your own schedule by creating work blocks aligned with your optimal windows of productivity. If you're super motivated in the morning, you may want to schedule a block of work time starting at 7 a.m., then take a long break at midday. Do your best work late at night? Then plan to have meetings in the afternoon and give yourself the mornings off.

Set Clear Boundaries

Once you've established your optimal schedule, try to avoid planning calls or meetings outside of your designated blocks of work time. You might even consider having work calls automatically routed to an answering service or voicemail when you're not working. Be sure to set expectations with clients, vendors and employees so

> It can feel like no one but you can manage your business, but it's important to bring on people you trust as your operations grow.

Change Is the Only Constant
Staying Flexible and Alert Can Help You Adapt to a Shifting Marketplace

L aunching a successful business requires a lot of work. Once you finally open the doors, literally or figuratively, you may be tempted to go on autopilot. But as recent history has demonstrated, drastic changes can happen unexpectedly—and rapidly. Thankfully, major economic upheavals like the COVID-19 pandemic don't come along very often. But the marketplace changes constantly in ways both big and small.

Here are ways to keep your business flexible enough to adapt when change happens to come from out of the blue.

Don't Let Paperwork Pile Up
It may seem like a minor detail, but keeping orderly and complete business records can be a big advantage when the winds of change start to blow. Understanding your current financial

Thinking about what comes next helps your business thrive.

status can guide how urgently you need to make changes and how quickly you'll need to enact them before a dip in revenues becomes an existential crisis.

Engage With Your Customers

Your market research shouldn't stop once you've settled on a business plan. In addition to staying on top of industry sources, you now have access to an ongoing focus group: your customers. Communicate with them to let them know your plans and get feedback on how their needs may be changing. Finding new ways to help your customers can deepen your relationships with them and increase their loyalty, especially in times of crisis. Gathering that information can be as simple as asking for it in person, via personal emails or phone calls, or through a survey.

Rethink Your Strategy

Some changes may require you to shift your target audience temporarily or permanently. For example, if you normally focus on tourists and people suddenly become reluctant to travel to your area, you may need to adapt your offerings to attract locals instead. Or difficult economic times might require a change in pricing strategy to keep your prices more closely aligned with what your newly cash-strapped customers are willing to spend.

Make Full Use of Your Resources

As markets change, stay on the lookout for ways to adapt your current resources to fulfill changing customer needs. For instance, you might reposition existing products or services to solve your customers' new problems. In other cases, you may be able to use your existing inventory, equipment or supply chain to introduce high-demand products or services. For example,

> **As new changes occur, you might want to dust off one of your old ideas and repurpose it to fit your new reality.**

consider retail clothing stores that pivoted to selling face masks, or manufacturers that started making protective equipment during the pandemic.

Don't Be Afraid to Try New Things

Whether or not your customers' needs are changing, innovative experiments can pay off. If you already have a customer base, trying something new doesn't have to be costly. Test out a different service or product on a small scale first. Offer samples to customers or employees and solicit feedback to help shape your ideas. If something doesn't work, you can always abandon it and move on.

You may find that some of your failed experiments were simply ahead of their time. As new changes occur, you might want to dust off one of your old ideas and repurpose it to respond to your new reality.

Change is inevitable. But if you stay flexible and understand the changing needs of your customers, you can make adjustments and keep your business well-positioned to not only adapt, but also thrive in good times or bad. ∎

PRO TIP

Keep thorough business records so you can clearly see your current systems, as well as where you need to adapt during times of change.

Being prepared for new circumstances will keep your business relevant.

A bakery might open a new location to serve customers in a wider geographic area.

Expanding or Acquiring Another Business
Have Sales Been Booming? You May Now Be Ready to Branch Out

I f your business has been a success and you're looking to grow, you have two options: Expand your existing operations or purchase another business. Both options offer potential new income streams, and both also come with their own risks and responsibilities.

Steps for Safe and Successful Expansion

Expanding your business requires revisiting some of the steps you took when you started your business. The U.S. Small Business Administration advises focusing on the following tasks:

▪ **Revise Your Marketing Plan** To reach customers in a new area, or to let existing ones know about your new products, you'll need an updated marketing strategy. This plan might include placing advertisements that target a new neighborhood, or sending out mailers to let customers know about your new offerings.

▪ **Review Your Finances** Expansion usually comes with costs. You may need to pay rent on a larger space, for instance, or purchase new equipment. Make sure that your current income, along with the projected additional revenue from expansion, will be able to cover these costs. If your ledger looks precarious, you may need to seek outside funding to help get your expansion efforts started.

▪ **Take Care of the Legal Stuff** Expansion often comes with new rules and regulations. For example, if you'd like to expand a restaurant to include a full bar, you may need to apply for a liquor license. Familiarize yourself with any new licenses, permits, zoning ordinances, fees or taxes that will apply if you expand. If you are branching out to operate

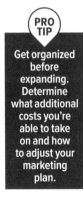

PRO TIP

Get organized before expanding. Determine what additional costs you're able to take on and how to adjust your marketing plan.

167

If your business is thriving, expanding can open up new income streams.

in a new state, you may need to file for foreign qualification to be able to do business there. You may also become responsible for collecting or paying new taxes.

Acquiring Another Business

Another way to grow as an entrepreneur is to acquire an already existing business. This approach can sometimes present less risk than starting from scratch, if the business has a record of success. Consider some of these tips for this approach:

▪ **Stick to What You Know** If you've had success in a specific industry, consider looking to acquire a business in the same field. Your skills and knowledge will translate more easily this way than if you were to learn all the ins and outs of a brand-new business in a completely new arena. What's more, you will be able to benefit from economies of scale when it comes to buying supplies, paying for services or even staffing operations.

▪ **Do Your Homework** You'll obviously want to know if the business has been profitable, but there's other information you'll want to look at, too. Have existing inventory and equipment appraised, so you know the true value of any assets you're taking on. Also look closely at all paperwork and legal documents, including existing contracts, debt disclosures, and five years of tax documents and financial statements.

▪ **Get Professional Help** Business brokers can help you locate businesses for sale that meet your criteria. Much like real estate agents, they work on commission (typically paid by the seller), so they have a vested interest in negotiating sales. You don't necessarily need a broker to work out an acquisition deal, but they are helpful for first-time buyers who are unfamiliar with the process.

Expanding a business takes all the hard work that got you started, with the benefit of the lessons you learned along the way. An expansion can be just the thing to take your company to the next level. ▪

Exit Strategies and Succession Plans
Preparing for a Transition Can Strengthen Your Business—Now and Later

At some point, you and your business will eventually part ways. You might be ready to retire, or want to sell it to start a new venture. And of course, something unexpected could happen—an injury, an illness or even your death—that could prevent you from continuing to operate your enterprise. An exit strategy or succession plan will lay out the necessary steps to ensure you, your family and your employees get what is needed when you're ready to move on.

> **PRO TIP**
>
> If you plan to pass along your small business to family members, include them in the process so everyone is on the same page.

Yet despite the importance of a succession plan, nearly six in 10 small-business owners don't have one. Many wait until they are near retirement, which might be too late to retain key management or mitigate problems such as the tax burden produced by a sale. Earlier planning can facilitate a smooth transition.

Know the Important Players

Before setting your exit strategy down in writing, it's important to understand who the key players will be in any business transition. Consider these:

- **Buyers** Even if you're not planning to sell your business, someone could make an offer. They may be wary if you have no succession plan.

- **Investors** If you have outside investors, they'll want to know your eventual exit plans to gain a clear understanding of how their stake in the business may change when you leave.

- **Family** Whether they work directly with you or not, your spouse and children have an interest in what becomes of your business, as it likely represents a large portion of your family's assets. If family members do work with you, an exit plan can be a huge help in heading off any potential disputes among them that may develop over who will control the business after you've left.

▪ **Employees** Be sure to include top employees in your succession plan to help retain them after an ownership transition. One or more of your staff members may even be solid candidates to buy the business from you.

▪ **Creditors** All businesses have outstanding bills. A succession plan lays out how they will be paid, so your heirs don't need to liquidate your business to pay off liabilities.

▪ **Uncle Sam** The government is likely to come calling when you transfer your business, whether by collecting gift or estate taxes from your heirs, or capital gains taxes from you and

Before setting an exit strategy down in writing, it's important to know who the key players will be in the next phase of your business.

other owners. Advance planning can minimize the tax burden on you and your family.

▪ **A Team of Experts** At the very least you'll want sound advice from a lawyer, a tax expert and your accountant. You may also look to enlist your personal financial planner or bank representative.

Next Steps

Organize a short-term plan known as a crisis protocol. This plan operates under the assumption that you could die or become disabled today—and describes in detail who would immediately take over the daily operations of the business. It might include a time frame after which a longer-term strategy kicks in.

With a short-term plan in place, you then need to decide on a long-term succession plan, which could take one of many forms:

▪ **Family-Based** It's common to pass along a small business to family members, but be aware of hurdles that can develop. There could be resentment from heirs who get left out. Some family members might prefer to sell rather than operate the business themselves. And your heirs might not share your skills or values. Include family members in the planning process to make your intentions clear and avoid misunderstandings later.

▪ **Sell to Partners** If your business already has partners, you may decide to divide your share among them. This approach requires what's called a buy-sell agreement, which spells out the terms when one partner exits. Have your business professionally appraised to calculate the value of your share and the amount your partners will need to pay you when you leave.

▪ **Sell to Management** The advantage of selling to long-time employees is continuity—your business will be run by people who know it well. Managers who are on an ownership track may also be particularly motivated to be conscientious and loyal. This strategy also requires you to obtain a valuation and write up a detailed purchase plan.

▪ **Sell to Employees** Employee-owned businesses have one big advantage: Every worker is vested in its success. That means less turnover and better relations between workers,

Selling to employees or family ensures workers are vested in the company's success.

management and customers. One common way to sell to employees is through an employee stock ownership plan (ESOP). It's basically a trust into which employees can contribute funds that eventually convert to ownership shares.

▪ **Sell to a Third Party** If your heirs or staff have no interest in taking over your business, it often makes sense to put the company on the market. Consider planning for this likelihood well in advance of retirement. Finding an outside buyer and working through the purchase process takes time. A new owner might also want you to stick around a while as a paid consultant.

Unfortunately, an all-too-common endgame for small businesses without a succession plan is liquidation—the assets are sold at a discount to pay off debts, and employees lose their jobs. A succession plan can help you, your employees and any family members involved in the business to avoid that fate. ▪

08 | **DIVERSIFY YOUR WEALTH**   01 | 02 | 03 | 04 | 05

Diversifying Your Wealth
Your Venture Is an Investment,
But It Shouldn't Be Your Only One

As an entrepreneur, it's natural to want to pour everything you can into your business, but personal finance experts recommend keeping a diverse investment portfolio. It can contain different kinds of investments, such as stocks, bonds, commodities, real estate and, of course, business ventures.

Many entrepreneurs struggle to adequately diversify their investments, and instead end up keeping all of their money tied up in their business. The problem with this approach is the possibility that your business could fail without warning—as happened to many small businesses during the coronavirus pandemic. If you have no savings outside of your business and disaster strikes, you could be left without a safety net.

Here are some ways to diversify your wealth as a small-business owner:

Start a 401(k)

Offering a 401(k) to your employees is a great way to both diversify your wealth and offer a desirable benefit to your staff. When you set up a 401(k) for your company, both you and your employees can use the plan to save for retirement. Most 401(k) plans offer a variety of mutual funds, each of which is comprised of a combination of individual bonds, stocks and money market investments. Entrepreneurs without any employees can create a solo 401(k) plan. These plans work exactly the same way as traditional 401(k)s and apply to only a sole proprietor and his or her spouse.

Buy Another Business

If you've had great success running one business, purchasing another could be a smart way to bring in more money over the long term. As with any investment, you'll want to do your research and make sure you can expect a return

Opening another business can bring in more money over the long term.

on investment that is worth the time and energy you'll have to put into running it. If you're looking for passive income, or a set-it-and-forget-it approach to investing, buying a second business may not be the right choice for you. Running a business takes a lot of work, and if it's not something you have the time for, you could find yourself stretched thin.

Invest in Real Estate

If you already own the building where you run your business, that property is part of your investment portfolio. Even if you closed up shop tomorrow, you'd still have a piece of real estate that you could lease or sell. While not every business owner can afford to buy property in the area where they operate, purchasing a commercial property can provide you with space to expand in the future. It can also offer a steady cash flow if you decide to rent it out to other business owners.

No matter how you choose to diversify your wealth, as a small-business owner you'll need to always keep a significant amount of highly liquid assets (like cash). Unexpected expenses come up all the time and not having cash on hand can disrupt your operations. If you're not sure how much cash to keep liquidated, or what portfolio mix is best for you, seek out the help of a professional financial planner. ∎

CHAPTER 09

Worksheets

Use these pages to help plan your startup
and keep track of your finances

Business Plan Prep
Create a Detailed Document so You Can Lay the Groundwork for Your Success

A comprehensive business plan is critical for success. It helps you identify your goals, secure funding, and even spot potential weaknesses in your model. It will also allow you to brainstorm solutions that will provide you with a road map for how to proceed. Use this handy worksheet to get started developing your business plan.

Draft a Mission Statement

What are your goals and objectives? What do you want your business to provide to your customers? Write a short, specific summary of what you plan to achieve.

_____

_____

_____

_____

_____

_____

_____

Describe Your Product or Service

What are you offering? What problems are you solving for your customers?

_____

_____

_____

_____

_____

Describe Your Ideal Customer

Who makes up your target market? How will you reach them?

_____

_____

_____

_____

_____

Analyze Your Competition

How will you differentiate yourself? What unique skills and strategies will you bring?

_____

_____

_____

_____

_____

Assess Your Financial Outlook

If you are requesting funding, include information here about startup costs and how much you're asking for. Describe how you will use the money and how it will benefit your business.

_____

_____

_____

_____

_____

Brand Development
Clear Branding Helps You Communicate Better With Your Customers

Your brand is a reflection of what you stand for, whom you serve and what makes you different. It ensures that when you communicate with your customers, your message stays on target. Use this worksheet to start crafting your brand.

Mission Statement

Your mission statement describes what your brand stands for, representing what your business does and why. It can bring your company's purpose into focus and help you define what you want to communicate to your customers. Write a one- or two-sentence mission statement that defines whom you serve, how you are unique and the value you offer.

_____
_____
_____
_____
_____

Your Customer

Profile your ideal customer. Be as detailed as possible, describing features such as gender, age, family status and values.

_____
_____
_____
_____

Your Communications

Once you've defined your ideal customer, identify what platforms you'll use to communicate with them, including traditional advertising, social media apps, direct mail, etc.

_____
_____
_____
_____
_____
_____

Your Brand Voice

Your brand "voice" is the consistent style you'll use when communicating with customers. Write a list of adjectives that describe your business' character, including how people should feel when they read your communications. Make sure these words can be applied to all of your customer-facing materials.

_____
_____
_____
_____
_____
_____

Market Research
Identifying Your Customers and Their Needs

When you have a business idea, you have to first make sure there are customers who want your product or service. Who are they? Which of your competitors do they already use? And what need will you fulfill that will entice them to switch? Use this worksheet to compile information about your buyers, your competition and what makes you different.

About Your Buyers

Age _____
Gender _____
Occupation _____
Income _____
Preferred Media _____

About Your Competition

Market Share _____
Time in Business _____
Advertising Channels _____
Main Selling Point _____
Location _____

About Your Competition's Offerings

Products and Services Offered _____
Price _____
Packaging _____
Why Is the Product Purchased? _____
How Often Is It Purchased? _____
What Could be Improved? _____

How Your Product/Service Is Different

What Need Does It Address? _____
Features _____
Price Point _____

Business Structures at a Glance
A Quick Look at the Entities You May Choose From When Setting Up Your Business

The structure you choose when establishing your business can have big implications for how your business is treated in the eyes of the law.

Your choice will determine factors including how you're taxed and legal liability. Consider these different legal structures.

Sole Proprietorship

FORMATION

•Easiest entity to form

•Even if you don't register as a business, if you perform business activities, you are automatically considered a sole proprietorship.

TAXES

•Business income is taxed as personal income.

•You must pay a self-employment tax of 15.3% on the first $137,700 of net income (per 2020 numbers).

LIABILITY

•You are personally responsible for business debts and legal obligations.

Partnership

FORMATION

•Businesses with one or more partners may consider limited partnerships (LPs) or limited liability partnerships (LLPs).

•LPs consist of at least one "general partner" with unlimited liability for legal obligations and at least one "limited partner" with limited liability.

•LLPs give all members of the partnership limited liability.

TAXES

•General partners and limited partners must pay personal taxes on business profits.

•General partners must pay self-employment taxes.

LIABILITY

•Personal assets are mostly protected from legal action against the company.

•No partner in an LLP can be held personally liable for the actions of other partners.

Corporation

FORMATION

•There are two types of corporations: C corps and S corps.

•C corps can have an unlimited number of global shareholders.

•S corps are limited to 100 shareholders, all of whom must be U.S. citizens.

TAXES

•C corps face taxes on both their profits and dividends.

•The money S corps make is not subject to corporate tax. Rather, S corps allow profits to pass through directly to owners' personal income.

LIABILITY

•Legal liabilities fall to the company, rather than the individuals who own it.

Limited Liability Company (LLC)

FORMATION

•LLCs are separate entities from the person or people who run them.

TAXES

•Profits are passed through to personal income and taxed as income.

•All members of an LLC owe self-employment taxes.

LIABILITY

•Personal assets are protected from any legal action against the company.

Cash Flow
Keep Track of the Money Coming Into and Going Out of Your Business

Cash flow refers to all forms of business income and output. Income can include revenue from sales, loan proceeds or transfers of your personal money to your business account, while output refers to cash you've spent, such as on operating costs, payroll or loan payments. Cash-flow problems can mean trouble for your business, but regularly producing a cash-flow statement can help keep you on track. Here's a sample cash-flow worksheet to get you started.

CASH FLOW

Opening Balance $ _____

Incoming Cash

Sales $ _____

Loan Proceeds $ _____

Transfers $ _____

Other Income $ _____

TOTAL INCOMING $ _____

Outgoing Cash

Merchandise Purchases $ _____

Other Purchases $ _____

Wages $ _____

Rent $ _____

Utilities $ _____

Insurance $ _____

Taxes $ _____

TOTAL OUTGOING $ _____

Closing Balance

Opening Balance Plus Total Incoming Cash Minus Total Outgoing Cash $ _____

Staying on Top of Your Budget
Track the Financial Trajectory of Your Business

Working with a budget allows you to compare your business income and spending to make sure you have enough to cover expenses and still turn a profit. Use this monthly worksheet to keep track of the difference between estimated and actual spending, so you can adjust accordingly.

Income

	Estimate	Actual	Difference
Product Sales	$	$	$
Income From Services Provided	$	$	$
Other	$	$	$
TOTAL	$	$	$

Expenses

	Estimate	Actual	Difference
Fixed Costs			
Rent	$	$	$
Business Insurance	$	$	$
Utilities	$	$	$
Payroll	$	$	$
Taxes	$	$	$
Variable Costs			
Materials	$	$	$
Production Expenses	$	$	$
Marketing Fees	$	$	$
Other	$	$	$
TOTAL	$	$	$

Totals

Total Actual Income	$	$	$
Total Actual Expenses	$	$	$
Net Income			
Total Income Minus Total Expenses	$	$	$

09 | PROFIT AND LOSS | 01 | 02 | 03 | 04 | 05 | 06 | 07 | 08 | 09 | 10

Profit and Loss
See How Your Revenues
Will Translate Into Profit

A profit-and-loss statement may be referred to as an income or operating statement, or simply as a P&L. Whatever you call it, this financial report summarizes your company's revenues, costs and expenses over a fixed period, such as a quarter or a year.

Revenue

Product Sales	$
Service Sales	$
TOTAL	$

Operating Expenses

Costs to Make Products (materials, labor, etc.)	$
Gross Profit (total revenue minus operating costs)	$

Fixed Costs

Rent	$
Utilities	$
Office Supplies	$
Other Costs	$

TOTAL	
Operating Income (gross profit minus fixed costs)	$

Other Expenses

Income Taxes	$
Other Expenses	$
TOTAL	$

Net Earnings

Operating Income Minus Other Expenses Total	$

Small-Business Resources
These Organizations Can Help
Guide You as You're Getting Started

Starting your own business can feel intimidating. There is a lot to consider, from writing a business plan to finding financing options. But you don't have to do it alone. Here are some resources to help guide you.

U.S. Small Business Administration (SBA)

The SBA is a federal agency that provides support to small businesses across the country. Its website offers templates and information on everything from writing a business plan to growing your business and expanding to new locations. It also offers free online courses on many different business topics and backs small-business loans. You can access these resources at sba.gov. Plus, the SBA offers in-person counseling, training and business development guidance at its district offices across the country. Find a location near you at sba.gov/local-assistance.

SCORE

A nonprofit resource partner of the SBA, SCORE is a network of volunteers who offer mentoring, webinars and online classes to entrepreneurs. Its online library of resources includes templates, guides and checklists for dozens of topics, like how to start a work-from-home business and how to make tax preparation go smoothly. Visit score.org and connect with a business mentor at score.org/find-mentor.

Business USA

Business USA is an online directory of financing options for small-business owners. It offers tons of information on free or low-cost financial support for businesses, including government loans, grants and information on travel loans and insurance. For more info, visit busa.org.

Small Business Development Centers

Each state has its own small business development center that provides free business consulting and low-cost training to startups and existing businesses. Some may also host local networking events and other ways to connect with other entrepreneurs in your community. Visit americassbdc.org to learn more.

IRS Small-Business Portal

This portal offers a wealth of tax information for small businesses, from filing taxes to guidance on record-keeping and deducting expenses. The portal can be found at irs.gov/businesses/small-businesses-self-employed.

09 | **RETIREMENT OPTIONS** | 01 | 02 | 03 | 04 | 05 | 06 | 07 | 08 | 09 | 10

Your Retirement Options at a Glance
A Quick Overview of the Retirement Accounts Available to Business Owners

Traditional and Roth IRAs

	Traditional IRA	Roth IRA
Contribution Limit	$6,000 ($7,000 for those age 50 and older)*	$6,000 ($7,000 for those age 50 and older)*
Deductible Contributions	Contributions are deductible if you qualify.	Contributions are not deductible.
Withdrawals	Withdrawals can be made after age 59½. Early withdrawals are subject to income tax and a 10% penalty.	You may withdraw contributions at anytime. Withdrawals on earnings can be made after age 59½. Early withdrawals on earnings may be taxable and subject to a 10% penalty.
Required Minimum Distributions (RMDs)	You must start taking RMDs by April 1 following the year in which you turn age 72 and by Dec. 31 each year after that.	None
Taxable Withdrawals	Yes	No, as long as you are over age 59½ and have held the account for five years or more.

SIMPLE, SEP IRAs and Solo 401(k)s

	SIMPLE IRA	SEP IRA	Solo 401(k)
Tax Status	Tax-deferred	Tax-deferred	Tax-deferred
Who Can Contribute	Employees and/or employer	Employer	Self-employed individuals and their spouses
Contribution Limit	$13,500 ($16,500 for age 50 and older). Employers may match 3% of employee contributions or 2% of employees' compensation up to an annual limit of $285,000.*	25% of an employee's salary or up to $57,000*, whichever is less.	$57,000*
Withdrawals	Withdrawals can be made after age 59½. Early withdrawals are subject to income tax and a 10% or 25% penalty.	Withdrawals can be made after age 59½. Early withdrawals are subject to income tax and a 10% early withdrawal penalty.	Withdrawals can be made after age 59½. Early withdrawals are subject to income tax and a 10% penalty.
RMDs	Yes	Yes	Yes
Taxable Withdrawals	Yes	Yes	Yes

*Based on 2020 numbers; for updated figures visit irs.gov.

Disaster Resources
Where to Turn for Help Preparing for a Disaster, or to Seek Disaster Relief

Natural disasters, pandemics and even cyber-attacks can wreak havoc on a small business. But you can mitigate the damage with smart planning, including knowing where to turn for help now and in the case of a true disaster. Here are some resources that can help.

Business Disaster Relief

U.S. Small Business Administration (SBA) The SBA provides low-interest disaster loans that can help businesses recover from declared disasters. These loans can cover expenses related to real estate, equipment, economic injury and personal property. Call 1-800-659-2955 or visit www.sba.gov/funding-programs/disaster-assistance

Personal Relief

Federal Emergency Management Agency (FEMA) FEMA provides relief to individuals in the form of financial assistance, direct services, housing, food and clothing. The agency does not help businesses that have been impacted by a disaster, but they do partner with the SBA, which offers low-interest loans to help businesses cover damages that have been incurred. Apply for assistance online at fema.gov, or call the FEMA Helpline at 1-800-621-3362

Cleanup

Environmental Protection Agency (EPA) Contact the National Response Center at the EPA to report oil or chemical spills. Call 1-800-424-8802

Occupational Safety and Health Administration (OSHA)

Cleaning up after a disaster, particularly one that involves flooding, can pose all sorts of safety hazards. OSHA offers a list of procedures for cleaning up safely after a flood. Visit www.osha.gov/OshDoc/cleanupHazard.html

Safeguarding Records

Internal Revenue Service (IRS) Protecting financial and tax records is critical to restarting business operations after a disaster. The IRS offers tips businesses can follow to protect their records in preparation for a disaster. Visit www.irs.gov/businesses/small-businesses-self-employed/preparing-for-a-disaster-taxpayers-and-businesses

Cybersecurity

Federal Communications Commission (FCC) The internet gives businesses access to important information as well as larger markets, but it almost makes them vulnerable to cyberattacks. The FCC offers cybersecurity tips and lists of government and private agencies that offer tools and resources. Visit www.fcc.gov/general/cybersecurity-small-business

185

A

Accessibility, business location, 42
Accounts
    managing, 84
    tracking information in, 82
Action plan, for disaster recovery, 129, 130
Advertising, 146–149
    franchises and, 69
Advice
    from experts, on succession planning, 170
    from franchiser, 69
    on recruiting and hiring, 102–103
Affordable Care Act (ACA), 109
Agreements, upon hiring employees, 125, 126–127
Allen, Paul, 54
Angel investors, 78
Appendix, in financial plan, 36, 39
Assets, 83

B

Backing-up, of records, 131
Balance sheet, 39
Bank loans, 77, 78
Basic business operation license, 86
Benefits, employee. See Employee benefits
Bookkeeper
    hiring a, 84
    setting up business as, 47, 48
Bookkeeping, business requirements for, 82–84
Brand/Branding, 142–145, 177
    franchise licensing and, 63
Brand recognition, 144–145
Budget
    analyzing/tracking, 117, 181
    building, 116–117
    for startup location, 40
Bundled pricing, 139
Burt's Bees, 56-57
Business brokers, 168

Business expansion. See Expanding your business
Business format franchise, 64
Business line of credit, 78
Business owner, insurance policies and, 90
Business plan, 14
    elements in, 36–39, 176
    market research for, 22–25
    templates, 36
Business structures/entities, 79, 80–81, 179
    record-keeping requirements for, 87
Business USA, 183
Buying a business
    additional business, 172–173
    existing business, 72–73, 168
Buying vs. leasing
    business location, 121, 123
    equipment, 132–133

C

C corps, 81
Capital. See also Startup costs
    access to, 28
    franchises/franchising and, 70
    low amount of, business options for, 46–49, 63
Career development, employee, 104, 106
CARES Act, 10
Cash flow, 114–116, 180
Cash flow statements, 39, 116
Caterer, 47
Certified public accountant (CPA), 84, 93
Change, adapting to, 163, 164–165
Choice
    limited, advantages of, 52–53, 58
    unique, 58
Cleanup, following disaster, 185
Coca-Cola franchise, 64
Commercial property insurance, 90

Commitment, to business venture, 21
Communication
    branding and, 144–145
    with customers, 154–157, 164–165
    disaster recovery and, 130
    employer-employee, 104, 106, 130
    franchisee-franchiser, 69
Community Impact Newspaper, 50, 52
Company description, in business plan, 36, 38
Competition/Competitors, 21
    analyzing, 152–153
    business location and, 42
    identifying, 25, 38, 150–152
    keeping current with, 150
Competitive pricing, 138
Consumer behavior, changes in, 28
Contracts, 125, 126–127
Coronavirus pandemic, 10
Corporations, 81, 179
    large, with small-business origins, 54–59
    record-keeping requirements for, 87
Cost-plus pricing, 139
Costs
    running (See Expenses)
    shipping, 120
    for startup (See Startup costs)
    up-front, in existing business acquisition, 73
Coulombe, Joe, 57–58
Credit cards, 77
Crisis protocol, 170
Crowdfunding, 14, 76
Customer relationship management (CRM) software, 157
Customers
    brand identity and, 144
    building rapport with, 149

identifying and reaching,
20–21, 154–157, 164, 178
(*See also* Target market)
price survey and, 137
Cybersecurity, 129, 185

D
Debt financing, 76
Demographics, business
location, 42–43
Development Centers,
small-business, 183
Digital advertising, 146, 149
Disaster recovery/relief, 185
strategy for, 128–131
Distribution franchise, 64
"Doing business as" (DBA)
permit, 86
Domain name availability, 35
Dream Vacation franchise, 65

E
Earnings, calculating, 94
Economic recession, startup
ventures during, 27
Employee benefits
competitive, 106
401(k), 172
required vs. optional, 107,
108–109
Employee handbooks, 126–127
Employee-owned businesses,
170–171
Employees
businesses owned by, 170–171
career development and, 104,
106
existing business acquisition
and, 72–73
hiring (*See* Hiring
employees)
managing and retaining,
104–106
succession planning and, 170
Employer identification number
(EIN), 79, 86, 120
Employment tax, 93
Enrolled agent (EA), 93

Entrepreneurs/
Entrepreneurship.
See Small businesses
Environmental Protection
Agency (EPA), 185
Equipment, leasing vs. buying,
132–133
Equity, tracking, 83
Equity financing, 76
Estimated quarterly tax
payments, 93
Evaluation, by franchiser, 69
Exccution, business plan, 36, 38
Executive summary, in business
plan, 36, 38
Existing business, buying an,
72–73
Exit strategies, 169, 170–171
Expanding your business
acquiring additional
business, 172–173
franchise operation, 70–71
steps for, 166–168
Expenses
setting against revenues, 94
short-term vs. long-term, 132
tracking, 83
Exxon franchise, 64

F
Failure rates, small-business,
18, 27
Family
as financial source, 76–77
succession planning and,
169, 170
Farmgirl Flowers, 52–53
Fast food chain franchises,
64–65
Federal Communications
Commission (FCC), 185
Federal Emergency
Management Agency
(FEMA), 185
Federal income tax, 91, 92–93
rates, 93
Federal licenses, 85
special, 86

FEMA (Federal Emergency
Management Agency), 185
Filing requirements, 87
Financial plan, 38–39
Financial records
backing-up, 131
basic bookkeeping and,
82–84
safeguarding, 185
Financing your business,
76–78
Fire Department permits, 86
Flexible scheduling, 108–109
Foot traffic, business location
and, 41, 42
Ford, Henry, 154
401(k) plans
for employees, 172
individual (solo), 97, 172, 184
Franchise disclosure document
(FDD), 63, 67, 68
Franchise/Franchising, 18
criteria for, 66
definition of terms, 63
single-unit vs. multiple-unit
operators, 70–71
types of, 64–65
Franchisee
defined, 63
and franchiser relationship,
66–69
role of, 66–69
single-unit vs. multiple-unit,
70–71
Franchiser
defined, 63
and franchisee relationship,
66–69
role of, 69
Friends, as financial source,
76–77

G
Garrett, John and Jennifer, 50,
52
Gates, Bill, 54, 57
General liability insurance, 90

H

Handbooks, employee, 126–127
Health Department permits, 86
Health insurance, 106, 109
Help, for small businesses. *See*
  Resources, small business
Hiring employees, 102–103
  additional, 101
  agreements upon, 125,
    126–127
  in franchise setting, 69, 71
Home-based businesses, 16, 18
  defined, 31
  insurance for, 90
  pros and cons of, 30–33
Home office deduction, 33

I

Income statement. *See* Profit-
  and-loss (P&L) statement
Income tax, federal, 91, 92–93
  rates, 93
Individual retirement accounts
  (IRAs), 96–97, 184
Influencers, 149
Infrastructure, at business
  location, 42
Insurance coverage, 88–90
  disaster recovery and, 131
Internal Revenue Service (IRS),
  183, 185
Internet
  advertisement
    trustworthiness and, 146
  cybersecurity and, 185
  domain name availability, 35
Inventory management,
  134–136
Investment portfolio, 172–173
IRAs, 96–97
IRS (Internal Revenue Service),
  183, 185
Isolation, working from home
  and, 33

J

Jazzercise franchise, 65
Job description, 102–103

Job franchise, 65
Job postings, online, 103
Joint ventures, 149

L

Landscaper, 47, 48
Leasing vs. buying
  business location, 121, 123
  equipment, 132–133
Legal issues, 124–127. *See also*
  Regulations
  business expansion, 167–168
  business structures and, 79,
    80–81, 179
  insurance (required), 88–90
  licensing, 63, 66
  trademarks, 35
Liabilities, 83, 179
Licenses, 85, 86–87
Licensing, defined, 63
Life coach, 48
Limited choice, advantages of,
  52–53, 58
Limited liability company
  (LLC), 81, 179
  record-keeping requirements
    for, 87
Limited partnership (LP), 81
Line of credit, business, 78
Liquid assets, 173
Liquidation, 171
Loans
  bank, 77, 78
  for purchase of existing
    business, 72
  SBA, 78
Local licenses, 85, 86
Local taxes, 93
Location of business
  checklist for, 40–43
  franchise expansion and, 70
  leasing vs. buying, 121,
    122–123
  location history and, 42
Loyalty programs, 154
Lukafit, 50–51

M

Mailing lists, 157
Manufacturing franchise, 64
Margin multiplier, 94–95
Market needs/trends
  adapting to changes in, 28,
    163, 164–165
  identifying, 38, 58
Market research
  for business plan, 22–25
  identifying potential
    customers, 20–21, 178
  pricing and, 137–138
Market studies, 22, 25
Marketing
  in business plan, 38
  consistent voice for, 144–145
  effective advertising for,
    146–149
  franchises and, 69
Marketing consultant, 49
Marketing plan, 38
  business expansion and, 167
Medical transcriber, 47
Microsoft, 54–55, 57
Monitoring, by franchiser, 69

N

Naming your business
  tips on, 34–35
  Trader Joe's example, 57
National Federation of
  Independent Business
  (NFIB), 90
Ndlovu, Mbali, 50–51
Net earnings (profit margin),
  94–95
Networking
  events, 157
  organizations, 25
New hires, cost of, 101
"New Normal," preadaptation
  to, 28
Niche job sites, 103
Niche marketing/markets, 13,
  50
Noncompete clauses, 126
Nondisclosure agreements, 126

O

Occupational Safety and Health Administration (OSHA), 185
Online job postings, 103
Operations, 38
    basic business license for, 86
    franchisee's responsibility, 69
    SMART method, 112–113
Opportunity(ies)
    as business plan element, 36, 38
    for current startup ventures, 26–29
Overheads, 31, 33
Owning a business, 14
    concept development, 20–21
    overview, 6–7
    rewards and risks, 10–15
    successful ventures, 50–59

P

Paid time off (PTO), 108
Partnerships, 79, 80, 179
    record-keeping requirements for, 87
    succession planning and, 170
Passion, for business venture, 6, 13, 19, 21, 47
Penetration pricing, 138
Performance reviews, 106
Perks, employee, 106. *See also* Employee benefits
Permits. *See* Regulations; *individual permits*
Personal credit cards, 77
Personal savings, 76, 78
Photographer, 47
Pricing strategies, 137, 138–139, 153
Problem(s)
    hidden, in existing business acquisition, 73
    solving a, as reason for startup, 13, 20
Product franchise, 64
Product liability insurance, 90
Product(s)

comparison between, 22–23
in franchise operation, ordering and maintaining, 68–69
limited selection of, 52–53, 58
unique, 138
Professional liability insurance, 90
Professional organizer, 49
Profit-and-loss (P&L) statement, 39, 182
Profit margin (net earnings), 95
Profitability, 94–95
Promoting your business, 38, 146–149

Q

Quickbooks, 84
Quimby, Roxanne, 57

R

Real estate
    investing in, 173
    leasing vs. buying, 121, 122–123
Record-keeping
    disaster recovery and, 131
    importance of, 163, 164
    requirements, 87
Recruitment, 102–103
Referrals, 102–103
Regulations, 85–87
    legal compliance with, 86–87
    zoning, 42, 86, 153, 167
Resiliency, 28
Resources, small-business, 22, 25, 183
    for disaster recovery/relief, 129, 131, 185
    market changes and, 164
Retention, employee, 106
Retirement, saving for, 96–97
    employee plans, 106, 109
Retirement accounts, 96–97, 184
Revenue, 94
    and earnings relationship, 95

profit and loss worksheet, 182
    tracking, 83
Review(s)
    financial, business expansion and, 167
    product/service, usefulness of, 157
Rewards
    of business ownership, 13
    financial, for employees, 106
    of home-based business, 33
Risk assessment, 129
Risks
    of business ownership, 13–14
    current, for starting a business, 26–29
Roth IRAs, 96–97, 184
Royalty fees, 69
Running costs. *See* Expenses

S

S corps, 81
Sales
    in business plan, 38
    pricing and, 137, 138–139, 153
Sales tax license, 86
Saving(s)
    personal, as financing source, 76, 78
    for retirement, 96–97
SBA. *See* Small Business Administration (SBA)
Scalability, 20
Schedule, setting a, 160, 162
SCORE, 183
Self-employment tax, 93
Selling your business, strategies for, 169, 170–171
SEP IRAs, 97, 109, 184
Service-based businesses
    franchises, 65
    with low startup costs, 46–49
Shavitz, Burt, 57
Shipping costs, 120
SIMPLE IRAs, 97, 109, 184
Simplified employee pension (SEP) plan, 97, 109, 184

Skimming, 138
Small Business Administration (SBA), 183
  business plan template, 36
  disaster recovery/relief, 129, 185
  loans from, 78
  "small business" definition, 16
Small businesses
  financing for, 76–78
  IRS portal for, 183
  major corporations beginning as, 54–59
  naming tips, 34–35
  resources for (See Resources, small business)
  SBA definition, 16
  statistics on, 16, 18–19
  success stories, 50–53
  types of, 16, 18
SMART method, 112–113
Social media influencers, 149
Social media manager, 47
Social media presence, 157
  advertising via, 149
  customer contact via, 149
  job recruitment via, 103
  marketing via, 145
Software tools
  accounting/bookkeeping, 47, 84
  CRM (customer relationship management), 157
  inventory-management systems, 136
  speech-recognition, 48
Sole proprietorship, 79, 179
  record-keeping requirements for, 87
Solitude, working from home and, 33
Solo 401(k), 97, 172, 184
Space, for business location
  growth and, 42
  leasing vs. buying, 121, 122–123

Special licenses, state and federal, 86
Sponsorship, 157
Startup costs, 18, 28
  financing of, 76–78
  franchises and, 66, 69
  home-based business, 31, 33
  service-based businesses and, 46–49
State licenses, 85–86
State taxes, 93
Stembel, Christina, 52–53
Stress test, 28
Success
  large corporate examples, 54–59
  measuring, 18–19
  small business examples, 50–53
  SMART method for, 112–113
Succession planning, 169–171
Supply chain. See Vendors

T
Target market, 38, 154–157
  adapting to change in, 28, 164
  branding and, 142–145
  connecting with, 154–157
  social media presence and, 149
Tasks
  delegating, 160, 162
  prioritizing, 160
Tax records, safeguarding, 185
Taxes
  business friendly locations and, 42
  on business structures/entities, 91, 92–93
  equipment deduction, 132–133
  estimated quarterly payments, 93
  home office deduction, 33
Trade associations/publications, 25
Trade fairs, 150
Trademarks, 35, 126

Trader Joe's, 57, 58–59
Traditional advertising, 146, 149
Traditional IRA, 96–97, 184
Training, by franchiser, 69
Turnover, employee, 104

U
Unemployment insurance, 88, 107
Unique choices, 58
Unique product, 138
Upfront costs, in existing business acquisition, 73

V
Vacation time, 107–108
Vendor accounts, establishing, 120
Vendors
  existing business acquisition and, 73
  finding and vetting, 118–120
  paying, 120
Videographer, 47
Visual identity, 144

W
Wealth, diversification of, 172–173
Woodworker, 48–49
Work-life balance, 31, 33, 160–162
Workers' compensation insurance, 88, 107
Working from home, 28
  options, 109
  pros and cons of, 30–33
Workload, setting boundaries for, 162
Workplace disability insurance, 88, 90
Worksheets, 175–185

Z
Zoning regulations/permits/variances, 42, 86, 153, 167

CREDITS

COVER Inked Pixels/Shutterstock **FRONT FLAP** Rawpixel.com/Shutterstock **2-3** jacoblund/iStock Photo **4-5** Rawpixel.com/Shutterstock; Brian A Jackson/Shutterstock; Alistair Berg/Getty Images **6-7** Slavica/Getty Images **10-11** Andrey_Popov/Shutterstock **12-13** Jacob Lund/Getty Images **14-15** Peter Griffith/Getty Images **16-17** G-Stock Studio/Shutterstock **18-19** Maskot/Getty Images **20-21** Brian A Jackson/Shutterstock **22-23** Tony Anderson/Getty Images **24-25** REDPIXEL.PL/Shutterstock **26-27** SDI Productions/Getty Images; tommy/Getty Images **28-29** leminuit/Getty Images **30-31** Westend61/Getty Images **32-33** 10'000 Hours/Getty Images **34-35** David Zaitz/Getty Images **36-37** andresr/Getty Images **38-39** Rawpixel.com/Shutterstock **40-41** yuoak/Getty Images; 1000 Words/Shutterstock **42-43** Thomas Barwick/Getty Images **44-45** Brian A Jackson/Shutterstock **46-47** 10'000 Hours/Getty Images **48-49** Alistair Berg/Getty Images **50-51** Lukafit **52-53** UfaBizPhoto/Shutterstock **54-55** Tada Images/Shutterstock **56-57** Vladislava_Solovyeva/Shutterstock **58-59** Kristi Blokhin/Shutterstock **60-61** oatawa/Shutterstock **62-63** kali9/Getty Images **64-65** Goran Bogicevic/Shutterstock **66-67** kate_sept2004/Getty Images **68-69** Travelerpix/Shutterstock **70-71** Robert Kneschke/Shutterstock **72-73** Drazen Zigic/Shutterstock **74-75** Alekseyliss/Shutterstock **76-77** Rido/Shutterstock **78-79** Africa Studio/Shutterstock **80-81** Jacobs Stock Photography Ltd/Getty Images **82-83** namtipStudio/Shutterstock **84-85** kate_sept2004/Getty Images; seksan Mongkhonkhamsao/Getty Images **86-87** ESB Professional/Shutterstock **88-89** Drazen Zigic/Shutterstock **90-91** wavebreakmedia/Shutterstock; cnythzl/Getty Images **92-93** SeventyFour/Shutterstock **94-95** Richard Drury/Getty Images **96-97** bbernard/Shutterstock **98-99** Nora Carol Photography/Getty Images **100-101** LumiNola/Getty Images **102-103** PR Image Factory/Shutterstock **104-105** Tyler Olson/Shutterstock **106-107** skynesher/Getty Images **108-109** Monkey Business Images/Shutterstock **110-111** donatas1205/Shutterstock **112-113** PeopleImages/Getty Images **114-115** Tom Werner/Getty Images **116-117** Jacob Lund/Shutterstock **118-119** Hispanolistic/Getty Images **120-121** Alistair Berg/Getty Images; sorbetto/Getty Images **122-123** Westend61/Getty Images **124-125** Jack Frog/Shutterstock **126-127** Vitalii Vodolazskyi/Shutterstock **128-129** theskaman306/Shutterstock **130-131** Rawpixel.com/Shutterstock **132-133** hedgehog94/Shutterstock **134-135** Klaus Vedfelt/Getty Images **136-137** sorbetto/getty Images **138-139** Hudzilla/Getty Images **140-141** Tawan Saklay/EyeEm **142-143** andresr/Getty Images **144-145** wera Rodsawang/Getty Images **146-147** primo-piano/Getty Images **148-149** d3sign/Getty Images **150-151** Thomas Barwick/Getty Images **152-153** Black Salmon/Shutterstock **154-155** Thomas Barwick/Getty Images **156-157** Luis Alvarez/Getty Images **158-159** azure1/Shutterstock **160-161** sanjeri/Getty Images **162-163** Westend61/Getty Images; DrAfter123/Getty Images **164-165** fizkes/Shutterstock **166-167** Maskot/Getty Images **168-169** fizkes/Shutterstock **170-171** Annie Engel/Shutterstock **172-173** Rawpixel.com/Shutterstock **174-175** voyata/Shutterstock **SPINE** JuSun/Getty Images **BACK FLAP** G-Stock Studio/Shutterstock **BACK COVER** namtipStudio/Shutterstock; David Zaitz/Getty Images

SPECIAL THANKS TO CONTRIBUTING WRITERS

MAX ALEXANDER

ERIN HEGER

MATT KUHRT

ANDREW PALMER

DONNA SELLINGER

PARAM ANAND SINGH

EMILY SMITH

CENTENNIAL BOOKS

An Imprint of
Centennial Media, LLC
40 Worth St., 10th Floor
New York, NY 10013, U.S.A.

CENTENNIAL BOOKS is a trademark of Centennial Media, LLC

All rights reserved. No part of this publication may be reproduced, stored
in a retrieval system, or transmitted in any form or by any means (including
electronic, mechanical, photocopying, recording, or otherwise) without
prior written permission from the publisher.

ISBN 978-1-951274-52-8

Distributed by
Simon & Schuster, Inc.
1230 Avenue of the Americas
New York, NY 10020, U.S.A.

For information about custom editions, special sales and premium and corporate purchases,
please contact Centennial Media at contact@centennialmedia.com.

Manufactured in China

© 2021 by Centennial Media, LLC

10 9 8 7 6 5 4 3 2 1

Publishers & Co-Founders Ben Harris, Sebastian Raatz
Editorial Director Annabel Vered
Creative Director Jessica Power
Executive Editor Janet Giovanelli
Deputy Editors Ron Kelly, Alyssa Shaffer
Design Director Martin Elfers
Senior Art Director Pino Impastato
Art Directors Olga Jakim, Natali Suasnavas, Joseph Ulatowski
Copy/Production Patty Carroll, Angela Taormina
Assistant Art Director Jaclyn Loney
Photo Editor Jennifer Veiga
Production Manager Paul Rodina
Production Assistant Alyssa Swiderski
Editorial Assistant Tiana Schippa
Sales & Marketing Jeremy Nurnberg

To all the queer kids,
who are exactly who they were meant to be

Contents

Author's Note   9

Chapter 1: The Suitcase   11
Chapter 2: So, Like, How Did You Know?   19
Chapter 3: Wonder Woman   35
Chapter 4: Boys, Boys, Boys   57
Chapter 5: Facing the Truth   79
Chapter 6: America, Home of the Brave   109
Chapter 7: Out   127
Chapter 8: Aftermath   137
Chapter 9: Fallout   145
Chapter 10: Jimmychooshoes   157
Chapter 11: The Purple Passions   181
Chapter 12: Busted   207
Chapter 13: What Mums Do   231
Chapter 14: Lesbian Paraphernalia   243
Chapter 15: Go Your Own Way   259
Chapter 16: Ad Wankers   265
Chapter 17: The Letter   275
Chapter 18: Mad (Wo)men   283
Chapter 19: Exploring Family   317

Acknowledgements   343

Author's Note

This book is memoir, and reflects my current recollections of experiences from the past. Some names and details have been changed to protect privacy, and some dialogue has been re-created. There will no doubt be some errors in my remembering, for which I can only apologise. Know that if you are in the book, you have been hugely important to my life.

Chapter 1
The
Suitcase

I stood on the side of the dark road, looking back down the hill to the lights of my family home.

'Well, fuck,' I said, juggling my laptop and the few other possessions I'd managed to grab in my hasty exit.

Hearing my voice out loud somehow made me feel a little better, breaking me out of my shock enough to search my pockets. Finally my fingers found the familiar shape of my phone, and a spike of panic receded.

I flipped it open and scrolled through to JACK CELL, then typed out a message, my fingers clumsy on the buttons.

UM, YOULL NEVER GUESS WOT JST HAPPENED

Forty minutes later, I heard the roar of my best friend Jack's muffler bouncing off the cliffs that leaned over the narrow road. As he rounded the last corner I recognised our favourite song, Nelly's 'Ride wit Me', blaring from the open windows of his souped-up 1986 hatchback. He'd saved up for it by working after school and weekends at the Mobil station up the road from his house, and it was his pride and joy. It had tinted windows, an aftermarket exhaust and a police radar to avoid speeding tickets. I took the piss out of him about being a bogan every time I saw it. But maybe not this time. This time he was my knight in a shining white Mazda Familia 323 GT.

Jack pulled a U-turn and turned down the stereo as he stopped the car, then leaned over to peer at me through the open passenger window.

'Mate, what the fuck?'

—

It was the Easter holidays, and my mid-semester break from university. The evening had started out ordinarily enough. Mum would always cook one of my favourite meals when I came home from uni for the holidays—so dinner that night might have been a leg of lamb with roast potatoes, or a piece of eye fillet with oven fries. Maybe even a fried egg for Dad too, as a treat. I can imagine him now: 'Good old steak, eggs and chips. Goody goody.' He would rub his hands together exaggeratedly, hunch his shoulders and grin at me. Dad loved Mum's cooking, even when she overcooked the meat or double-salted the broccoli.

After dinner, still hungover from a big night out, I flopped on the couch and buried my nose in a book, hoping to be left alone.

'Lilly? Lil. Lilly, I'm talking to you!'

'What?'

I'd ignored Mum for as long as possible, my irritation with her incessant chatter growing.

'I'm asking you whether you want to go into town tomorrow. I want to look at shoes but you could pick out a new T-shirt and pants. Or we could go to Farmers first, get some basics . . .'

I zoned out again.

'Lilly . . .'

'Mum, I'm trying to read, okay. Can we decide tomorrow?'

There was a pause. 'More like you're hungover. I heard you clomping around at three a.m. this morning,' Mum said.

I sighed. *Here we go.*

'I thought I was pretty quiet, all things considered,' I said.

Mum huffed. 'You can't drink like that forever, you know.'

'Mum, I'm nineteen. I'm in my drinking prime,' I replied with a grin.

I was a third-year student at the University of Otago, its

campus in the southern New Zealand city of Dunedin. The university was known for its drinking culture more than anything else, and I had embraced that wholeheartedly. I travelled back to my parents' house every semester break, something that at nineteen I was still young enough to describe as 'going home'. Home, to a seaside suburb in a South Island city where I'd grown up. Home, to Mum's cooking and her soft towels and to my younger sister, Jenny, and to my dad, and our fluffy cat. Although I enjoyed those familiar comforts, my priority during the holidays was to go out drinking with Jack. We'd gather with his ragtag gang of buddies at someone's house to smoke darbs and pre-load—him with a twelve-pack of Flame beer, me with a $7.30 bottle of Aquila sparkling wine. Then we'd hit town, squeezing into packed bars, ordering two-for-one Mudslide Shakers or shots of shitty tequila, or 'Quick Fucks' if we didn't want to be quite so hardcore. The combination of Kahlúa, Midori and Baileys looked cool and didn't taste half-bad either. Around 2 a.m. I would usually slip away from my friends unnoticed, avoiding the inevitable 'Stayyyyy, Lilly, just half an hour longer, staayyyyy'. I'd fling myself into a taxi, which would drive me the $60 journey home and was paid for with Dad's taxi charge card.

'Have you thought about what you're going to do when you finish university, Lilly?' my dad chipped in from behind his newspaper.

I sighed. 'Dad, c'mon. It's Sunday, can we just relax and not get into my career prospects today?'

'It doesn't hurt to plan ahead—we're not going to financially support you forever,' Dad said.

'No,' Mum seconded knowingly, sending a plume of steam shooting up from her iron.

'I know that!'

'You only have one full semester left,' Dad said, stating the obvious.

I didn't know why they couldn't just chill about this topic. With the confidence of someone who'd never had to worry about money, I knew I would figure it out when the time came. With my parents there as a safety net.

'Seriously, can you guys just leave me alone,' I said, putting my book down and preparing to leave the lounge. 'I don't need you giving me shit right now.'

It was the wrong thing to say, and that's when things really kicked off. It was a big one—one of those fights that dredged up every negative feeling and cause of conflict that was between us, old or new. But this story isn't about that fight. It's about what happened after the fight, and how my life changed forever because of it.

As the argument wound down, reaching the kind of impasse where there's a whole lot of tension in the air but nothing left to say, I escaped to the other side of the house. After I'd left for university my parents had downsized to a small home, so this consisted of stomping a few metres and closing the door to my sister's room, where I was sleeping while she was away on a school trip.

I called Jack to vent.

'They are so fucking mad,' I said into the phone, pacing the room. 'Man . . .' I laughed. 'Imagine if on top of this they found out I was into girls.'

'That would go down like a bag of sick,' Jack replied emphatically.

After saying goodbye to Jack and hanging up, I strode confidently back out to the kitchen, feeling vindicated. I plonked myself down at the table and flipped open my laptop, plugging the phone cord in so I could connect to the internet.

When Mum stepped into the room I took no notice. But when I heard her say 'Lilly, have you got something to tell us?' in a low tone, and I looked up to see the expression on her face, my stomach dropped.

I immediately understood what she was talking about. And that I was so, *so* fucked.

Because I knew that being gay was not a viable option in my family.

What happened next has survived in my memory as a series of sensory elements and emotions. It's as though my brain has tried to block out the detail but hasn't protected me from the feelings: dread, terror, nausea. It's easy to bring back the ghosts of that memory even today, sixteen years later. I remember the soft night-time lighting of the room and the TV murmuring in the background. I remember the shape of what they said.

'It's unnatural . . .'

'How could you . . .'

'What did we do wrong?'

'. . . sick . . . not normal . . .'

It began with Mum, who kept storming away into the other room then boomeranging back as she thought of another point to make about this humiliation and betrayal. 'How could you even know?' she spat. 'You've never had a proper boyfriend!'

Dad had got up from his comfy chair in the lounge, and now he piled on: '. . . ungrateful . . . after all we've given you . . .'

His anger was different, pure rage meeting my mother's icy upset. He called me nasty things, swept something from the table near him onto the floor.

It could have lasted five minutes; it could have been 40. Time seemed to slow down and speed up at the same time. I couldn't speak or think. I just sat stupidly at the table with my head bowed, pressed hard into the wooden chair, wiping at the tears and snot running down my face with my fingers. My heart roared in pain. Finally, there was a long, loaded pause, one that grew more dangerous by the second. I didn't dare look up, afraid of what I'd see in their faces.

Then Mum said: 'You need to get out.'

And that's what made me finally look at her, uncomprehending.

She seemed to steel herself, and declared in an escalating voice, 'You need to leave, now. Just . . . get out of here.'

I finally clicked that she meant for me to leave the house . . . right now. But it was dark outside and nearly bedtime; where would I go? I looked to Dad, but he wouldn't meet my eye. So I pulled myself up from the table on legs that didn't feel like my own, getting them tangled in the chair as I tried to extricate myself. I started shakily gathering my laptop and charger and other stuff at hand.

'No,' Mum said. 'Don't pack. Just go.'

Using a small reserve of defiance, I finished grabbing

everything on the table, gripping it to my chest in a tangle of cables and papers. I shuffled between Mum and the kitchen bench towards the front door, and she leaned back into the wall and turned her head away slightly as I passed.

Thankfully my wallet and a few other things were sitting on the bench by the door, and I scooped them up too, shoving things into any pocket I could find. I glanced back and found both Mum and Dad watching me, coiled tightly as though making sure I didn't try to take anything that wasn't mine on the way out. Like I was some stranger who had infiltrated their house. Perhaps that's what I felt like to them—now that I wasn't who they thought I was.

When I reached the front door Mum spoke again, sounding a little shaky. 'I don't ever want to see you again.'

In shock, I could barely process what she'd said. My brain seemed to have a time lag. But finally I managed to tune in to what she said next.

Dad would text me tomorrow with a time I could come by to pick up my things. I was not to come by whenever I wanted. I was not to come back into the house. My suitcase would be waiting for me on the side of the road tomorrow.

Chapter 2
So, Like, How Did You Know?

**The agony of becoming. This is what she experiences.
The young girl. She would like to be someone,
anyone else. She wants, vaguely, to be something
more than she is. But she does not know what that
is, or how one goes about doing such a thing.**
— *Green Girl*, Kate Zambreno

When I was a kid, two of my favourite books were *Lost Girls: Adrift!* and *Lost Girls: Alone!* by Linda Williams Aber, about a group of girls shipwrecked on a tropical island. One girl cuts her foot on coral and falls into a fever, and the leader of the group nurses her back to health. She stays attentively at her side, wiping the sweat off her brow and soothing her whimpers. Oh lord. This sparked a long period of dreams (or were they fantasies?) where I would imagine the big sister of one of my friends—her name was Angelica—nursing me back to health. After I'd injured myself saving her life first, of course.

I had a crush on her sister Violet too, and at school lunchtime I would often suggest that we play a game I'd made up called 'manhunt'. It was a version of tag where, if you were captured by Violet, you'd be put into a wooden hut in the playground dubbed the 'jail'. I was a small kid, and when I was nabbed Violet would pick me up to carry me there. The feeling of being pressed against her chest by her strong arms is what ensured that I was caught over and over again.

There were movies that would have given me many clues as to my sexuality, had I had the maturity to untangle my reactions to them. I was nine or ten when I first saw the cult classic *The Goonies*, and despite all the other things to love in that movie—a ragtag bunch of kids getting into trouble, booby traps, inventions, pirate treasure—it was Andy, the older girl with her red hair and yellow letterman jacket, who stayed with me afterwards. I wanted to be the one who dived in after her when she was made to walk the plank, to swim her to safety and then loop her bound hands over my head so that I could kiss her with such confidence. I didn't think too deeply about it, but I knew that it was something to keep squirrelled away deep in my brain. When I discovered that the same actress, Kerri Green, was in the film *Lucas*, too, it was the first time I remember developing an obsession with someone.

The title character of the film, Lucas, doesn't understand that because of key structural differences between him and Maggie, Kerri Green's character—he is fourteen, she is older; he is nerdy, she is popular; he collects bugs, she dates the football player—he'll never be with her. I identified with Lucas strongly. He would never win the girl just like I'd never win the girl, because that wasn't how the equation of life worked. Still, I made my cousin play her VHS tape of that movie nearly every time I went over to her house. I couldn't stop dreaming of a different world.

By my teenage years, watching movies mostly became something to do alone, in my bedroom. I knew I shouldn't talk too much about my favourite actresses in movies, not in the way my sister, Jenny, went on about Devon Sawa from the *Casper* movie and Peter Andre's abs (were they really implants? The mystery has never been solved). A home video of Jen's tenth birthday party shows her and her giggling mates playing a game of 'pin the lips on Leonardo DiCaprio', while thirteen-year-old me skulks in the background wearing tartan cargo shorts and a shaggy mullet, scoffing at them from a distance and feeling left out somehow, even though I had no desire to pin my lips on Leo.

Splayed across my sister's bedroom walls were 'hot hunk' posters pulled from *Girlfriend* magazine, while every surface in my bedroom featured framed photographs and corkboard montages of my female friends. It was something I sensed was neutral territory. But the prevailing message I got was obvious: boys were the way forward, and I was expected (by myself and by others) to 'get there' eventually. The thing was, I went to a single-sex girls' school and boys simply didn't feature in our lives much—apart from those pesky school socials. At the first and only social I attended, at age fourteen, I was horrified to see couples making out inside to the thumping beat of 'Butterfly' by Crazy Town, and dry-humping outside against the terracotta brick walls. I'd called Dad to come pick me up early.

I had more important things to do during these years anyway, like lifting weights every day over the summer holidays so that the coach would let me into our school's 'A' soccer team. And other kinds of thing that anyone who was a tomboy might identify with: building huts, trying to turn anything with wheels into a go-kart, creating apocalypse-ready campsites in the hills like they did in my favourite book, *Tomorrow, When the War Began*, raiding the dress-up box and usually ending up with a moustache and top hat on, playing tackle rugby with the boys and being told off for being too rough, and always, always wearing a baseball cap.

By the time I got to my mid-teens the topic of boys was prevalent, but I still didn't get it. I'd become close with a girl named Amber, and even though I couldn't understand her overwhelming desire for the teenage male, I thought I could learn something about how I was supposed to feel.

Amber fit my understanding of what adults meant when they called young women 'boy crazy'. She talked about boys constantly, to a point that seemed obsessive . . . and yet they were so interchangeable! Someone could be in one day and out the next due to any number of perceived slights. The first year that most of us got cell phones with text-messaging capabilities, Amber created her own set of rules around how guys were supposed to communicate with her. I was gobsmacked when one day she decided to dump one poor sod because he didn't text her back within fifteen minutes.

Every morning in our form room I would question Amber about her latest boy goss, and she was pleased to have an audience—even if that came along with a lot of teasing and eye-rolling from me. Sometimes I would change the lyrics to a song and sing it to her—like the 'Mambo No. 5' lyrics changed to 'One, two, three, four, five. Boys, you can run but you sure can't hide. Amber's on her way and she's after her prey . . .' etc. Other notable songs included 'Hooked on a Feeney' about her current boyfriend Simon Feeney (a bastardisation of 'Hooked on a Feeling'), and 'That Don't Impress Her Much' based on the Shania Twain song, although that one was the least imaginative of the bunch.

I began scouring second-hand bookstores for Mills & Boon romance novels, which she adored and claimed she was going to write herself one day; I presented her with a huge box of them on her birthday. Although I never felt an attraction towards Amber the way I began to later that year for an older girl in my soccer team, my friendship with Amber was the beginning of a pattern, one where I would give thoughtful gifts to my closest female friends—gifts that showed how much I understood them. While they were thinking of boys, I was thinking about them.

My encouragement of Amber's crushes also functioned as a

cover for me. Egging her on meant the attention was always on her boy dramas rather than on my lack of interest in the male gender. It meant I was talking about boys without ever talking to boys. I could be involved in this strange pull towards boys without actually feeling any pull towards boys. But eventually that wasn't enough. I knew I needed to work harder to solve this mystery. I wanted to know what it was like to kiss someone, and most importantly I needed to be able to say I had kissed someone. I knew I couldn't turn sixteen having never kissed a boy. Steps needed to be taken to rectify the situation, and that meant finding a way into a social scene where boys were around.

I began to work towards getting a first kiss by squeezing my way further into the group of friends I'd dubbed the First Ladies. The First Ladies all lived locally in posh suburbs and they had parents who would put up marquees for their birthday pool parties, supplying catered nibbles and everything. Before then I'd primarily hung out with the boarders who lived at school during the term. With the boarders I spent a lot of time doing active things, or watching movies in the TV room (although I never understood why they loved *Dirty Dancing* so much), or dancing on the wardrobes in the dorms to 'Barbie Girl' by Aqua. But once I'd decided it was time to grow up, it was clear I needed the friendship of the First Ladies. Their parties had boys invited. Their parties ran late and included booze and flirting, I presumed, and all kinds of other things I needed to be a part of. This had to be the social circle that would provide me with a solution.

My first attempt to find a pash was at my friend Penny's

house. She'd been left alone one weekend with just her older sister to babysit—who didn't give a shit what we did as long as we didn't get in her way. She was scary, and super cool. When I arrived at Penny's there were already boys there, but to be honest I didn't notice. I had been drawn instead towards my first experience with a far more tantalising prospect: booze. I started pouring vodka and orange juices that got steadily stronger over the course of a couple of hours, and after half a bottle the room was spinning. I crawled up the stairs towards the bathroom, but just as I was almost there a guy jumped over me and slammed the bathroom door in my face. I puked on the carpet and passed out, and Amber spent the rest of the night sticking her face in my face to see if I was still breathing. Needless to say, Pashing: Attempt One was not a success.

Pashing: Attempt Two took place at a proper party at a First Lady's house, with boys from the private boys' school down the road in attendance and a dress-up theme. I knew I had my costume down: I would go as Pamela Anderson from *Baywatch*. Bleach-blonde wig, red *Baywatch* togs my friend had got on a family trip to Venice Beach in Los Angeles, which were just a teensy bit small. Bulging water bombs down my togs as fake boobs, and bright red lipstick. Perfect.

'Are you sure you want to go to your first party with boys dressed like this?' my mother asked me.

I didn't know what she was talking about—of course I did! It was an amazing costume! And despite some nervousness I had a great time at the party . . . for the first hour or so. Then someone stole my wig, one of my boobs popped and I spent most of the night holding back my friend's hair as she chundered into the downstairs toilet. Attempt Two: fail.

By the beginning of my second-to-last year of high school I still hadn't had my first pash, or even a flirtation. I was desperate. Then, another of the First Ladies announced a party. I had two primary goals that night—get a bit pissed for courage and find a pash. By midnight I had achieved the first goal (had been a bit overzealous, even), and I had my sights set on one boy, for no reason other than I sensed that I could make it happen. Unfortunately, Harry Gibbs was useless at making the first move, seeming content to sit next to me in the outdoor marquee and rub his head against mine, which is only sexy if you're a character in *The Lion King*. Finally, my patience ran thin, and I grabbed him by his surprisingly large, rough hand and pulled him into the darkness of the garden. When I raised my face and stood on tiptoes to kiss him, he stuck his tongue in my mouth, which was alarming enough, then he began weaselling his hand between the waist of my skirt and my skin.

At first I reacted without thinking, sucking in my breath to let him get his hand down there—even though I didn't want it. It was just my instinct to let him do what he wanted to do, even though my alcohol-fogged brain was flashing a warning light. I'd had no idea this was going to happen—we were supposed to kiss so I could tick that off my list. I hadn't thought much further than that! I let him wriggle his giant man-hand around for about five seconds before I came to my senses and yanked it back out. Horrible.

The night was winding down, so we stumbled upstairs and

passed out on a mattress on the floor with a number of other people. In the morning I came downstairs trailing Harry and, without thinking, thanked my friend's mum for having 'us'. Apparently that was the magic word that made Harry think he was in with a grin. I'd set events in motion without realising it.

Things continued to get out of hand from there. I made it back home a couple of hours later and sank into bed, grumpy and exhausted. All I wanted to do was sleep and watch TV and ignore everyone. But soon I heard a knock at the front door upstairs.

Seconds later, my mum called out for me. 'Lilly, you have a visitor.'

What the fuck? When I got to the top of the stairs I was greeted by the sight of a smiling Harry Gibbs standing next to my bemused-looking mother. I didn't hang out with any boys and they certainly didn't turn up on my doorstep unannounced. Under Mum's very interested but suspicious gaze I greeted Harry unenthusiastically. 'Oh. Hi. What are you doing here?'

I pulled him downstairs to my bedroom without even introducing him. I had no idea that taking a strange boy to my bedroom and closing the door could be perturbing to a parent.

'Um, I'm just going to watch TV, okay?' I said.

He agreed and I reluctantly moved over to make room for him on my single bed. I could smell the stale alcohol coming off him, which was even more of a reason to keep my face turned away. I was highly aware that if I tilted my head even just a little bit too far in his direction he would try to kiss me. Unfortunately my TV was at the foot of the bed so turning on my side would have made it difficult to see. I ended up lying with my bum on the mattress but my body twisted away, my arms wrapped protectively across my chest. I tried to breathe shallowly. I looked at his meaty hand, which was resting on my hip, daring it to move somewhere untoward so that I would have a reason to jump up and tell him to go.

There was no conversation—he was no conversationalist and I gave him nothing to work with, responding only in grunts or monosyllabic words. And so we watched Ricki Lake in what I felt was screamingly awkward silence.

Meanwhile, outside my bedroom, my mum was getting more and more worked up about there being a boy in her daughter's bedroom. She kept coming out onto the balcony that connected our two rooms to 'hang out the washing'. She didn't dare come right up to my window but I kept catching the edge of the towels in my peripheral vision as she flapped them around vigorously, making sure I knew she was there. It was the only thing that made me smile during those torturous 45 . . . no, he was still there . . . 60 . . . why wouldn't he leave . . . 76 (!) minutes.

When I finally got him to leave—after leading him to the front entrance, enduring a wet kiss to my closed lips and shutting the door behind him—I felt immense relief. I knew I was about to face a lot of questions and quite possibly be in trouble with my mother—which I was—but that was nothing compared with the anxiety I now felt about what was going to happen with Harry Gibbs. And those fears came true. Somehow during this interaction we had become boyfriend and girlfriend.

Harry began calling me every evening, which was a dating ritual that I knew about but had never really considered. I was certainly not one of those teenage girls who talks on the phone for hours every night, and our first conversation went something like this: 'How old are you? What's your birthday? What's your school like? Who are you friends with? Where do you live? Yeah, our house is real nice eh.'

That was the first two minutes. Then we moved on to more like: 'Oh yeah? Cool. Yeah. Nah. Yeah, I quite like that. Yeah, I like music too. Kind of. I mean, not heaps, but yeah. Music's good. Yeah, nah. Yeah, food's good, I like food. Cool. Yeah. So. Cool. Um. Yeah . . . so . . . um . . .'

I hung up after a torturous amount of time, thinking, *Ugh! What the hell was that?*

But apparently Harry thought it went swimmingly, and he began calling me every night. I dreaded each of these phone calls and would become more and more anxious as our prearranged time of 8 p.m. drew closer. My evenings became laden with an additional kind of homework outside of essays and worksheets: frantically trying to think of topics to talk about with Harry, and writing them down in a list while watching the clock with mounting nerves. It was difficult work because he and I were nothing alike. He came from a farming background, I was a townie. He'd repeated Year 11 because he failed School Certificate. I actually enjoyed exams. He was into me. I was not into him. Harry did have nice tanned skin and I quite liked to touch his shaved head because it was lovely and soft. But that was about the extent of my feelings around all that.

Harry and I were together for what felt like the longest six weeks of my life. We would meet up in the weekends at the house of whoever was hosting drinks, and each time without fail he would bring me a dispenser of Smints and a $6 bottle of Golden Gate spumante. While these attempts to get me into bed were sweet (except, like, what was he trying to tell me with the breath mints?), they were unsuccessful. One night we slept on the floor of my friend's dad's empty house, and I got as far as touching him through his underwear for about twenty seconds before I rolled over, uninspired, and fell asleep. Even a complete lack of parental supervision and an overnight stay with his girlfriend couldn't get him laid.

There were a number of less-than-satisfactory encounters with Harry that made me more and more certain I needed to get rid of him. Because Harry and many of our respective friends came from farms in the region, in the weekends we'd often head out of the city to party. Or, in one case, to what was supposed to be a party but ended up being me and fifteen boys in a woolshed, where I threw back sparkling wine in desperation while they sculled Double Brown beer and took turns seeing who could crack the stock whip. I refused to get into the car with Harry because of how much he'd had to drink, and I curled up in a pile of straw until the early hours of the morning, when he deemed himself sober enough to drive.

Sleeping in not-beds became a habit during our month-and-a-half-long whirlwind romance. But it wore thin very quickly, particularly when Harry began lying to me about having accommodation. One weekend we drove south to the remote town of Twizel to support our schools' rowing crews in the Maadi Cup. Harry had promised me that his grandmother lived there and would be delighted to have us to stay. Instead I found myself sleeping in my car with Harry after the grandmother's house never materialised, waking in the morning with a sore back, rancid breath and condensation rolling down the insides of the windows.

'Ha, smells like fish tacos in here!' one of the girls from another school exclaimed when she came outside to see us, having actually slept inside the house we were parked by. I cringed at both the crude language and the sexual association.

This girl was just one of a few who I'd sensed might be into Harry. To be honest, I wondered why he was with me at all when he had these other girls as options. Worse than how I kept trying to uphold standards such as not drink-driving and sleeping in a bed, I was proving to be a prude. We hadn't even got to second base.

Everything unravelled in a way that seemed inevitable at the farm party to beat all farm parties. Carloads of teenagers convoyed out to a rural property, where we had been given the expansive free reign of the shearers' quarters, the cowshed and the surrounding paddocks. As the girls arrived they drove slowly over the grass to park their cars in a row, boots filled with sparkling wine and Vodka Cruisers, sleeping bags, and warm jackets to put over their nicer outfits when the temperature dropped at night. Meanwhile, at least every third carload of boys thought it would be funny to drive far too fast into the paddock and pull the handbrake on, carving up the grass and encouraging what would, by morning, be a quagmire of sheep shit and mud, cigarette butts and bottle caps from Speight's and Export Gold stubbies.

I drove out with Harry, as was expected of me, although I would have much preferred to be with my friends. With them I could have joked around or sung loudly to 'Say My Name' by Destiny's Child rather than sitting in silence with John Denver singing 'Country roads, take me home, to the place I belong, West Virginia . . .' or listening to 'The Gambler' on repeat. (Although I will say, this was helpful to me because knowing all the words to 'The Gambler' was essential for social occasions such as these. Inevitably at some point in the night this song would come on and everyone would gather around in a circle, arms draped around each other, singing every word of this song religiously.)

After we parked, Harry went off to find his friends. Night fell, the bonfire flames grew, people began falling prey to the slick mud of the paddock and I still hadn't had any interaction with Harry. He didn't want to hang with me, and I didn't want to hang with him, although from a distance I did notice a girl from one of the other private schools flirting with him. He seemed responsive. I was 90 per cent indifferent, 10 per cent 'Should I be caring about this?'

At around 2 a.m., Harry appeared from the darkness, grabbed me and hustled me into the back seat of my car. He got on top of me, mouth wet and hands everywhere. His cold hands went under my top, and I shrieked and pushed him away.

'Harry! Get off me!'

'What? What?' he kept saying, his beer breath hot on my face.

'It's not going to happen!'

He pulled himself up and left me lying in the back seat.

The next morning I climbed out of the car and joined the people milling around the burnt-out fire. I spotted Harry sitting very close to the girl he'd been flirting with the night before. But I didn't care. I knew that last night had been a tipping point, where I either had to take it further with Harry or break things off with him.

I let Harry drive me back into the city in my car, and by the time we got into town it had started raining hard. The traffic was moving slowly, and I zoned out with my head against the window. BOOM. We struck the car in front and jolted to a halt.

'What the fuck, Harry?' I said.

'I'll sort it, I'll sort it,' he said, getting out of the car in a panic. I watched through the watery windscreen as he negotiated with the driver in front, then he came back towards my car.

'I'll be back in a second,' he said, reaching inside to grab his wallet.

'What? Harry, what's going on?' I said, but he had slammed the door and run off into the rain. I watched anxiously, sure that the other driver was going to come to my window demanding answers.

Five minutes later, Harry reappeared and handed something through the window of the car in front before swinging back into my car, soaked.

'What happened?' I said.

'Don't worry, I sorted it,' he replied.

'What do you mean you sorted it?'

'I gave him two hundred dollars, it's cool,' Harry said.

'But I have insurance . . .'

'Don't worry!' Harry said. 'It's sorted.'

We made it back to Harry's boarding house, where I happily said goodbye to him for what we both knew would be the last time as boyfriend and girlfriend. Getting behind the steering wheel, I drove the car home carefully, gearing myself up to face the wrath of my parents when they saw the large dent in the front bumper. I found out later that Harry had a suspended licence for drink-driving, which explained the $200.

My mother was as relieved as I was to see the back of him.

Chapter 3

Wonder Woman

**I know who I *was* when I got up this morning, but I think
I must have been changed several times since then.**

— Alice's Adventures in Wonderland, Lewis Carroll

I now had an ex-boyfriend in my past whom I could bring up
at appropriate moments when I was hanging out with my
friends. So, in a way, I guess having a boyfriend had been a
success.

But I was halfway through my second-to-last year of high
school, and, although I had lots of great friends and was

regularly invited to parties, I still felt out of place in the world of boys and sex and flirtation. I couldn't connect with the male gender, finding them pretty boring and predictable. They made me feel like I was boring too, because I was too nervous to share the things I cared about or to crack jokes. When there's no dialogue your value becomes based on how you look, and then I resented them for reducing me to that.

Unfortunately I needed boys. The school-ball season arrived, and having a male partner was essential. There was a range of events to navigate, like the balls from the boys' schools, which were primarily formal wear, and our own dress-up ball in the middle of the year, which was less formal but no less important. The next year I'd have a leavers' ball to go to as well. It was . . . a lot. All of a sudden there were new social expectations. Avoiding the school dances of earlier years hadn't been a big deal. But balls were different. They were inextricably woven into the social fabric of being a teenager, and there was an unspoken knowledge that the more balls you went to in a year the more socially adept you were, because it meant you'd been invited by boys from other schools. It seemed weird that being desired by a boy was apparently the marker of popularity to strive for. But I bought in.

It was common for all the teenagers from the high-decile schools to stay in motels on the night of a ball and, for some reason, Central Park Motel was by far the favourite choice. Its textured plaster exterior was a dirty light grey that had perhaps once been white, and its interior design was particularly loathsome: puke-coloured carpets clashing with floral polyester bedspreads that always seemed to hook on to your skin somehow and were likely never washed. But still, staying there was a tradition, and we loved that place in the sarcastic way that teenagers choose to like things that are a bit naff. After zipping ourselves into full-length strapless satin dresses—bold purple or Barbie blue or hologram orange being the trend—and curling the twists of hair that hung down the sides of our faces around our fingers with a final spritz of hairspray, we would totter on strappy high heels across the uneven cobbles to the room of whoever's parents had sprung for a suite. There, we would slurp cheap bottles of spumante or Mad Jacks not-quite-rum with the kind of desperation that comes with drinking on a deadline. As the taxi vans rolled into the courtyard and began honking, we would chuck back our final drinks, strap hip flasks to our thighs and flood into the courtyard to meet the boys. Girls drank separately from boys before the balls. That's just how it was done.

It was difficult to find my date in these moments because I'd usually only met him for the first time that night. One of my friends had always set me up with one of their boyfriend's mate's mates who was as useless with the opposite sex as I was. Remembering the guy's name was one thing; I was lucky if I could even remember his face.

Anyway, it wasn't these dates I was excited to spend time with. It was the two girls I was growing closer to with every social event. I wasn't fully 'in' with Bridget and Coop yet—at my school's dress-up ball that year, they split a room while I had one to myself next door. I was still working out how to be comfortable with sharing personal space. Bridget and Coop were mates with all the First Ladies but they were a little rougher around the edges in a way I found interesting and reassuring, because there was something about spending time with the core group of the First Ladies that wasn't quite me. They dressed beautifully but without character, watched what they ate and dated nice (boring) boys from the private school up the road. I felt like my jokes always went too far or just didn't land at all with them. Friendship is an odd thing. When you spend time with your bestest friends, it's like you're being lifted up and borne along on a light breeze. The conversation flows and you can revel in being yourself. But some friendships are like a headwind; you have to lean in a little harder to keep your balance. I often felt off balance when I socialised with the First Ladies. When friends make you feel like this, I think you either judge yourself and all your failings, or you judge them. I was probably guilty of the latter.

Bridget and Coop were different. They were silly and unpolished and not PC at all. They also had this physical ease with one another that fascinated me. I wasn't like that at all. I would quietly enjoy everyone else's hijinks from the sidelines, watching carefully and throwing in the odd piece of dry wit. I was best in a one-on-one conversation rather than in a group of high-spirited teens. I certainly wasn't at ease with myself, and I'd never initiated a hug with anyone my own age, though I desperately wanted those hugs. That was not what I'd grown up with in my family, not who I was. But, then again, I was still trying to figure that out.

I think what I loved most about Bridge and Coop was that they weren't self-conscious, so I became less self-conscious. I could relax around them. I could pretend to be like them and I knew they wouldn't see through me or, if they did, they wouldn't make me feel embarrassed for trying so hard. After our school ball ended that year, I found myself back in their room. Our other friend JJ was there too and the three of them were rolling around in the queen-sized bed being drunken idiots, saying funny things and imagining the alarm clock was sending them a message from space, while I sat in a chair nearby, laughing. One by one they dropped off to sleep, bundled together and completely at ease with themselves. I quietly snuck out of the room back to my own, and that was the moment I decided I had to become more like them.

Over the next few months, that's what I did. I invited them around to my house often, where they would lean over the kitchen bench, their legs swinging behind them, chattering and helping themselves to the food Mum had put out, thanking her and joking with her in equal measure. I tried to be more like that, more teasing and charming with people who were my elders or whom I didn't know well. I tried to engage more, to be more a part of the group, and I was. But I was also always the person behind the camera, filming Bridget as she danced to our favourite song from Geri Halliwell's first solo album after leaving the Spice Girls, or Coop as she mugged for the camera, her dimples catching my eye every time I watched the footage back on the small screen of my handheld video camera. I enjoyed getting ready to go out at night as a group, the others flinging their clothes around the room or rummaging in my wardrobe to find me the perfect outfit, which caused me anxiety but gave me validation at the same time. Mum would herd us together in the kitchen to take a group photo before we went out, and when I reviewed those photos years later, I looked like I belonged. It was these friendships that gave me new confidence and a growing self-awareness that even though I was never the loudest in the room, I could be other things. Maybe I was the glue that held people together or maybe I was the stable, considered one. I realised that could be a valuable role too. I was the one who looked after everyone's debit cards when we went out on the piss, and being given that responsibility made me feel accepted for who I was.

Most importantly, these friendships taught me intimacy, the kind I had seen between Bridget and Coop and JJ and wanted so much for myself. The girls began to stay over during the weekend, particularly Bridge and Coop, and we would snuggle up in my queen bed together in the mornings, or at night, or sometimes just in the afternoons as we lazed around. Occasionally my mum or dad would come downstairs, and although my mum has a brilliant poker face I could tell Dad was taken aback. After the girls left, then would come the comments.

'It's weird how you girls cuddle up together like that.'

'It's a bit of a strange friendship you have with those girls . . .'

'Do you all have to be in the same bed together? It's not normal, surely.'

I didn't care—couldn't he see that I was normal *because* I

had started cuddling with my friends? It made me feel so good and no snarky comment could stop me. But it was during this year, my Year 12, that my relationship with my parents began to deteriorate. I was creating an emotional landscape in my other relationships that was foreign to them and to how we were as a family.

Around this time I also met Jack, my first real friend who was a boy. Jack and I both took part in a ten-day sailing experience on a ship called the *Spirit of New Zealand*. It was designed to help school kids learn more about themselves, and I hated nearly every moment while I was there. Being squeezed into tiny canvas slings to sleep in, the disgusting food we had to prepare ourselves, being forced to jump into the winter ocean every morning at 6 a.m. and mostly that I never, ever got a moment to myself. But Jack and I had bonded one day as we gathered the sails at the top of the 31-metre-high mast, and we became fast friends once we got back home.

We were always completely platonic, which I found to be a relief. I could finally relax around a boy. Once, in the first weeks of our friendship, he'd come to visit me at home and we'd tried to hold hands and stare romantically at the ocean together, because we felt like that's what we were supposed to be doing. But we'd both simultaneously come to the conclusion: 'Yeah, nah.' We were always just the best of mates. My parents loved Jack too. One weekend when my parents were away, I'd had Bridge, Coop, Jack and a few others over to drink, and Jack filled the stairwell leading down to my bedroom with real pine Christmas trees after the rest of us had gone to sleep. The next morning we'd had to climb through over 30 trees, laughing, to get up the stairs. It took me hours and hours of vacuuming to get rid of the pine-needle evidence and wipe the scuffs off the walls before my parents came home. But even if they'd found out what he'd done to their beautiful home, they would have forgiven him. Jack was like the son they never had.

Between my friendships with Jack and with the girls, things were going pretty well in my life, I thought. But after a while I couldn't keep pretending to myself that there was nothing unusual going on with the way I felt about one of them: Alison Cooper. I think most people have known a Coop. She was the kind of girl who charmed everyone she met, especially parents. Coop thought nothing of stripping off her top in the car on a hot day, driving in her bra and not giving a damn who saw. She danced with abandon, laughed easily and loudly, threw her arm around friends without a second thought. She didn't appear to have a self-conscious bone in her body, and I saw her as everything I wasn't but wanted to be. When Coop turned her attention on me she made me feel like the best person in the world; I would have done anything to get more time under her spotlight.

One night, near the end of Year 12, we arrived back to our room at Central Park Motel after yet another underwhelming school ball. I'd been getting closer to Coop for about six months by then, and we had progressed to not only sharing a motel room, but also sharing a bed.

Tossing my ridiculously small and impractical handbag to the floor, I collapsed onto the bed in a huff.

'Get up,' Coop said, pulling me off the bed. 'We're going dancing.'

'What? No, I can't dance! I've never been to town before. I don't have an ID!'

'C'monnn, Lilly.' She tugged on my arm and laughed at me, as she was apt to do. 'Don't worry about the ID thing. Let's dance!'

She stuck her tongue out and pulled her signature dance move, where she would squat and throw her fists out in a slow circle, tongue peeking out of the corner of her mouth. I took one look at her sparkling eyes and knew that I would dance. I would do anything she told me to.

Coop charmed the two of us straight past the bouncers at a bar in town, and, once inside, she didn't give me time to panic or second-guess myself. She just pulled me through the crowd and straight onto the dance floor. She twirled me and laughed and busted her own moves like she didn't care how she looked or who might be watching. Coop danced for herself, and she made me let go of my inhibitions and dance too.

I'd never really danced much—still haunted by an intermediate school disco with Saint Kentigern's boys from Auckland many years before. I must have been about eleven, and before we'd left for the disco I'd asked my father, 'Dad, how do I dance?'

Good old Dad, he'd tried to help. 'Well, you just plant your feet on the ground and keep them in one place. Then you kind of move your upper body to the music, like this . . .'

When I tried to copy his (terrible) advice, what came out was an unbalanced bop with punching robot hands, but it was deemed a success and I was sent off to the disco. My moment arrived when one of the boys asked me to dance. I got all my courage together to say yes, but while we were dancing I looked up to see two of my teachers pointing down at me from the upper balcony. No doubt they were just exclaiming over how cute we looked, but to an insecure kid dancing for the first time, it was devastating. I was sure they were laughing at me. In my lasting embarrassment I hadn't danced in public since that day.

My first dance with Coop wiped that memory from my mind. Everyone else in the bar was just a shadowy figure to me, but Coop was in full colour. I copied her moves even if I couldn't quite replicate her self-assurance. Song after song we danced and, although I worried, she never seemed to get bored of dancing with me. We rolled into bed after 3 a.m. and had to be up only a few hours later to make the soccer game we were both playing in, but we giggled and joked the whole way there. It had been the best night of my life. No one had ever been able to pull me out of myself like she could.

Because of this infatuation, my friendship with Bridget took a few knocks. We had been a pretty tight trio and now I only wanted my cuddles from Coop. Bridget and I still wrote each other emotional letters about our friendship, but now I also began writing letters to Coop—letters that became more intimate and intense and probing as the months passed.

Coop was on my mind 24/7, but we didn't see each other much at school because we were in different classes. It didn't help that for much of the year she was a competitive athlete, busy every day after school. So I manufactured ways to see her. I knew her timetable and I began to change my route so that I'd 'happen' to run into her in between classes—even if it meant running from one side of the school to the other before 'casually' walking around a corner. 'Oh, hi, Coop, fancy bumping into you . . .'

I'd often visit her at the stadium after school, and sometimes I'd bring her home to my place for the night, no matter how late she finished or how early she had to be back at school. It was my chance to be her white knight, the person who gave her a break from the stresses of sport and schoolwork and her family.

She told me in letters how much that meant to her, and how she was usually afraid to let people get close but I was breaking down her walls. Those words made me shiver with emotional ecstasy. But I had other motives too. I created every opportunity I could to sleep in the same bed as her and to hold her in my arms, even when she was still in her stinky thermal top from training. We laughed together about her sweaty pits, and the fact that it didn't bother either of us was just further confirmation to me that we had something special. I couldn't get enough of the intimacy, and I began to blur the boundaries of friendship. One night at my house she was cuddled into the crook of my arm in bed as I lay on my back, and I turned to be face to face with her. She stiffened but ultimately relaxed into the embrace, and we went to sleep breathing each other's air. In the morning she asked me what it was all about in a suspicious tone and I gave her some excuse about wanting to be more comfortable, which she seemed to accept. This new form of intimacy between us became normal and frequent, and I didn't think about what it meant, just how it felt.

We were a couple of months into Year 13, our final year of high school, when one evening as I was saying goodbye I turned to her and said, 'You know, not that I'd kiss a girl, but, if I had to, I'd choose you.' As I walked away I felt sick. I knew I'd crossed an unspoken line.

My confession lurked in the undercurrents of our relationship, and I could feel a change between us. I just didn't know if she felt it too. Before anything was addressed, Coop went away to a national tournament for a week, and her absence was painful. The weekend she got back my parents were away and she came to stay, both of us promising to look after my thirteen-year-old sister. Instead we got drunk and taught Jenny about alcohol, feeding her sips of things like Amarula and sambuca that we poured in careful nips out of the bottles in Mum and Dad's liquor cabinet. They always hid the key in the same place on the top shelf of the pantry, next to Dad's pack of Rothmans Blue, which he smoked in a hidden corner of the balcony when he thought my sister and I were asleep. Fuelled by the combination of at least four types of alcohol, we all danced together in the darkened lounge to one of the bad house songs we were into at the time. Dancing with Coop had become one of my favourite things to do. When my sister disappeared downstairs, Coop and I moved outside to the balcony, where we listened to the ocean roar below us. The conversation turned naturally into a 'deep and meaningful', and what I'd said about kissing her finally came up.

'I couldn't, just, like, lean over and kiss you right now or anything . . . but, y'know, if I haaaad to kiss a girl, I'd *probably* choose you,' I clarified unnecessarily.

I have no doubt that Coop could see through that statement, but she took it in her stride and we eventually moved inside and draped ourselves over the couch. I closed my eyes, leaning my head back against the cushion, and we both lay there peacefully for a while, comforted by the repetitive thud of the music. Then I felt a pair of soft lips on mine for a long second. It was really only a peck, but the distance between a friendly peck on the lips and one with the promise of something more is infinite.

My sister came upstairs at that moment, tipsy and rambling, and we decided it was time for all of us to go to bed. Nothing else happened, but when I held Coop in my arms that night, my heart pounding, I knew there was no going back. I didn't want to go back.

The next weekend, Coop came to stay again and we got into bed with an understanding that this night would be different from all the others.

'I can't do this,' I said, practically hyperventilating.

But I knew that I had to make the first move this time, and eventually I did. I leaned over and kissed her, properly this time. Our lips seemed to fit together perfectly, and the shock of feeling her tongue against mine was quickly replaced by a sizzle I'd never felt before. It was more than physical, though. I felt an enveloping sense of peace.

After a few seconds I had to break away, overwhelmed.

The air was crackling with expectation, and after a while she kissed me again. Everything was so soft. Her lips. Her well-washed T-shirt, and her thighs when they slid between mine. We kept falling asleep with our lips still pressed together, until finally one time when I opened my eyes I could tell that the light had changed and dawn was coming. We'd kissed the whole night.

Coop stayed over even more often after that, and I think it was only because my parents liked her so much that they didn't ask questions. I knew that they were still a bit weird about the physical intimacy they'd seen between me, Coop and Bridget. But I got the feeling that they'd focused any suspicions about 'unnatural' or 'strange' behaviour on Bridget mainly, so they relaxed as Coop came to stay more frequently and Bridget less often. Little did they know, they had the wrong culprit. But Coop had charmed them, as she did so many people.

Every time Coop stayed we kissed for hours and fell asleep intertwined. But I never dared to do anything more—not to take layers off, not to go below the waist. We had drawn this arbitrary line in the sand. For me it was because I was in no way ready to address the bigger picture of what this meant for who or what I was. I didn't want to think about it . . . I didn't even want to think about thinking about it. Instead I gave my thoughts only to how good it felt and how much I loved this girl.

That meant grand romantic gestures, and lots of them. I wrote her a song to the tune of the Cat Stevens song 'Father & Son'. I made her smash a wall clock and told her that when I was with her time stopped. One day after school I let myself in to her house while she was at training and plastered glow-in-the-dark stars on the ceiling in her bedroom. That night I waited for the time I knew she'd go to bed. Finally, the text came.

OH MY GOD I JST TURND OFF MY LIGHTS AND SAW WOT YOUD DONE. YOURE AMAZING. I LOVE YOU.

I went to sleep with a smile on my face and what I was sure was true love in my heart.

Our pattern of emotional dependence continued, but slowly that which had been so rewarding and validating became intertwined with threads of angst and unhappiness. Sometimes I had the self-awareness to wonder if I made myself feel upset or angry about things just so I'd have an excuse to be comforted by Coop. But I couldn't stop. I needed her.

Mostly my emotional turmoil was characterised by the tempestuous relationship that had developed between me and my parents, who all of a sudden seemed so different to me and didn't understand the things I cared about. I was becoming acutely aware of their prejudices now that one of them related to me. It wasn't just negative comments about gay people that made my ears prick up; anyone outside of some arbitrary set of standards was at risk of their criticism. And I guess I understood subconsciously that, one day, that could be me on the other end of it. I knew I was hiding a big, dangerous secret.

Sometimes after intense make-out sessions with Coop I'd get stabbing cramps in my stomach, a build-up of both sexual tension and anxiety. One day, about two months into this new version of our 'friendship', I asked Coop to take off her top. I promised I wouldn't look, because that might mean something we weren't prepared to acknowledge. She hesitated then agreed. And, I have to admit, I did peek. She was stunning. But even as I revelled in the feeling of touching her skin without restrictions, my unease about having made such a bold request grew. I burst into tears. She put her top back on and followed me across the room, gathering me in her arms and comforting me as I apologised profusely. What was I doing?! Why did something good stress me out so much?

Coop and I never talked on any level about what our relationship was or what we were doing. We could describe our feelings at length and we shared declarations of 'I love you' freely, but we ignored how far we'd strayed from the path of friendship. We never spoke about what went on when the lights went out. 'Best friends'—that was the phrase we used often in our letters.

Even though Coop spent many weekend nights in my bed, it never felt like enough and I missed her acutely during the week. And so I began my old manipulation tactics to try to see her more often, like the nights when I'd convince her to meet me in a lonely car park halfway between her house and mine, where she'd sit on the hood of my car and put her arms around me. We'd share a cigarette and I'd tell myself that a few precious minutes together outweighed the pain I felt when I had to tear myself away from her again.

Midway through my final year of high school—about four months since Coop and I had taken our relationship to a new level physically—our school's dress-up ball was approaching, and as the prefect in charge of social activities I was tasked with organising the whole thing. Ironic, given how out of place I'd always felt at school balls. Coop, Bridget, JJ and I, and our respective dates, had booked a motel apartment for the night of the ball, and I'd managed to steer the situation in such a way that Coop and I were sharing a room alone. This was no mean feat considering that her date for the ball was her ex-boyfriend, who I was 100 per cent certain wanted to get back together with her. I couldn't wait to spend some time with her, as both of us had been so tied up recently with extracurricular activities— Coop had been training daily and I'd been flat-out too, juggling prep for the ball along with school and playing in multiple sports teams.

Finally, the night arrived and I threw on my outfit. Mum had sewn it for me a few days earlier after I'd gone to her nearly in tears, upset that I'd been too busy to think of a great costume. Mum was always good for things like that, from dressing me up as the Mad Hatter for Book Day in Year 4, complete with top hat, to sewing my ball gown from scratch in Year 12. Given little time, though, my shapeless animal-print cavewoman dress wasn't her best work. Poor Jack, my partner to the ball, didn't fare much better. I'd convinced him that going to the ball in a bear costume, including a headpiece that fastened with Velcro under the chin and whiskers that Mum drew on with eyeliner, would be cute. At the pre-drinks I watched on glumly as Coop and her ex-boyfriend, dressed as Wonder Woman and Superman respectively, flirted and looked fantastic in their latex outfits. Coop's brunette hair was lightly curled and she had on bright red lipstick for the first time. I thought she'd never looked more beautiful. But although I knew her lipstick would be on my pillow at the end of the night, I couldn't help but be slightly worried. How long would Wonder Woman be happy hiding in a dark cave with me when she could be out there flying proudly through the sky with Superman?

I think things started unravelling around the time of that school dance. Having to watch the way those ball dates threw their muscular arms around the girls, and flirted openly, and made out publicly, grated on me. I wanted to do that, even though I couldn't fathom ever being able to.

It's also not in my nature to be secretive, so I was beginning to test the boundaries of my relationship with Coop. Like the time I ran into her in a deserted corridor after school was out for the day, and pushed her against the wall for a kiss. No one saw us, but Coop had sprung away from me, shaken.

'Don't do that,' she'd said in a panicked tone, and I'd felt chastened.

Coop began to pull away in ways so subtle that I didn't realise what they were at the time. She didn't respond to my letters for days, or did so in scrawled half-thoughts that didn't address everything I'd said to her. She would apologise, but feeling like you have to apologise to someone all the time is a warning sign in itself. Eventually it turns into resentment. She certainly didn't like it when I would pace through school at lunchtime to find her and pull her away from our friends to ask her why she hadn't responded to my letter. Why wasn't I her priority, like she was mine?

But the more Coop became distant or absent-minded, and the less time I could spend with her because of our schedules, the more my focus on her sharpened.

'The way you express yourself so well is intimidating, and I feel bad that I can't give you the same back' is the kind of thing that began creeping into Coop's letters. I ignored it; she was perfect in whatever she did. Other times it was things like 'you're so intense'. This is sometimes seen as a positive descriptor, but really it's not. 'Intense' is too close to 'nuts' and 'clingy'.

Saying goodbye to Coop in August when she left for the world championships in Europe was the hardest farewell I'd ever faced, and she was going to be away for two whole weeks! Torture. At least when she came back I'd get some quality time with her, I thought, because we'd be staying together in a motel for our soccer team's national tournament.

Coop arrived at the soccer tournament a day later than the rest of us, coming straight from her championships to ours. I raced to her room as soon as I heard she was there.

'Hi!' I said, pulling her into a hug. 'Oh my god, I missed you so much. It sucks so much that we're not staying in the same room, eh?'

'Oh, it doesn't really matter, does it?' she said, pulling away hastily. She turned to the younger girls who were in the room and began hamming it up, making them laugh. I stood there staring at her in confusion, but she wouldn't meet my eye.

Then it was time to leave for our game and, instead of making sure she got a seat next to me on the shuttle like she usually did, I watched her disappear into a different van. I was confused, and dark tendrils of apprehension began to creep through my stomach. Something was really wrong.

At our warm-up my gaze kept flicking to her as we criss-crossed our legs through ladders on the ground and sidestepped around cones, looking for some sign of her state of mind. She wore her orange bandanna over her head, which I had always thought brought out her dimples. That was the same. She fastened the Velcro straps on her goalie gloves fastidiously, starting again if anything was the slightest bit wonky. That was the same. She didn't look at me once. That was not the same.

As we pulled on sweatshirts and put our smelly shin pads away in our bags after the game, I watched her again, waiting for her to give me her special smile, or to do anything that would indicate that we were still bound in some way, even in friendship. But there was nothing.

I don't know when I finally got the chance to talk to her, whether hours later or days. She didn't make it easy to get her alone. But when I asked her what was wrong, she said 'Nothing!' with an incredulous smile. I pretended to let it go with the ease with which she'd laughed off my question, even though it was all I'd been thinking about. I didn't want to be 'intense'. In the days after that, I tried the tactic of not talking about it and just acting like we once had as best friends, approaching her with feigned casualness. In response she was overly polite, as though I was that person who thinks they're your friend and you're nice to their face but laugh about them to your real friends once they're gone.

Where we had once always sought each other out, now she was avoiding me. Day by day that realisation grew bigger and more painful. After a week, when I gave up playing along and cornered her for an explanation, she continued to act as though I was imagining everything. I tried pushing hard enough that she became angry—even that would have been better than her sham ignorance. She acted confused about why I thought something had changed or pretended she couldn't understand why I was so upset or told me I was overreacting. It made me feel crazy. She left me feeling like I'd dreamed up or misread our whole relationship.

Finally I got the closest thing to a straight answer I'd ever get. She said that being away from me had given her some much-needed space and perspective away from my analysing and all those feelings. She'd realised that our relationship was unhealthy, which was a horrible thing to hear. There was nothing in my world to tell me she was wrong about that except my feelings for her. There was no such thing as the 'It Gets Better' movement or coming-out videos on YouTube. No Tumblr, where everything on your feed can be pictures of girls kissing if you choose. No pop stars coming out as bi, no Hollywood stars playing gay for pay, no celebrities giving speeches saying that who I was should be celebrated. All I had was my personal experience, and I was too full of my own shame to disagree with Coop the way I wanted to. And a small part of me knew that she was right. We'd worked our way into an emotional vortex where everything was 'so much' and we had to feel everything 'so deeply'. But that was the only way I could keep her close to me—by proving I was the only one who truly understood her.

At home one night I stepped out onto the balcony outside my room and called her in what felt like a last-ditch effort, praying that she would pick up. She answered, which was a good sign, but then responded to everything I said in monosyllabic statements.

'Coop,' I finally begged, letting go of any dignity, 'I need you. You can't do this to me. I need you so much.'

And in a flat tone she replied, 'Yeah, but I don't need you.'

Chapter 4

Boys, Boys, Boys

I seem to have run in a great circle, and met
myself again on the starting line.
— *Oranges Are Not the Only Fruit*, Jeanette Winterson

Robbie was a sweet guy with a rower's body, nice skin and a cute upturned nose. I don't remember flirting with him or how we started the slow ascent from simply being two inhabitants of the North Four floor of University College into something more. I don't remember our first kiss. But I remember opening the door of my room one afternoon to find rose petals scattered across the bed with a sweet note. That's when I knew it was destined to be: I would have to have sex with him. Because that's what I should want to be doing, right? That's what any normal girl would want in this scenario. Coop had obviously been a bump in the road, and this wasn't Harry Gibbs trying to get on top of me in the back seat of a car. It was rose petals and romance, and it was well past time to get rid of my virginity. I was in my first year at uni, for god's sake. And living in the University of Otago's hall of residence where all the cool kids went—UniCol. I needed to keep up. I was desperate to pass the lose-your-virginity milestone, but in the same way I had been desperate to have my first kiss two years before—because that's what you did. I didn't long for Robbie. I just longed to get it over with.

One night there was an unspoken agreement and we found ourselves back in his room after the pub, a little tiddly but not too drunk for a change. It was hot and dark and as he lay on top of me and kissed me I thought to myself, *Well, this is it, here we go*. But the feeling of wrongness grew and grew the more clothes we shed, until it became as wrong as anything had ever felt. And, at almost the last possible moment, when we were both naked and my virginity was about to be farewelled, I stopped him, pushing at his chest with a growing urgency.

'I'm so sorry, Robbie,' I said, sliding out from under him. 'I can't do this.'

I mumbled more apologies to the bewildered boy as I gathered my things as fast as possible and slunk out. I made it to my room down the hall and burst into tears. Because if

I couldn't do it with Robbie, couldn't feel it with Robbie, how could I possibly hope to ever feel 'it' the way I was supposed to? Worse, I knew how it could feel, but the person who'd given me that feeling was a girl—a girl whom I'd kissed for hours until I was literally dizzy, who gave me stomach aches because I had wanted her so much. When I held her in my arms, it had felt the most 'right' anything had ever felt. The two experiences couldn't have been more different.

In the UniCol dining hall the next night, I stared at Coop. The girl that I couldn't get out of my mind or out of my life. Not only did Coop live in the same new city as me and go to the same university as me, but she also lived at the same goddamn hall of residence as me, just 100 metres away in UniCol's South Tower. Coop was in my life nearly every day: in the dining hall, in the movie room, in my friends' rooms when we were drinking and in the hallways. She turned and walked the other way when she saw me in the hallways. Nearly six months had passed since she'd broken my heart. In a way I was the closest to Coop that I had ever been. But also the farthest.

I knew I'd been too clingy over the last few months of high school after Coop had ended things with me, doing passive-aggressive things like handing her a mixed CD of songs that expressed how I felt and trying to pass it off by saying, 'Oh, it's just some new songs I thought you might like.' Of course she saw right through me, and I was surprised by how angry she was at my attempt to manipulate her back into loving me. I played the songs to myself instead: Matchbox Twenty's 'If You're Gone' and Gabrielle's angsty 'Out of Reach'. I also liked Nelly Furtado's 'I'm

Like a Bird' because I felt like it really captured who Coop was. Yes: she *was* like a bird. Of course she *would* fly away—how did I not see that before? I would play the CD in the car as I drove home from school, crying so hard at times that I could barely see the road. I tried to capture some of those tears in a vial so I could wear them around my neck, like Angelina Jolie had done with a vial of her husband Billy Bob Thornton's blood, but they evaporated—gone, just like my relationship with Coop.

Because no one had known what was really going on between Coop and me, there was no one I could turn to for support. This isolation, paired with the heartbreak, really changed me, and I lost some of that more outgoing, sparkly persona that I'd worked so hard to create.

'She doesn't smile much, does she?' Coop's mum said about me one day when a bunch of us were hanging out at her house over the summer holidays, before we all took off for uni. I couldn't just stop hanging out with Coop, could I? She was supposed to be one of my best friends, and our other friends would have noticed if things between us changed too much. For her part, Coop wasn't cold to me in public, not in an obvious way. I just never felt her true warmth again. All her charm now seemed like pretence to me, her smiles just fakery. She teased me like she teased all her friends, but it felt like she was goading me on, knowing that I couldn't do anything but play along and pretend everything was okay.

I fantasised about going up to Coop's mum and shaking her by the lapels as I screamed in her face, 'I'm not smiling because of *your daughter*. Your daughter broke my fucking heart, do you understand?'

One weekend during that endless summer between the last day of high school and the start of university, I had chucked my sleeping bag in my car to head out to a farm owned by Coop's ex-boyfriend's parents for a massive party—this was the guy who had dressed as Superman to Coop's Wonder Woman at our school ball. It was still early in the evening when I stepped out of the barn to find somewhere to pee and saw Coop chatting with her ex. When she looked up, she held my gaze for a few seconds before turning to him and pulling his head down into a ferocious kiss. I walked past, pretending it meant nothing but feeling like I was dying. Later that night, my booze-addled brain told me that maybe I could score a point back against her by pashing her younger cousin Dave. But when Coop heard about it the next day as we all sat around the embers of the bonfire nursing hangovers, she laughed uncontrollably. I'd got mud and sheep shit all up the back of my clothes for nothing.

After that I'd tried to stay away from Coop for the rest of the summer, and I guess I'd naively thought that by the time we got to university we'd be friends again, even though my heart still flipped when I saw her. But it seemed that Coop had become angrier over those months. I didn't know why she was so angry because she wouldn't speak to me, but I could see her carrying it around. We had made practically the same friends at UniCol, and that meant we spent a lot of evenings in the same room, pre-loading on peach schnapps and cheap sparkling wine before town. Eventually our friends picked up on the tension. A couple of my closest mates even asked what the deal was between the two of us. I shrugged and said nothing. But inside I was still mourning my first love, and my best friend. I'd lost both with a suddenness that left me reeling.

After the first few months at UniCol, I had come to accept that we would never get our friendship back. I did try one last time to clear the air between us. I slipped a note under the door to her room when I knew she was inside, then ran away, feeling ashamed of myself for being so weak to still care so much. In the note I said that I would never forget what had happened between us and that it had been really special to me. But I was being 'intense' again. I never got a response. Well . . . in a way I did.

One night our core group of friends—all girls—were at The Moa, a rundown pub a few blocks away from UniCol. Like many first-years we followed the cheap drinks around town—every day of the week there was a drink special designed to encourage binge drinking. The Moa's drink special was $2 Corona bottles on a Wednesday, and we were there to take advantage of it to the best of our abilities. The mood was high. Coop was there, and we'd reached an uneasy, unspoken understanding that we could be at the same social occasion without interacting. But tonight was different. I was on the dance floor, pissed, dancing with abandon, when Coop crossed the room and began dancing with me. It was like old times. She caught my eye and smiled at me and we danced around with the others in glee, like only a group of drunken teenagers can. I felt a surge of happiness. This was all I wanted from her, and she finally understood. I tossed my head back and smiled, dancing just like she had taught me to do, and that's when Coop stepped close to me and spoke.

'What?' I yelled over the music. 'I can't hear you!'

She came closer and shouted in my ear: 'You know, my sister saw a really good counsellor last year. I can give you the number . . .' She stepped back and looked at me expectantly.

'What?' I said, confused, thinking I'd heard wrong.

She stepped close again. 'Come on, you're pretty fucked up. It's obvious you need to see a counsellor.'

'What?' I said again, stopping still in the middle of the dance floor. I felt sick. Her smile now read like a wicked smirk, one that seemed to widen the longer I stared at it. I burst into tears explosively. I bent over and grasped my knees, wailing, struggling to breathe.

Coop must have been taken aback by my outpouring of emotion, and she disappeared into the dark as my concerned friends came rushing over and held me upright. I was so hurt by what Coop had said that the floodgates opened; all those months of tension and upset and trying to be brave came pouring out, and I just could not stop crying. I must have really scared the shit out of my friends. I was usually the level-headed one, and they couldn't even get a word out of me to tell them what was wrong. One thing they seemed to understand was that it had something to do with Coop, and they shepherded me out of the pub, two or three of them flanking me on each side. As we stepped out into the cold I looked up for long enough to see the other half of our group of friends, the ones who were closer to Coop, surrounding her near the side of the building. I think she was crying too, and a couple of them shot me the evils. I had unintentionally split the group in two, causing them to choose sides even though no one knew what was going on.

It seemed I hadn't healed quite as much as I'd thought I had, and now Coop had ripped the scab off. I still hadn't told anyone what had really gone on between Coop and me, and I fobbed off renewed attempts by my friends to find out what the deal was after that night at The Moa. Her words had really, really shaken me. I wasn't fucked up. I didn't need counselling! No one had counselling, not in New Zealand, not unless you were actually fucked up, suffering depression or something.

Eventually I resolved that Coop had hurt me for the last time and I was over trying to build some kind of bridge with her. I would no longer find meaning in soppy songs about love lost. No. I turned to the Roman poet Catullus instead, whose 'Lesbia' series of poems I was studying in my classics paper. I found these poems particularly meaningful for their tale of forbidden love— the rapture of togetherness then the fountain of bitterness and anger as one lover pulls away. I would soliloquise to myself in the mirror with clenched fists and pointed fingers.

> I hate and love. If you ask me to explain
> The contradiction,
> I can't, but I can feel it, and the pain
> Is crucifixion

It was a huge step forward.

With this change in mindset I realised that I had lost focus on an important goal: sleeping with a boy. The near miss with Robbie had put me off for a few months, but now, after the Moa incident, I decided I needed to forget about Coop and renew my quest to be like the other girls. I'd never had any problem pashing boys—I kissed a lot of them that year, drunk, and I even enjoyed it sometimes. But I knew it wasn't enough. One-night stands were something that everyone else seemed to be able to do without a second thought, either with strangers they met in one of the uni pubs or with one of the other 400 students in UniCol. There was no shortage of choices, and much time was spent hanging out in one of UniCol's common rooms, giggling over everyone's escapades. I figured if everyone else could do it, so could I.

One night I hooked up with a boy in the Captain Cook Hotel, one of our regular haunts. He was older, maybe not even a student. Much like all those times in the past—getting a date to the school ball, finding someone to have a first pash with—his looks and personality were beside the point. I had a need, and he could potentially provide a solution.

When he asked me back to his flat I agreed readily. But when I sat, swaying, in the back of the taxi I realised I was really pissed. Too pissed. We got to his flat and started fooling around. Suddenly we were in his room and in his bed and clothes were stripped, and he became quite sexually aggressive. I freaked out. I realised how dangerous this was, and how awful and humiliating. When I told him no and started putting my clothes on, finding it difficult to even lift my legs to put my boots on, he was mad. His sure bet was a certain dud. And he was an arsehole about it, not wanting to call me a taxi. But I made him, because I was too drunk to punch the numbers on his home phone myself.

I decided to get the fuck out of there and wait outside, and he didn't give a shit about that, just stumbled back to his room and slammed the door. But when I got outside I was hit by a sudden paranoia that he was going to come after me and force me to finish what I'd started. I took off down the hill, not knowing where I was but assuming I couldn't be too far away from North Dunedin, where all the students lived. I just had to keep going down, and eventually I'd hit familiar territory. But I was wasted, and every second street I turned down suddenly changed from a downhill into an uphill or a dead end. What had I been thinking, not waiting for the taxi? It was now after 4 a.m., with very few streetlights or cars around. I gritted my teeth and kept going, wincing at my feet blistering in my knee-high boots—the kind of boots that, ironically, were dubbed 'fuck me' boots. I'd left my socks behind. After over an hour I seemed to be getting closer to the bottom of the hill, but I was still a long way away from home. There was a sour alcohol taste in my nostrils and my mouth was tacky with dehydration, but at least I'd managed to stop weaving across the pavement now that my drunkenness had become a hangover.

And then, a potential saviour. I heard a loud exhaust, the unique calling card of bogans, and turned to see headlights coming towards me. Making a snap decision, I stuck my thumb out and the car pulled over. Three boys yelled out the windows, asking what I was doing. I studied them as closely as I could, looking for any potential red flags beyond their Offspring T-shirts and baggy jeans. They seemed friendly, if a bit pissed, and I tried to joke with them about having a failed one-night stand. They laughed good-naturedly, so I got in the car. And thankfully they dropped me home.

When I made it in the doors of UniCol the sun was coming up and I happened to run into Bridget, my old best friend from high school who also lived in UniCol. Things hadn't been the same between us since I'd got involved with Coop and begun keeping that secret from her, but I collapsed in her arms, sobbing. I was shocked at my own recklessness. Then and there I decided it was over. No more trying to be normal, not if it was going to be like this.

I scared myself so badly that I didn't try to lose my virginity with a boy for another sixteen months.

But I hadn't got away without consequence. The week after that one-night-stand disaster, I was leaving the Cook when a group of boys started yelling insults at me. It was him. Him and all his mates. They hollered 'Frigid bitch!' and so on after me as I walked away from them, trying not to show how shaken I was. Then, a few days later, I was leaving that same pub, pissed yet again, and it happened once more. I walked outside and there he was, standing on the pavement, smoking. I pretended I hadn't seen him and walked away; once again he shouted something degrading at me. But this time he didn't have all his mates with him. So, emboldened by booze, I turned around and walked back to him.

'Hey!' I said. 'You know, like, I know maybe you think I led you on and I'm this frigid bitch, and I'm sorry for not having sex with you when you thought I would. But you're being a real dick. In fact you're acting like a creep, and it scares me. Does it make you feel good, to know you can scare a woman like that? Is that what you want?'

He was taken aback, as was I. I didn't know I had it in me. He even apologised.

'Thank you,' I said and walked away. And I did see him again, and ignored him, and he ignored me. And I felt good about that.

I'd like to say I learned my lesson from that encounter and stopped getting myself into bad situations because of booze. But if drinking was a major, we were all studying for a Bachelor of Boozing with a minor in unforeseen consequences. Our favourite haunt for morning drinking, afternoon drinking and also night-time drinking was Gardies, a pub that was the unofficial UniCol hang-out. Gardies was our version of the bar in the classic TV show *Cheers*, except instead of regulars sitting on bar stools we were regularly falling off bar stools. We particularly loved Wednesday nights because of 'toss the boss', which was yet another invention of the Otago University student culture designed to encourage binge drinking. 'Toss the boss' night meant you could order your drink and wait for someone behind the bar to flip a coin—if you called the toss correctly you got the drink for free. We were ordering bottles of wine at a time, so there was a lot at stake—$11.40 to be exact. That's how much a bottle of Riverlands sauvignon blanc cost, our favourite wine (not because we were discerning but because it was the cheapest). If you were unlucky and they'd run out, you'd be stuck with Corbans, which tasted like piss and was deemed a rip-off at $13.60. However, on 'toss the boss' nights we ladies really drank for free because the bar staff had seriously underestimated their clientele. They had only one dedicated coin-flipper on what was the busiest night of the week, so there was ample opportunity to slink off between the bartender handing over your bottle and the coin-flipper noticing you. Because we were canny, broke-ass booze hags, this was an opportunity we never let slip past.

One such night I had my Riverlands cradled protectively against my body as I pushed my way through the crowd when I looked up to see a familiar face. Harry Bloody Gibbs. I hadn't spoken to him since our passionate high-school love affair of six weeks had ended. It seemed that time hadn't dulled his insatiable desire for me, because he engaged in some heavy flirting and we managed to actually make conversation for five minutes (a new record) before I went off to find my friends. I didn't think of him again for the rest of the evening.

But the next morning, I woke up to a disturbing sight. A sock, crumpled in the corner of my room. Just one lonely thick woollen sock. It sounds innocuous, but this was certainly not my sock. This was undoubtedly, undeniably, a man sock. I sat staring at it for quite some time before I shuffled out of bed, threw on a hoodie and stumbled down to the common room on our floor, still feeling the Riverlands $11.40 sav coursing through my veins. I relayed the story of the sock to my North Four floor-mates, who were hanging out watching TV and eating packets of two-minute noodles.

Robbie the Nice Guy, he of the flower-petal scattering, came in and overheard. 'It was some guy you knew from high school,' he said. 'I'd just got home when you came out of your room and asked me to help you get rid of him. He was in your bed!'

'What?' I gaped.

'Yeah, he was nearly naked in your bed and wouldn't leave. You were really upset.'

'What the fuck?' I said. 'What happened?'

'I told him he had ten seconds to get the fuck out of there then I started counting down. You should have seen him trying to get his clothes on in a panic,' said Robbie, laughing.

That explained the sock. (Why are socks always the things left behind in failed sexual encounters?) I thanked Robbie weakly. He really was a nice guy. But, fuck! It turned out that Harry had waited until someone else used their swipe card to get in the front doors of UniCol, then he'd snuck in after them. I have no idea what happened when I opened my door to him as I'd been so drunk, but I can only assume that, true to form, he hadn't planned anywhere to stay during his visit to Dunedin and thought that my bed would be the best spot—and that, who knows, he might finally get lucky with me this time. I couldn't believe his audacity. Harry Gibbs, still causing trouble all these years later! But at the same time, I was worried for myself. Yet again my extreme intoxication had put me in a bad situation.

Despite my new-found wariness and a vow to stop leading boys on lest I face a more serious consequence next time, there were some circumstances that were outside my control. In the New Year period before I'd moved to Dunedin for uni, I'd met a nice farmer boy in a bar in the cute ski town of Wanaka and we'd shared a drunken pash. Jack always called him 'the Sheepshagger', so let's just go with that. For nearly a year following, every time I went back home—where the Sheepshagger also lived—he and I would meet up at a bar with our mutual friends, and I'd inevitably kiss him. He was a little smitten with me, but I'd never really had to worry about it because we lived in different cities. But now he was coming down to Dunedin with a carload of mates and my first thought was, *Shit. Now we're going to have to sleep together.* I mean, it had been nearly a year that I'd been holding out on him! I had my own room, no parents to be seen!

My fears were confirmed when I texted him and asked where he was staying. His response:

HNVT FIGURD THT OUT YET, WILL PROB JUST SEE.

Yep. He was definitely hoping to seal the deal.

There's a line in the book *Sweetbitter* by Stephanie Danler that goes: 'It is a strange pressure to be across from a man who wants something that you don't want to give. It's like standing in a forceful current, which at first you think is not too strong, but the longer you stand, the more tired you become, the harder it is to stay upright.'

I knew that I couldn't stay upright any longer, and I spent the rest of the day in a state of anxiety. One minute I resolved to do it, to stop being a pussy and just bloody do it, and the next I had visions of getting in my car and driving all the way to Invercargill (once described by one of the guys from the Rolling Stones as the 'arsehole of the world') just to have an excuse. But the night rolled in, and after a couple of mugs of Aquila I decided to stop worrying about it and just see what happened.

I arrived at Gardies and was reunited with the Sheepshagger. He had a gentle nature and a cute, chubby face. I did think he was a lovely guy. But after a couple of hours of being there, feeling his heavy, clammy man-hands wrapped possessively around me, his sausage fingers digging into my beer-induced love handles, I couldn't hack it anymore. Every minute that ticked by was taking me closer to a scenario that I knew, deep down, I wouldn't be able to go through with. So, in the pre-closing-time commotion, around midnight, I disappeared out the back door into the night. In the end, wasn't it kinder to let him down now, before the 3 a.m. closing of the next bar, when expectations would be even higher? I felt guilty, but I ignored his texts until the morning then made an excuse about being too drunk and passing out. I made sure to never kiss him again.

I was a good way into my first year of university by then, and despite some obvious missteps in terms of trying to lose my virginity, overall I was satisfied that I was progressing in other ways. Towards what, I wasn't quite sure. What was the end goal of being me? I couldn't think much beyond objectives like being more comfortable in social situations. Dressing in a way that made me appealing. Being able to capture the attention of a room as I told a story. Appearing charming and at ease at all times. That was enough to think about. There wasn't space for other things. Like what my relationship with Coop had meant. Why I couldn't have sex with a guy. Why I was so interested to hear that there was a girl who lived in UniCol's South Tower who had told everyone she was bisexual. Why I was so dismissive when I heard that she'd bragged about having a double dildo. *What an attention-seeker*, I'd thought. Even though I couldn't stop wondering what a double dildo was, and I craned my neck to look at her when I was in the dining hall. Even if I was into girls, she wouldn't be my type, I decided. Her hair was too curly. Her confidence carried with it indicators of being desperate for attention.

While I wasn't ready to put those pieces together and look at the picture they created, since the incident at The Moa I had been feeling a lot of pressure to come clean to my closest friends about the obvious weirdness between me and Coop. Not pressure from them, although they had asked a number of times. It was pressure coming from inside me. I had such great new friends, and I wanted to show them as much of myself as they showed me of themselves. The secret was driving me crazy. I had to share it with someone.

I decided to tell my two best friends at the time, Fiona and Emma. I have never felt such acute fear in my life, before or since, as I did in that period between deciding to tell them and actually doing it. There's a particular brand of fear that comes with telling someone something about yourself—something you are, something you really care about or something you've done. At the core of it is a fear of rejection. When it's something you can't change—like being gay—I think that fear of rejection is even stronger.

I took Fi and Emma to Cobb & Co., which was only a chain restaurant but felt fancy by our broke-student standards because it had tablecloths, even if they were made of plastic. Once we reached the restaurant we sat down in a booth, me on one side, them on the other. They were curious as to why they were there but also distracted by the promise of a meal out, and they immediately pored over the laminated menu, which was sticky from the hands of countless children who'd gorged on Cobb & Co.'s signature child's drink, the Pink Panther (Sprite, ice cream and red food colouring). I ignored the menu, unable to concentrate on anything but getting this done, and wrung my hands under the table as I watched my friends attack the basket of complimentary nibbles. Finally, I just had to spit it out.

'Hey, so . . .'

They looked up at me, cheeks stuffed like chipmunks.

'I invited you guys here because I wanted to tell you something that's really huge for me, and it's got to the point where I need to share it with someone . . .'

I really had their attention now. They could sense something juicy.

'You know how things have been weird between Coop and me this whole year? Well, that's because . . . we used to be more than just friends.'

They stared across the table at me blankly. I clarified, thinking they didn't understand. 'Like, we used to hook up kinda.'

'Oh,' said Emma. 'It all makes sense now.'

Fi didn't say much. I wasn't sure she really understood, and then the waitress arrived to take our orders. After that, the conversation changed direction. I was confused and a little disappointed. Was this not a big deal to them? Because it was a fucking huge deal to me. Now it just felt anticlimactic. Was this really the only reaction I'd get to the biggest secret I'd ever held in my life, something I'd carried for a year?

But then, over the next few hours, I felt a surge of relief and happiness. It felt so good to tell someone, and they didn't even care! All that worry for nothing. Later that week, Emma confided something in me too—her mum was gay, and she'd practically been raised by two women. What the fuck? I'd really picked the best people to tell!

Or had I?

By the end of the week, somehow everyone in our group of friends knew about Coop and me.

This in itself was devastating. But I almost couldn't think about them, and what they thought of me and how they might treat me differently and how our friendships might change or be lost. I could only think about what this meant for Coop. Because I had inadvertently 'outed' her. The worst thing I could do to her. The worst thing you could do to anyone not ready to face that aspect of themselves. Especially if that person sees a same-sex experience as just a thing that happened to them rather than a part of their sexuality. Now I was the one hiding from Coop in the hallways.

I managed to avoid her for two days. Then one night I was at a bar called Two Bears, standing in the dark near the dance floor, when someone shoved me from behind. I caught myself on a high table nearby, wine from my overfilled glass slopping everywhere. As I turned around Coop stepped up and screamed in my face.

'Fuck you! Fuck! You!' She kept pushing me painfully against the wooden edge of the table. I thought I'd seen every version of Coop there was, but I had never, ever seen her like this, feral-eyed and furious.

'I'm sorry, I'm sorry!' I kept saying. And I think I tried to explain that I had only told Emma and Fi, but somehow that seemed just as bad as if I'd told everyone. How could she understand why I had needed to tell people I thought I could trust? Why I needed my closest friends to know something that felt like it might be a super big part of the person I was trying to become? She couldn't understand. It wasn't the same thing for her. It was something she wanted to forget. It was something she wanted to hide.

I absorbed every word and every shove she gave me. I felt she was owed that. I let her scream at me until she turned and disappeared into the crowd. The next morning I had a line of bruises across my back from the table.

She wasn't the only casualty of everyone finding out about us, of course. The revelation also affected Bridget, the third in our tight friendship trio from high school. Bridget must have been given a whole new perspective on our friendship. Perhaps she now understood why I'd withdrawn from her as I got close with Coop. Maybe she was also grossed out. After all, the three of us had shared numerous beds together, and she and I had also been very physically affectionate and close. Maybe she was hurt that I had hidden something from her. Maybe she felt like we had played her for a fool, sneaking around behind her back and giggling about it. I never found out because we didn't really speak after that, even when we were drinking together in our mutual group of friends. I understood. I deserved that.

But the question remained: who had spilled the beans?

I soon found out from Emma that it was Fi. She was in fact one of the worst people I could have told, because—with hindsight—she is the most terrible secret-keeper the world has ever known. But she's also the kind of person who's hard to stay mad at. I can't remember if she's ever apologised—if she did it wasn't until years later. She simply didn't understand the magnitude of what she'd done. The implications. It was the first time I learned on a personal level how dangerous ignorance can be.

Chapter 5
Facing the Truth

**And the day came when the risk to remain tight in a
bud was more painful than the risk it took to blossom.**
— Author unknown

I hadn't kissed a girl for ten months, two days and four hours.
But now here I was, piled into a booth with six others at
Winnies pizza bar in the alpine party town of Queenstown,
and I sensed my luck was about to change. Across from me
sat a girl called Annie, who had a slow, sexy smile and eyes that
talked. People have often asked me how women pick each other

up—how do you know if the other person is gay? Or bi? Or even just interested? Much like with guys, I think it comes down to the act of looking. I was looking at her, and at some point she started looking back. By the early hours of the morning, many drinks later we ended up squashed against the wall of the booth with tension crackling between us. Her hand found its way onto my leg, we kissed in the toilets, and when she left that night with her boyfriend I knew I'd do anything to see her again.

I was pretty stoked with myself to have kissed a girl besides Coop. And what a contrast: while the first experience had been an emotional one wrapped up with a physical element, this was pure sexual attraction. We had absolutely nothing in common, but after that night Annie would regularly send me dirty text messages and I felt like a new world of sexual liberation had opened up. Here was someone who wasn't ashamed. Someone who wanted me and wasn't afraid to say it.

It also meant that I finally had another solid clue about my sexuality—a sign that it hadn't been just Coop. I was into girls. Not that I was necessarily a lesbian or anything, but there was something there. That's what the evidence was telling me. I still wasn't ready to figure it out completely, to face it and put a label on it. For now it was enough to just focus on this super-hot girl who wanted to sleep with me.

Annie came to Dunedin for the weekend soon after, boyfriend in tow. When we went out that night he sat between us on a three-seater couch, and Annie and I held hands literally behind his back. It felt taboo, and that was electrifying. We excused ourselves numerous times to 'use the loo' and made out furiously in the cubicle, but in the end what could I do? She went home with her boyfriend and I went home very, very frustrated.

A couple of weekends later I convinced four friends to make a 'spontaneous' road trip to Queenstown. Really I just needed them to share the petrol cost, and when we got into town that night I texted Annie to meet us at the bar. After she arrived we hung around long enough to chuck back a few drinks before I told the others I was going home because I was tired. They couldn't believe it; no one ever went home early or without the whole group. I was breaking unwritten rules of conduct. But I didn't care. Annie and I raced back to the cheap motel room I was sharing with the others. The room was filled with bunk beds except for the one precious double bed, which Fi had dibbed. But I figured she was owed a little payback for not keeping my secret about Coop, so Annie and I got in. This was it—I was finally going to lose my virginity, and with a girl! The others were bound to be out until the early hours of the morning, dancing the night away as they always did . . .

Fifteen minutes later, when Annie and I were down to our underwear, there was hammering on the door. I couldn't believe it. It was my friends, drunkenly laughing and yelling for me to let them in. After I'd finished swearing I chucked on some clothes and finally opened the door. When Fi stumbled in she couldn't understand why Annie was there, nor why we were in the double bed when she had clearly baggsed it as hers. It's amazing what people don't see even when it's staring them in the face (with hardly any clothes on, to boot). Annie made her excuses and left, and I grumpily clambered into my top bunk bed.

My sexting with Annie escalated after that, until one weekend after a barrage of texts with adult content, I thought, *Fuck it*, and I drove to Queenstown again. It was only four hours away after all. A mere trifle. Totally worth it. So what if it would blow my weekly allowance? I could just squirrel away extra food from the UniCol dining hall for a few days. When I got to Queenstown, I checked into a room at a backpackers, texted Annie and waited. And waited. Annie had decided to go out of town with her boyfriend. Cool. We were destined to only ever be star-crossed not-quite lovers.

While I still didn't completely know whether I was gay or bi or what after the Annie encounters, I was now fairly certain that this wasn't something that would go away. But I still wasn't ready to confront it head on. So with my sexuality slowly processing in the background, I carried on with life. My end-of-year exams came scooting up quickly, and then they were done, and so was my first year of university. Leaving me 100 per cent still a virgin, but 100 per cent more experienced with girls. And approximately 3000 per cent chubbier, as were all of my friends. It was a cliché, the old 'fresher five' kilograms that first-year students put on, but I was actually quite proud that by slumping as I sat on the pub couch I could now sit a pint of beer upright on my stomach without holding it.

That summer I worked for Dad, at the company he'd started in his early twenties. In the morning my job was to file papers, but I was far too efficient and by the end of the first week I had nothing left to do except beg the staff to let me make them cups of tea. I had no internet access, this being the transitional time of the early noughties, so I did what millions of people have done when they're insufferably bored: I played *Solitaire*. It was the only game on the computer besides *Minesweeper*, which I never understood how to play.

Every day I longed for the afternoon to come because that was when I got to change roles and do a job that Dad actually had a need for, not one he'd made up because I'd begged him for employment. Being a motherfuckin' badass courier driver. Every afternoon I would pull myself up into the driver's seat of a big, dirty Ford Transit van to deliver packages to various businesses around the city. I would shed my corporate wear and go out on these courier runs wearing stubbies and a white ribbed singlet. In a way this uniform was a weird choice, but it spoke to my frame of mind. I wore it because it made me feel capable and strong and slightly masculine—like I could fit into this world of men in warehouses wearing steel-capped boots, who were doing manly things like driving forklifts too fast. To show the guys that I could lift every package they gave me. Some things, like a roll of carpet, I would pretend I was fine to carry until I got out of sight, when I would let it plummet to the ground and stagger around panting before dragging it the rest of the way to the van. At the same time, I wore a tight singlet because I wanted the men at these warehouses to think I had feminine sex appeal. I wanted to be wanted by them, because it made me feel powerful. And it made me feel more powerful to know that I didn't want them back. Because I wanted girls. I wanted girls? This thought kept flickering at the edges of my consciousness, occasionally flaring brightly in moments of self-awareness. A version of my sexuality that wasn't straight was creeping into my everyday thought processes, gaining fuel and growing stronger.

After a month or so I ditched the job (poor Dad), loaded up my station wagon with a surfboard and a few stolen bottles of Mum's sauvignon blanc, and hit the road. I spent the rest of my summer holidays in the North Island visiting all the new friends I'd made at uni and using up any money I'd earned from my short employment. I made liberal use of the petrol charge card connected to Dad's business. Looking back, I understand how privileged I was to have a whole summer holiday funded by my parents, even though I was eighteen by then and didn't even live at home. But I didn't think about that then, not much. All I knew was that I was going to have the best summer ever, and I did. It was a summer of friendship that felt so different from the year before when I'd been licking my wounds over Coop and feeling so desperately alone.

At the end of this liberating break I shoved all my stuff in my car again and headed back down to Dunedin to move into my first-ever flat. There's nothing like the first time you live alone with your friends in a real house with no rules beyond those of common decency—and most of us who went to Otago barely upheld those. I was so excited when I arrived that I hopped the fence, jumped through the window and landed on a pile of my friends who were hanging out on my flatmate Maya's bed. The bed base cracked and we all shrieked as we hit the floor. A few days later during the university's legendarily debauched Orientation Week we lit that bed base on fire in the middle of the Castle St and Howe St intersection. If there was an epicentre of the student-run part of the city, it was here. And we lived right in the middle of it, in a flat called the Haunted House.

The Haunted House was one of Dunedin's most legendary student flats. A wooden structure of ill repute and nil insulation, much like its contemporaries the Palace on Ellis, the Pink Pussy and the Castle on Leith. Each one was its own brand of shithole, with holes in the walls, toxic carpet, mouse infestations and pipes that froze every winter. One month our sewer pipe exploded, scattering used toilet paper and everything else you can imagine over the backyard. After that we had to dry our clothes on the far end of the clothes line, except that this was a fruitless task in itself: nothing ever really got dry during the cold, wet winter months that uni was in session. Still, to live in one of these houses was considered a privilege.

The Haunted House was two stories high, with a turret on the corner upstairs room where Fi slept and a tiny balcony that we could squeeze a couch and about eight people onto when we had rare days of sun. The flat towered over the infamous Castle and Howe intersection, only a block away from the even more infamous Gardies pub. Every night around 11 or 12 p.m. when Gardies closed we had to suffer through the noise of hordes of blotto students streaming down the street, often running over the top of cars that people had been stupid or naive enough to leave parked on Castle St overnight. Halfway through the year, someone from the city council came up with the idea to paint angled parking lines down Castle St so that people would park with the car's nose to the kerb. This meant that cars were no longer lined up nicely, bonnet to boot, for drunken parkour wannabes to clamber over, and so the practice stopped. We were grateful for that; however, there was still much more to contend with, living on that street. For example, any possible night, but particularly Thursdays, Fridays and Saturdays, if there was a light on in our flat people would yell at us from the street: 'Haunted House girls! You should be out fucking drinking!' or 'You don't deserve to have that house, you bitches!'

Legend had it that no female had ever lived in the Haunted House before, and here we were, six girls. This was, in fact, the angle we'd taken to convince the landlord to choose us as that year's tenants from dozens of applicants. We sat down and wrote him a letter that made us out to be responsible and mature, but also funny and good-natured. The kind of girls you'd want to have a beer with—maybe even two. We knew it was a fine balance. Total nerds would never get such a famous flat because the street had a reputation to uphold. But crazy party fiends weren't desirable either.

We ended our letter with: 'We give you our guarantee that the flat we return to you at the end of the year will be in excellent condition, but certainly with a little more history.'

We broke that 'excellent condition' promise pretty quickly. If we left any kind of legacy after our year in the house, it was perhaps the record number of broken windows. For the first few months we lived there, people would throw bottles through the windows late at night in protest of girls living in the house (once it was actually a kumara). It set the tone for that year, one where I was constantly woken up, abruptly, in fear. If not because of the crashing of glass, then because of the guys that my flatmates would bring home nearly every week and encourage to 'go visit Lilly' as I lay asleep in bed. I would wake to the sound of blaring voices in the hallway and lie frozen in suspense, praying that I wouldn't hear my door handle turning. Or, worse, I wouldn't wake until the weight of a body would tilt my mattress or a heavy hand would touch me. I got a lock on my door, which made the drunk boys angry, and there were times when they would rattle the handle or kick at the door for long minutes.

Amid the chaos and fun of being a student flatting at Otago it was easy to put aside the issue of my sexuality . . . at first. But as the year went on the routine of getting pissed and going out to the same pubs to spend hours on the dance floor began to wear on me. Sometimes I would stand there in the overpacked bar, watching everyone laugh and flirt, and I resented how easy it was for them. The reality of how hard it was to be a girl who wanted to kiss girls was in my face every night, as I watched heterosexual hook-ups happen from nothing more than a loaded look across the bar. How on earth would I find even one girl who might think of kissing me? I spent a lot of time gazing around, sizing up girls, hoping that one of them would catch my eye across the room and recognise my glance for what it was. I dreamed of a girl giving me a smile that meant she'd seen me and wanted me.

Anywhere from three to five nights a week I stood in these bars while my friends were off dancing, hoping that tonight the game would be different. The longer I looked, the sadder I got, until I felt very sorry for myself indeed.

To enjoy myself when I was out I needed to be really drunk. The problem with being really drunk is that your inhibitions are shot, so you can imagine what happened: sometimes I found myself flirting with girls. The difference between two drunk girls who are just having a good time together and two drunk girls who are flirting can be virtually indistinguishable, which is problematic for the budding lesbian. In drunk-girl world, arms are thrown around each other, compliments fly and hugs are plentiful. Touch is the communication currency. And it's not just between good friends. Because of the culture of Otago Uni, where 99 per cent of us were imports from other areas of New Zealand and a tide of drunkenness flowed through the city daily, bonds were formed quickly. You had a night on the piss with someone and they could become your bestie by drink number six. I had to be careful. Firstly, I had to keep my feelings in check and remind myself that any physical attention I received was not meant like that. Even harder than that was managing my own behaviour, for I knew that beyond a certain point (or drink) I would give myself away. I began trying to monitor my behaviour, keeping my hands to myself and not hugging. But sometimes I slipped and I flirted, and I enjoyed it, then when I realised what I was doing I felt shameful and dishonest. Sometimes I would get it in my mind that my cover was blown, and I had to get out of there immediately. On these occasions I would end up walking home in the dark, crying as I weaved across the footpath.

My self-vigilance began to bleed into my everyday life, and it was holding me back from being myself around my friends, too. I wanted to be open, and I wanted to be a more physically affectionate person, but I felt like I couldn't even give my friends hugs. My emotional distance from the people around me grew, even if it was only in my own heart.

The catalyst to change came in second semester, when my flirting finally crossed the line. Lucy was in both my psychology and my gender-studies papers, and we'd struck up an acquaintance walking to lectures together. She had long dark hair and dark eyes. This, combined with the way she would pull up the fur-fringed hood of her jacket around her face, made her look like a Russian femme fatale. That was my private fantasy, anyway. One night we ended up out on the town, very drunk after splashing out on cocktails at Pop Bar in the Octagon, and things got cuddly. We were holding hands between bars, sitting with our arms around each other, and for a second I thought that it could have been something. At the end of the night we walked home together and before we parted to go to our respective flats I kissed her on the cheek. I saw her face change in sudden realisation, and she backed away. I held in the tears until I'd locked my bedroom door behind me. I berated myself for letting my guard down. Lucy and I stopped walking to lectures together and she began sitting with other friends. The new awkwardness between us wasn't just coming from her; I felt too embarrassed and ashamed to pretend that nothing had happened and forge on. The idea of addressing it with her and laughing it off was . . . not even an idea. I was years from that level of confidence in who I was. I still didn't know who I was, what I was.

However, one positive thing came out of that incident: it gave me the kick up the bum I needed to get my act together. I didn't like feeling this way and I didn't like who I was becoming, either. So, for the first time, I was really honest with myself: I was attracted to girls, it wasn't going anywhere, and I needed to do something about it. Three big statements that made my tummy twist in knots. But the question remained—if I wasn't straight, what exactly was I?

I began researching, trying to figure out where to start on my quest for enlightenment. It wasn't as easy as it would be in today's world, where internet access can be as simple as picking up your phone. Back then, if I wanted to use the internet I had to go to the university library and wait in a queue for one of the twelve computers assigned for 'casual personal use' rather than assignments. The time limit was only ten minutes—it took me longer than that to walk to the computer from home. My other option was to check out books, but there was a greater risk of discovery. I developed a detailed plan to get around this, which I believe still holds water today. First, walk past where the queer books are kept, casually glancing into the aisle on your first pass. If there's no one in there, loop around and approach again. As you get closer to the LGBTQ section, peruse the shelves casually as though you're looking for a particular reference number nearby. Whoops! You've stumbled upon the gay books, what a surprise, this is such a coincidence . . .

But hold on—before you step closer, make sure you have a book from a nearby section in your hand. That way, if someone suddenly walks into your aisle you can flip through the decoy book as though you'd picked it up and then just drifted closer to the queer section, unknowingly. Furthermore, make sure you put the book back while the other person is there, so they know you weren't actually looking at the homo books. Then continue looking at the books next to the books you actually want to look at for a good 30 seconds. Keep breathing: it's important not to draw undue attention to yourself. If you sense suspicion from the intruder, pick up another non-threatening book, flick through it, then snap it shut with flair, conveying through body language that you have found just the one you were looking for. Hurrah! Then leave, and do not look back—this is something only a guilty gay would do. However, if you're lucky and no one interrupts you (but, please, stay vigilant at all times), scan the titles in the queer section, identifying the ones you want to take. Do not pick them up until you have decided which ones you will take, otherwise someone could approach quietly and bust you holding something titled *Queer Theory* or, even worse, one with a purple cover showing an artistic rendering of two women intertwined. Now, have you mentally made your picks? Okay, grab them, quick, and get out of there. Wait for your heart to stop pounding as you walk away, because you're going to need to feign nonchalance to the librarian at the issuing desk. This is 2003, and there is no self-service issuing. Hold on, you don't want to approach the librarian with just a handful of lezzy books, do you? Silly—you're going to need to get out some other books to throw her off the scent: safe books about plant life in the Paraguayan jungle or the Treaty of Waitangi. Something nice and dull. Did you make it? Congratulations! Scurry back to your room, close the door and start learning how to be a gay-mo.

Books were actually not an overly successful route for me. The majority of queer books in the library were theory-based or just outdated. But I hit pay dirt one day on the uni computers: a lesbian film called *The Truth About Jane* was coming to Dunedin, and it was coming soon. I'd never been to a lesbian film at a theatre before—it hadn't occurred to me that such a thing might even exist. I was excited, but the thought of going also gave me an acidic feeling in my stomach. On the day of the film I held off leaving the house, paranoid that I was going to turn up early and have to wait around, which would have been too much to bear. Instead, I was almost too late. When I got to the cinema, housed in a retro building, I pushed through the swing doors with a neutral face, pretending that I went to these things every day, no big deal. It wasn't like I'd spent an hour trying to find an outfit that didn't scream 'straight girl!' but also didn't scream 'trying to look less straight!' I could tell that everyone was already inside by the level of noise coming from one of the theatres. Shit. I walked in and was trying to take in the overwhelming sight of nearly a hundred women laughing and shouting to each other, when a deep male voice interrupted my daze.

'Excuse me, honey, I need your ticket . . .'

Startled surprise must have flown across my face when I looked up into the eyes of the person who had spoken: a muscular black man dressed in a neon pink Carmen Miranda two-piece, complete with basket-of-fruit headpiece, a long skirt with a slit up the side and six-inch heels. What was such an exotic thing doing here in Dunedin, a tiny city at the bottom of the world, with that American accent and self-assurance? I was taken aback, but managed to smile and fumble my ticket over. I made a mental note: *Work on your poker face, dammit. Be cool, Lilly, be cool!*

The only seats left were, predictably, right near the front. I made my way down the aisle, feeling dramatically conscious of all those eyes on me, and when I reached the row I had to scoot along past ten people to get to the free seat in the middle. My crotch had never been so close to a lesbian's face before.

'Excuse me, sorry to push past, excuse me,' I said.

'It's okay, love, you can push past me any time,' a craggy voice rasped. Oh god.

But when I finally got to my seat and settled in, my nervousness began to give way to an unusual sense of peace. There was an atmosphere of warmth and good humour, with people throwing balled-up pieces of paper at each other and calling out. I realised that these women were relaxed, able to be completely open about who they were in an environment that felt safe to them. Maybe one day I would be like them. I let the wave of noise wash over me, and I leaned back in my seat and allowed myself a little smile.

The Truth About Jane (spoiler alert) tells the story of sixteen-year-old Jane, wry but earnest and kind-hearted, who falls for the new girl at school and has a whole lot of first-time experiences, including heartbreak. But the real story centres on Jane's relationship with her family and in particular her mother—including her mum's shock and inability to be accepting when Jane tells her she's gay. It's a Lifetime movie, so it's deliciously soppy, and comes complete with a philosophical yet dry narration from Jane.

When the film was over, I walked home stupefied. Every feeling and thought Jane had talked about in the film could have been my own. The disconnection from others, the feeling that everyone else 'got it' while she didn't, and the sudden enlightenment when she kissed a girl for the first time—I knew these feelings intimately. The realities of what I stood to face in not being straight were suddenly highlighted too. Jane doesn't face an easy road to acceptance in the movie, and deep down I knew that my own was unlikely to be much easier.

A line from the movie stayed with me, and when I got home I scribbled it deep in a secret notebook: 'Who she was was exactly who she was always meant to be.'

It was a sentiment I kept close to my heart over the next few years, and it gave me strength. Did I already sense how much Jane's mother was like my own? I think so. But I had no idea then just how much my own life would come to mirror that movie.

———

During my research, I'd found out about the university queer group . . . 'queer'—god, it seemed like such a radical word.

I couldn't say it out loud. I carried the email address for the group around with me for two weeks, but began losing confidence. I started worrying that once I talked to someone about this whole thing, I wouldn't be able to take it back. I'd be stuck with this other version of myself that I still wasn't sure was really real. Was I ready for that kind of huge commitment? And what had seemed so obvious after leaving *The Truth About Jane*—'I'm *so* a lesbian!'—was now all confused again. Sometimes I would think to myself, *What are you doing? You've never even had sex with a guy. Just get that out of the way first, then you'll know more, one way or the other.*

But then I would think back to that horrible encounter with the guy I went home with when I was trying to be 'just like everyone else'. I never wanted to feel like that again. Sure, I still wanted to have sex for the first time and get it over with, because still being a virgin by this point—over halfway through second year—seemed ridiculous. But then, I didn't think having sex with a guy was going to be the answer. I made a few last, desperate attempts to triple-check that I wasn't into boys after all, like the night I was plodding my way home from a bar and met a boy on the road just two blocks from home. Without saying much more than a hello, I ended up pashing him up against a fence. Thankfully, Emma—who was my flatmate that year—was only a couple of minutes behind me. When she came across our shadowy figures going at it she told me to come along now and leave the boy alone. I followed her home like a lost puppy.

Emma was the only one who knew what was going on with me. Since our meeting in Cobb & Co. when I'd spilled the beans about Coop and me, she'd become my sounding board. I knew I could trust her, and I needed her unflappable approach to help calm me down. During this period, when I was trying to get up the courage to email the university queer group, UniQ, I would often burst into her room in a tizz, full of self-doubt. She was usually curled up in her purple La-Z-Boy—never at lectures—reading a fantasy novel and trying to soak up the weak Dunedin sunlight that came in through her large (and sometimes broken) windows. Every time I slammed through her door, she would patiently put down her book, fold her hands in her lap and say something like, 'Yes, Lil, what is it now?' Her nonchalance about the whole issue gave me the encouragement I needed to go on, and I finally decided I would do it. I would email UniQ.

To set my plan in action, I first opened up a brand-new Hotmail account to send the email from. There was no rational reason for this, but in my mind it was necessary to keep my anonymity, and my regular email address had my full name in it. The second problem was those damn computers for 'personal use' in the library. Not only did I have just ten minutes to type and craft and send the email, but also the computers were right in the middle of the main thoroughfare of the library, where people walked behind your screen almost continuously.

I waited in line at the library, my whole body tensed. When it was my turn I tried to make my small build appear bigger, hunching over the screen to protect it from potential peeping toms.

The email went something along the lines of: 'I'm questioning my sexuality. I think I might be bisexual, but I'm not sure, but is there someone I can talk to about it? But if that's not something you guys do, that's cool, no worries.' I'm sure that the way it was written betrayed my nerves.

Forty-six and a half agonising hours and four trips to the library later, I had a response from the girl who ran UniQ. I stared at it, sitting in my inbox. I could have sworn it was pulsing, or maybe that was just my heartbeat in my ears. After a good minute, I opened it.

Hi, Lil

Thanks so much for getting in touch. I've talked to Gavin, my co-coordinator, about your email, and you're in luck! There's a women's group called 'Blossom' starting up in a couple of weeks. Would you be interested in going along? There'll be lots of young people there like you, newly out or still figuring out their sexuality. I'll put you in touch with the facilitator if you like. But perhaps you'd like to come to the UniQ office and meet me first?

    Best,

    Jo

What. The. Fuck. How could she be so casual? My first reaction to this email was outrage. Obviously this chick had no idea what a big, huge, fucking . . . *massive* thing this was for me, sending an email like that. Who was this 'Gavin' person she'd talked about me with, and who said she could do that? Furthermore, what was this about going to a group, this 'coming out' group full of bloody lesbians? Who said I was coming out? How dare she use the 'CO' phrase. I wasn't coming out, I was just casually enquiring as to what she thought about my ongoing and overwhelming desire for the same sex and wondered if we could, maybe, y'know, chat about it . . . on an abstract level, like. I mean, this could all be a big misunderstanding—I didn't know! Coming out, ha. The idea of it.

I'm not sure what I really expected from her response because it was perfectly supportive and relaxed, but I had a knee-jerk panicked reaction.

'Emma! Emmaaaaaa!' I came running home and burst into Emma's room waving the email, which I had printed out with sweaty palms, ready to jump on anyone who tried to claim it from the library printer. That piece of paper was as important and damning as any contraband material I have smuggled, before or since.

Emma looked up from her plush purple throne. 'What?'

'I got an email back from this chick, and she wants me to go to a coming-out group. A *coming-out* group, Emma! I'm freaking out!'

'Lil, I think you're freaking out,' she responded.

After talking me down from the ledge, Emma gently suggested that the girl's proposal wasn't really so outrageous. It still didn't mean I had to commit to an identity. Emma had a point, and I began unravelling my reaction. What was it about the idea of meeting others that had me so afraid? I know I was worried about what this girl, Jo, would think of me. Would she look at my long blonde hair, my UniCol hoodie and the way I blended in so easily with all the heterosexuals walking the campus, and go, 'That is one confused straight girl.' Would she and the real gays at UniQ laugh about me when I left, like, 'Who is this girl, thinking she can be part of this world she doesn't belong to?' I realised, also, that it would be the first time I presented myself to a stranger as something other than straight. All the women at *The Truth About Jane* screening had been a precursor, but that hadn't been half as scary as the thought of looking a gay person in the eye and communicating 'I'm like you'.

With Emma's support, I got up the courage to email Jo from UniQ back. We arranged to meet. On the day, I gave myself 30 minutes to make the ten-minute journey from our flat on Castle St to the UniQ office, which was smack dab in the middle of campus. Of course I was terribly early, so I passed the time walking nervous loops through the library food court, past the psychology labs, through the commerce building and back. Eventually I stomped up the twenty steps to the office and peered through the glass door. A girl with curly hair and a kind face saw me and waved me in.

'Hi! You must be Lil. I'm Jo. Come in, have a seat.'

I sat on the well-worn couch, wringing my hands. I could tell Jo had noticed. She'd probably had numerous terrified youngsters through her office, although she didn't look more than a few years older than me.

Jo was nice and non-threatening, and she took it well when I, nervously and with more than a hint of accusation in my tone, asked her who she'd shared my email with. She assured me that no one else had seen it—she'd just talked through how to respond to me with Gavin, the guy she ran UniQ with. I relaxed, slightly.

'Now, do you think you might like to go to this group, Blossom? I know it's scary, but you'll meet other girls there you can talk to. The woman who runs it is lovely. She's British.'

Jo told me to go away and think about it, but when I left the UniQ office that day I already knew that I would go. And I knew that I would change because of it. I had grown up thinking my life would be one way, and that I would be a 'normal' person just like everyone else. Not that anyone thinks of themselves as normal, but I didn't know that yet. I started liking the thought that I might be just a little different from everyone else.

We were a tight-knit flat that year, me and the five other girls who lived in the Haunted House. When you first go flatting there's a magic to it, living with your friends instead of your family, and you're more cohesive too—cooking together and socialising with your flatmates every day. We got on the piss as a flat three or four times a week, mutually suffered through numerous hangovers, went to lectures together and didn't go to lectures together. We laughed at Fi's matching hair-straightener burns on both sides of her forehead and talked our flatmate Kate down when she was determined to take all her clothes off on Nude Day at Gardies. Boys brought home to our house as one-night stands were regularly subjected to other flatmates bursting into the room the next morning, screeching 'Who do we have here?' and trying to pull the covers off. If one of the girls had hooked up with a boy and gone back to his house, the rest of us would sit on the balcony the next day and wait until she came shuffling down the street in last night's clothes, just so we could sing 'walk of shame, walk of shame, didn't even know his name' at the top of our lungs. Sometimes other people sitting outside their flats would join in and the song would echo down the street.

Living in each other's pockets the way we did, I knew I was going to have to find an excuse for leaving the house on Wednesday evenings to go to the Blossom meetings. Fortunately an excuse fell into my lap when I found out I had my soccer team's break-up dinner on the same night as the first meeting, but it also caused a dilemma—I could tell my flatmates I was going to the soccer dinner, but which event would I really go to? I decided I could do both. In romantic comedies guys date two separate girls on the same night all the time, and that always goes smoothly, right?

In the normal world, having to leave a group dinner early is nothing unusual, but the Dunedin culture was different. When you committed to a boozy evening, with each person bringing a bottle of wine to polish off at the restaurant, you were in it until the very last drop. I would be breaking the code to leave my teammates at the table.

The night arrived and, after picking half-heartedly at my teriyaki chicken for a while and pretending to drink, I got up from the table and announced that I had to be somewhere else. I was immediately bombarded.

'Second Year, sit your arse down!' shouted my team captain. Others joined in.

'Where are you going?'

'What could be more important than this?'

I couldn't answer any of these questions, so I just mumbled something about it being really important and got out of there before they held me down and poured cheap wine down my throat. I had ten blocks to walk, and I already knew I was going to be late. I powered along the pavement to an unfamiliar part of town until I reached a doorway tucked down a side street. My heart thumped with every step up the narrow wooden staircase, and as I reached the top of the empty old office building I followed the light and voices. I looked at the watch strapped to my sweaty wrist—yep, I was a good fifteen minutes late. Still trying to catch my breath, I hitched up my fishnet stockings, tightened my side ponytail and pushed through the doors.

The six girls slouched on chairs and couches around the room looked up at me, standing in the doorway, and the conversation stopped.

'Um, hi. I'm Lil, ah . . . sorry I'm late,' I managed.

'Hi, Lil.' An older woman standing at the back of the room smiled and stepped forward. 'Come in and take a seat. Don't worry about being late.' This must be Pip, the woman that Jo from UniQ had told me about.

'Thanks.' I looked for an empty seat, then paused and brushed myself awkwardly. I felt the need to explain myself because I was standing there, in front of a bunch of openly queer young women, admitting my sexuality to others for the first time, wearing a pink tutu, torn stockings and fingerless fishnet gloves pulled up to my elbows. My face was garishly made up with heavy black eyeliner, liberally applied blusher, red lipstick and bright green eyeshadow. 'And, um, I've just come from an "eighties" dress-up dinner, I had to sneak out, um . . . I don't actually dress like this normally.'

I smiled nervously, pinched my tutu between my fingers and gave a little curtsy. The expectant atmosphere broke and everyone laughed, relieved. They hadn't been able to figure out whether I was in dress-up or if my outfit was my own personal style. But I was still glad I'd decided to ditch my cone bra on the walk over.

I found a seat and waited for my turn to introduce myself and say why I was there. I was still sweating, my pulse was still racing, but I had made it. Things were going okay.

'You should be careful. Maya asked me why you're always going to "soccer practice" the other day,' Emma warned me one morning after I'd been going to Blossom for about a month. I had a moment's panic, but then scoffed. I didn't believe that Maya, of all people, would figure it out. When I'd told her about my past with Coop one night in a crowded pub, she'd thrown her hands to her cheeks in surprise, gaping at me dramatically. 'What?!' she'd cried. 'You're joking!' I couldn't believe she hadn't heard already, since Fi had spread my secret pretty quickly.

At the time I'd been satisfied that someone else thought it was as big a deal as I did. But I also suspected that Maya wouldn't be the most understanding person if she found out the full extent of my exploration into the gay world. Although I was a little worried that she was suspicious of all the soccer practices I'd made up, I'd also been to four confidence-boosting coming-out sessions by then. I realised that I didn't care what she thought. Let her be suspicious.

It was a sign of the change within me. I felt happier. I was excited about the possibilities in my life. And, mostly, I was learning to be a less judgemental, more open person. This wasn't easy. I'd grown up in a family where there was a lot of critiquing and snap judgements of others, and not a lot of open discussion about people different from ourselves. I hadn't been exposed to many other cultures or ethnicities, and certainly not other sexualities. I had grown up in a place steeped in traditional South Island values. And there was probably also a part of me that was proud of being an ex private-school prefect, sports captain and all-round popular kid. So when I met the girls at Blossom, I majorly looked down on them.

On that first night at Blossom, when everyone introduced themselves, I had sat there judging each and every person. *Oh gawd*, I thought to myself as I looked at these people with their short-cropped haircuts and uncool clothes. One girl didn't even have shoes on and was wearing men's denim shorts that fell past her knees and had daggy bits hanging off the bottom. Another had the wildest head of ginger hair I had ever seen, and I immediately pegged her as an overconfident dickhead. Gender studies, gender studies, drama, social work, gender studies. As I listened to everyone's majors I practically snorted. What a bunch of clichés. I felt much better about myself after meeting everyone else. I had this: I was the coolest person there. Well, except for Priscilla maybe. I eyed her across the room. She and

Pip both ran the group, but Priscilla was just a couple of years older than the rest of us. I fell in lust instantly. She was such a contrast to my mainstream self—tall, curvy and tattooed, she wore her jet-black hair pulled back in a ponytail with a heavy fringe and a big strip shaved out of the side (this was ten years before this haircut came into fashion and every third straight girl had a shaved patch). Priscilla even had a lip ring at the side of her mouth, which she would chew on in a way that drove me to distraction throughout the six weeks of the group.

I left Blossom after the first meeting with a whole bunch of mixed feelings. On the one hand, I was so excited. We'd talked about gay stuff and lesbians and just, like . . . gay stuff! It was amazing! In all nineteen years of my life I'd never once talked through my feelings for other girls and now I was! With other girls who also liked girls! And understood my complex emotions around it! Wow! On the other hand, I felt disappointed. I'd thought that the group would satisfy that little bit of me that didn't fit in with my other friends. I didn't think I was asking for too much—just one cool new gay friend would do. But I didn't fit in with the Blossom girls either, any more than they would have fit in with my friends. I was saddened that I hadn't found people who were like me: 'normal, but just happen to be gay' was how I described it. These girls were all, like, super gay. I wasn't, like, super gay. Just a bit gay, maybe. Probably.

But as the meetings went on, I started realising that my prejudices and insecurities were affecting the way I saw those girls. As we sat and shared, week after week, I came to see them as real people rather than the caricatures I'd judged them as.

During my life I'd heard all those phrases that ignorant people say, like, 'If lesbians are into other women, why do they try to look like men?' and up until then I'd secretly wondered the same thing. When people had said things about God creating men and women as physical opposites so that they 'fit together' and for procreation, therefore it was the natural thing and anything else wasn't natural, I had disagreed with them without knowing how to articulate why. At Blossom, I began to address each of these pervasive cultural statements and to untangle why they were wrong. I was taking on a queer side to my own identity, which made me think more about how those statements made me feel as a non-straight person. They seemed wrong now that I could hold them up against new frames of reference: actual queer people, including more masculine-presenting people like Zoe and Danny from my group. Knowing them made me realise that everyone has their individual reasons for presenting themselves however they do. Or they don't. Maybe they're just dressing in a way that is comfortable, and it's the rest of the world who's analysing them about it.

I also realised that my reaction to people like Zoe—she of the baggy men's shorts and bare feet—was first and foremost a judgement because she didn't dress to a standard I deemed acceptable, or in a way that was 'normal'. But my reaction was also tied up in feeling intimidated by how comfortable she was with herself. Zoe dressed how she wanted to dress, not like me. I dressed in skirts and heels when I wanted to look 'nice' because that's what everyone else I hung out with did. Zoe was also open and unpredictable, while I liked to control everything around me. Just being around her made me take a hard look at myself. I was becoming more and more aware of my own privilege, from my private-school education to my body type, right down to the fact that I had never had to worry about money my whole life. This revelation was uncomfortable and slightly embarrassing. But it was also freeing.

Two girls from the group, Sarah and Kirsty, officially became my first-ever lesbian mates. It was different hanging out with them. I felt a level of comfort in their company that I had sometimes struggled to find with my uni friends. And in the end the things I had judged Sarah and Kirsty on initially—such as the way they often talked about gender and identity, and how society functions—became the things that I cared about the most too. It wasn't their problem that they knew who they were and had found their areas of interest. It was mine. Back then I was only just beginning to realise what I was passionate about, and I judged the passions of others.

When the last session of Blossom rolled around, I was devastated. Now that I'd started talking about all these things, I never wanted to stop! I'd met girls with a range of identities. I'd heard some heart-warming stories and some very sad stories. I'd learned about the inequalities that queer people faced under the law, but also how far we'd come. My political side had been awakened, and I felt a new radicalism pulsing through my veins.

We had a night out together, all of us, to say goodbye. I would see many of them again, as the queer community in Dunedin was small, but I knew I probably wouldn't stay in close contact with most. And that was okay. There would always be a bond now. I felt newly protective of the gang of misfits I had been a part of, and I would have defended them fiercely to anyone on the outside who dared to judge, as I had when I'd first walked in the door of Blossom. Wasn't I—someone who passed as straight in my heteronormative university world but wasn't straight—a 'mis-fit' too? I might not have found exactly the new friends I wanted, but I had found something better—a confidence in who I was and what I could be. Slowly, because of that group, I learned not to worry so much about 'fitting in'. I was beginning to define my life by my own terms.

Chapter 6

America, Home of the Brave

It takes a long time sometimes, as a lesbian lady, to
realize that a girl who loves your love doesn't necessarily
love *you*. Sometimes it's malevolence on their part,
sometimes it's that you're not even speaking the same
language because your heart and your body have a whole
different vocabulary than girls who don't like other girls.
— Heather Hogan

I f I could make it 'out' in America, I could make it 'out' back
home in little ol' New Zealand. That's what I figured as the
end of my second year of university rolled in and I prepared
for a three-month working holiday in the ski fields of
Colorado. I'd decided that when I got to America I was going to
put a new version of myself out in the world; one that was more

open and confident. And bisexual. If that went well, maybe I could keep that person when I got back to Dunedin for my final year of university.

To kick off my coming-out tour I told my friend Katija, who was going to be my travelling buddy for the trip. And it was a great start. In fact, Katija quickly and lastingly became my biggest supporter, undaunted by my newly defined sexuality and ready to defend me against anyone who showed the slightest hint of disapproval. In a way Katija's response was perfect: she treated me exactly the same, but she also treated me differently. By that I mean she asked me questions about how sexuality worked, how I felt about women, who I liked and so on. Questions to get to know me better and to understand better a sexuality that she didn't share. She didn't just clam up like a lot of other people would in the near future, stammering out an 'Oh, cool, I'm fine with it' and then never speaking of it again. I felt really happy to have her by my side as I went into this experiment—both in being 'out' and in doing my first big overseas trip alone without adult supervision.

After a week in Los Angeles and San Francisco we landed in the dodgiest neighbourhood in Denver, Colorado, where we slept cuddling backpacks full of valuables against theft. We were driven out of our hostel before the sun rose by our roommate, a Buddhist monk who prayed loudly in the closet until 3 a.m., when Katija yelled for her to close the door or shut the fuck up. Having watched the manager cough uncontrollably into the complimentary bowls of cereal laid out in the communal dining area, we decided to skip breakfast and catch the first bus out of town, no matter where it was going. And that's how we found ourselves in the ski town of Vail, Colorado, where my adventure as an openly bisexual nineteen-year-old really began.

Why bisexual and not something else? I felt that, for now, that was enough. I wasn't quite ready to let go of the safety of opposite-sex attraction, even though I felt the pull of women like a siren song. For me, choosing to identify as bisexual was a way of stepping outside the closet while keeping a hand on the doorknob.

When Katija and I got down from the Greyhound bus onto the heated pavements of Vail, we marvelled at our surroundings. Snow tumbled across roofs, lights twinkled from under carved wooden eaves and fir trees were dotted strategically for maximum cuteness. The mountains towered above us, so close that you could practically hear the swish of latest-season skis slicing through powdery snow. It was like nothing I'd ever seen in real life—more like something from a Christmas movie.

As we manhandled our suitcases and snowboard bags over the cobbles, panting immediately in the high altitude, we were passed by people wearing expensive winter gear, which I judged by the amount of real fur used around hoods and cuffs and perched on top of women's heads in hat form. No one carried skis—they didn't need to. They could simply step out of their snow-side chalet and onto the mountain or be ferried from the door of their hotel to the base of the ski lift. I looked at them with envy as we left the village behind to cross a busy freeway lined with dirty snow, stopping often to juggle our things and strip off layers. Eventually we arrived at the Roost Lodge, the cheapest (but not cheap) accommodation in town, relegated to a suitable distance from the premium accommodation. Despite the startling honking of air horns from passing eighteen-wheelers, the lodge still looked cute to me, with burnt-ochre cabins framed by drifts of glistening snow. We quickly realised that every other foreigner who had plans to work and party in Vail over the season had sniffed out this place too. Young people poured out of their cabins, laughing and drinking and cramming into the spa pool. We'd finally arrived, and now we had to beat all these others to jobs and more-permanent accommodation.

I was the first to find success a few days later, when I nabbed a hostess gig 12 miles down the highway at the Beaver Creek Tavern, seating Americans who had trouble deciphering my Kiwi accent. This became a problem when they repeatedly failed to understand my warnings that ski boots would be slippery on the wooden parquet floor. There was a reason we called it 'the dance floor'—because of the way people would windmill their arms as they skidded across it. There were two broken wrists during my time at the helm. Katija, meanwhile, became the world's worst childminder at the Beaver Creek ski school. She regularly turned up late, stinking of booze, and more than once she was found cuddled up asleep in a pile of kid's plush toys in the playroom.

We found more-permanent lodgings in East Vail, just as our money was running out, thanks to a pair of overly friendly Argentinian boys who approached us in the library. They convinced us that living with them and two of their friends would be just perfect for us, sexual favours included. ('Lilly, if you ever want me to go down on you, I promise I am very, very good at it,' one of them reassured me one evening.)

On our first night in the house, after we'd all polished off a 5-litre box of Franzia wine, Katija and I gave in to their attentions and I pashed not one but three of our new roomies, while Katija rolled around on the floor with the fourth. At the end of the night I was so drunk and stoned that I had to pull myself down the stairs on my stomach and crawl into the bedroom I was sharing with Katija to collapse on my semi-inflated air mattress.

We soon welcomed more flatmates into the house: two beautiful, spoiled Brazilian princesses who had never lived away from their family homes, where they had maids to clean up after them. That made eight flatmates split between three rooms. Our house of madness was complete.

I was ready to get out there and start meeting some girls, but first I had to put my label of 'bisexual' to the test. Our male flatmates were predictably titillated, and the Brazilian girls thought it was kind of disgusting.

'No, Lilly, it is not right,' one of them said to me.

But I found real acceptance with our seven Australian neighbours living down the road. I'd met a few of them when they'd come into the Beaver Creek Tavern looking for jobs—three gorgeous sun-kissed Aussie girls with long limbs and an ability to knock back piss like I'd never seen. Their place became my sanctuary away from the never-ending house music, strobe lights, drug taking and communal-area masturbating of my own flatmates, and my sexuality was never treated as a thing. They teased me about girls just the way I teased them about boys, and their easy acceptance warmed me.

It was during our first week in Vail that I met Lacey. Katija and I were sharing a pitcher of beer at a cowboy-themed bar when we noticed that the girl having an awkward first date at a table near us was a fellow New Zealander. We struck up a conversation and the poor boy she was with soon faded into the background. I never even noticed him slink out.

Katija, bless her soul, had become the best wing-woman anyone could wish for, and she somehow raised the topic that I was trying out the new identity of bisexual.

'Hmm,' Lacey replied, then gave me a teasing smile. 'So, are you attracted to me?'

There are a number of red flags about this response, and had I not been so young and naive I would have immediately pegged Lacey as being Trouble. But I looked at her glossy brown hair and flawless skin, and all I thought was, *Yeah, duh.*

I knew not to respond verbally in such a way though, because I'd learned by then that sometimes straight girls just liked to flirt. So I kept my cool and did the best that I could when put on the spot with such a thorny question: I laughed in an 'oh, *you*' manner. I really didn't expect what was to come.

Five minutes later, I got up to go to the loo and when I came out I passed Lacey in the hallway.

'Hi!' I said cheerily as I walked past.

'Oh, hi, have you just been to the bathroom?' she responded.

'Yep.' I carried on my way back to the table.

Half an hour later, I went to the bathroom again, peed quickly and washed my hands. This time as I walked out, Lacey came screaming around the corner.

'Whoops, almost got me!' I said cheerily as I sidestepped her, eager to get back to my beer.

The third time I went to the bathroom, I stepped out of the stall and Lacey was waiting.

'I just have to get this out of my system,' she said, then she pushed me up against the wall and kissed me, long and hard, but soft at the same time. When she pulled away I stared at her, stunned.

'I followed you to the bathroom, like, three times,' she said.

Still I stared at her, trying to gather myself. She had come after me? To kiss me? She wanted me? It was the first time a girl had ever pursued me so aggressively. This kind of thing didn't happen in real life, surely? But it had. When we parted ways that night, Katija and I to East Vail and Lacey to the apartment in Beaver Creek that she shared with seven others, I rode the 2 a.m. bus home in a blissful, lust-filled fugue.

Life in Vail was busy but simple. Working, partying and the occasional day on the slopes. Every morning I would throw on as many layers as possible and make the trek to the main highway to catch the bus to Beaver Creek Tavern. Soon Katija came to work there for the occasional hostess shift too, and she got even more crap about her strong Kiwi accent than I did. One day a particularly rude American guy came in with his wife, and Katija asked him if he would like a table for two.

'Table for tew? Table for tew?' said the jerk, imitating Katija's accent. 'If you can learn to speak English I'd like a table for two!'

'Well, if you learn some manners I might give you a table for two,' Katija had replied. She was my hero.

In the afternoons I would hang up my Tavern apron and walk down a level to my second job at Surefoot, a fancy ski-boot store where, in return for welcoming customers and listening to them bitch about their sore feet, I was given a season's ski pass. Then, once Surefoot closed, three nights a week I would go to my third job at a fine-dining restaurant down the highway in the town of Edward. There I ate untouched desserts off people's plates, got into trouble for putting a tablecloth upside down so the tag was showing, and looked forward to the end of every night when we'd closed the restaurant down—tables reset, dishes cleaned, food prep done—and were given a complimentary beverage. Most of the people in the kitchen were Mexican and they would always laugh at me for my choice of Baileys and milk as they sipped their top-shelf tequila. Taking the piss out of other people transcends language barriers.

On the nights I wasn't working at the restaurant, I would traipse through the snow to Lacey's apartment, just across the highway from the lower Beaver Creek car park. We would hang out at her place, which was packed with just as many people as mine. Sometimes I liked her flatmates more than her because they always paid attention to me and talked to me like a normal person. Lacey's attitude towards me was inconsistent—at times flirty and warm, making me laugh with her audacious honesty, but on other occasions making me feel super unwanted. That made me question whether we were even friends. Whether she even liked me. I started falling into similar habits as I had with

Coop after she'd dumped me—desperate to manipulate Lacey into wanting me. This included cheeky teasing that sometimes verged on being mean as I grew more frustrated, and gift-giving, which probably only served to make everything more awkward and to push the balance of power in Lacey's direction. I knew I was allowing myself to be manipulated, subsisting off scraps of attention, caring too much. But I couldn't stop myself. Even the smallest glimmer of hope feels like a shaft of light to a person buried in rubble, and I had to keep digging.

Occasionally, after one of the epic parties at my place, Lacey would stay with me on my single air mattress. She was always much nicer to me when we were one-on-one. Those nights were difficult in their own way, to have the feeling of her body pressed up against mine while knowing that if I tried to kiss her I would ruin it all. Instead, I'd patiently obey when she'd ask me to stroke her hair to help her go to sleep. A warm, sweet-smelling girl in my arms was better than no girl at all, I would tell myself.

It didn't take long for all this to become torturous. I could never quite get enough from her, but I got just enough to keep me hanging around. Whenever I'd decide that I'd reached my limit, she would draw me back in with an intimate personal story that made me feel like I was special to her—not like all those silly boys she was always flirting with. Katija and the Aussie girls didn't approve of Lacey much. As straight women they seemed immune to Lacey's charms. All they could see was the way she was leading me on and, as my friends, they didn't like it.

One evening Lacey came with me to the Aussies' house, and

after a few Jägermeisters she began flirting with their flatmate Nick. He was the youngest of all of us at only eighteen, and the girls were particularly protective of him.

'What's Lacey up to?' one of them asked me as we watched Lacey and Nick roll around on the dirty linoleum in the kitchen. Nick couldn't take his eyes off her.

'She's had a lot to drink,' I said apologetically. I felt responsible for her because I'd brought her along, and it was clear to all of us that she was just teasing him. Inside, I was hurt. I pulled myself up off the couch to go smoke cigarettes with the boys, blowing smoke out the chimney because it was too cold to go outside. Before Lacey had got so drunk, we'd been having an emotionally intimate conversation and I'd felt like I was special to her. But she had to know that this would hurt me, so what was she up to?

Sometimes I managed to stay away from Lacey for a good couple of weeks, but she was often on my mind. While I was waiting for the bus home from Beaver Creek at night, I would listen to my iPod and dance around the deserted bus shelter to keep warm, jumping from bench to bench and swinging around the poles, thinking of Lacey and singing a Stacie Orrico song that was popular at the time, 'Stuck.' I was stuck on Lacey, and despite my best efforts, I just couldn't stop thinking about her.

There was still one problem I hadn't managed to figure out while I was in Colorado: losing my virginity. Lacey would be the catalyst to change this, but not in the way I'd hoped.

It was New Year's Eve, and it seemed like every foreigner in town was heading to a huge house in Vail known as the Mansion, which was occupied that winter by a good two dozen Australians, South Africans, Argentinians, Brazilians and Kiwis, sleeping up to six in a room. I was looking forward to seeing whether the epic Mansion parties lived up to their reputation, and I excitedly slogged through the snow towards the house with a couple of bottles of wine tucked into the large inside pockets of my ski jacket.

By 10 p.m. I was drunk; by 11 p.m. too drunk, and I attempted to reel myself in by drinking a glass of water in the kitchen. It was here that Lacey met Matt. Matt was a nice-looking Aussie guy I'd met back in LA, who'd ended up in Vail for the winter season too. We'd hooked up a handful of times—a drunken pash in the LA backpackers' swimming pool, OTT make-out sessions in the back of the 2 a.m. drunk bus. We'd had a good month of semi-regular hook-ups by then, but he still hadn't been able to convince me to go home with him. By the time I'd lurched into the kitchen, Lacey and Matt had already met and they were soon throwing meaningful glances and teasing comments back and forth. Ironically, they were perhaps also trying to make me jealous—Matt so that I would finally sleep with him, and Lacey so that I would continue to want to sleep with her.

But then Lacey took it too far. Making sure the crowd of boys around us were paying attention, she leaned over to me, grabbed my face and tried to kiss me. I resisted her instinctively, despite my inebriated state. I was instantly furious that she could lead me on for so many weeks then only want to kiss me for male attention. I pushed her away and stood up.

'Fuck you, Lacey,' I said. 'I am not your fucking plaything. Fuck. You.'

That—but imagine something less coherent and more slurred.

People in the kitchen hooted and cheered as I stormed away in fury. I stumbled into the depths of the house until I found an empty bedroom, where I sat down in the dark.

There was a knock at the door, and Matt came in.

'Are you okay?' he asked. Something in me broke and I pulled him onto the bed, kissing him aggressively and taking my clothes off. *Fuck this, just fuck it,* I thought. Being gay was too hard, girls were fuckers and life would be easier if I could just sleep with boys. I was determined to go through with it this time and I didn't care if I wanted to or not.

I tried to have sex with Matt. But I was so drunk . . . *so* drunk. I tried to give him a blow job, something I'd never done before, but through my stupor I realised that it was awful and he was going to think I was really crap in bed, so I stopped. I told him I was a virgin. He was surprised and suggested that perhaps we shouldn't do this. 'Yes, we should,' I said. 'Keep going.' And I tried, I really tried to have good ol' heterosexual intercourse with him. But we'd had barely any foreplay, and it just wasn't working, physically, for either of us. My body just wouldn't let me go there. Finally I conceded defeat and collapsed on the bed. Technically I was no longer a virgin, by the smallest margin. But I didn't feel any sense of relief, just sadness and defeat. I told Matt I was okay and he left, closing the door behind him. I stayed, lying on a pile of someone else's clothes in the dark while the party thumped on around me.

A few weeks later, I was standing in the middle of a pounding club called 1885, named after the altitude level. Every Tuesday, 1885 offered a $10 all-you-can-drink deal, and the floor would flex and buckle with the sheer weight of the people packed into it. Unsurprisingly, given that 99 per cent of the clientele were foreigners in Vail for the ski season, I ran into Lacey.

We chatted, if you call yelling into each other's ears chatting, and somehow Matt came up. 'Oh, yeah, Matt, I slept with him,' Lacey said, looking around the bar and chewing on the straw of her watered-down cranberry vodka.

'Huh?' I said, sure that I had misheard over the music. 'You slept with Matt, my Matt?'

'Sorry,' she yelled back. 'I didn't think you'd care?' And she really didn't. I could see the surprise in her eyes.

How could I explain to her that it didn't matter to me that she'd slept with a guy who had kind of been my hook-up? I didn't care that Lacey had slept with *Matt*, I cared that Lacey had slept with someone who wasn't me, someone she had just met and had no emotional connection with.

The next morning I lay on my shitty airbed, feeling the hard floor underneath me and listening to my flatmates' exuberant conversations in Spanish coming from upstairs. I realised that if Lacey didn't understand why I was really hurt, there was no way I could explain it. She would never be with me the way I wanted.

I don't believe Lacey intended to string me along or to hurt me. But she was nineteen, like I was, an age when any girl is exploring her sexuality—its boundaries and capabilities. I think part of it was that she was testing out her power. And I was in a phase of huge learning and openness, which is maybe why I put up with it for so long. I know that we had an emotional and physical attraction, but for whatever reason, she didn't feel the same way for me as I felt for her.

Those two experiences—trying to sleep with Matt and then Lacey sleeping with Matt—marked a turning point for me. They helped me to decide 'no more' and to understand that I needed to walk away from things that caused me pain. In some ways I was successful. I never attempted to sleep with a guy ever again, although I did kiss quite a few more because sexuality is never tidy and sometimes you just want to kiss someone. I also began really trying to get over Lacey. I stopped visiting her at her apartment, and I got on with the joy and madness of living, working and partying for the winter season in Vail.

With a month and a half left in Colorado before I had to fly back to New Zealand for my third and final year of university, I quit my jobs at the Beaver Creek Tavern, the ski-boot store and the fine-dining restaurant, and started working at the Lion's Den in Vail. One of the Aussies from the house down the road, Jules, got me the job, saving me the constant trek between places of employment. Jules and I spent a lot of time together and I maintained a low-level friend crush on her. She was such a charismatic, messy character. We would start our shift by drinking Jägermeister downstairs in the bathrooms, then get steadily drunker as the evening went on by preying on our tables full of impressionable men, encouraging them to buy rounds of shots, plus one for ourselves, plus one for the musician playing live (which we would also drink). The higher their bills, the bigger our tips. The more we flirted, the bigger our tips. New Zealand doesn't have a tipping culture, and I enjoyed the way the tipping system in the States allowed for our manipulations.

It was at the Lion's Den that I met Kasey. She was a tiny blonde girl from the American South, with dimples as American as apple pie. I loved her accent.

Kasey was a server, like I was, and one night at after-work drinks with Jules and a few others she began flirting with me outrageously. We ended up in a bathroom stall together where she told me she was bisexual, and, more specifically, that she loved boobs.

'I don't have very big ones though,' she said, pulling up her top. I blinked in surprise at the sudden sight of breasts, before pulling up my own top.

'Yours are about the same size as mine,' she said and leaned in to kiss me.

It was only the second time I'd seen a girl topless, one who wanted to kiss me anyway. The other time had been when I'd promised Coop that I wouldn't look, but had, and had been struck with a shame so powerful that I'd burst into tears seconds later. I'd grown since then, but there was still a part of me that felt as if being with a girl had to be a big secret, something you didn't talk about, or you did in the dark with the light off. I was blown away by Kasey's openness and her nonchalance about her sexuality. Of the girls I'd kissed so far, she was the first to give herself a label. It was so nice to meet someone I could relate to in that way. She was unapologetic about who she was and I took a little piece of that attitude away with me. But, sadly, Kasey and I never amounted to much. While we continued to flirt, the make-out session in the staff coatroom that I'd proposed came to nil and Kasey's flirting with the hunky male bartender at work escalated, until finally at one of my own parties I was forced to watch her making out with him. I decided it was time to Shut. It. Down. I was smart enough to realise that my currency value was weak compared with men's when it came to Kasey and to Lacey. My experiences over the previous four years had begun to teach me the lesson that people are either into you enough or they're not. There's nothing you can do about it and trying to force it through some kind of manipulation of yourself—your looks, your attitude, your personality—or through manipulation of them never works out in the end. I made a conscious effort to not wait around for their approval or attention for the rest of my time in Colorado.

By time I left the States I had kissed two girls and five boys, and I certainly knew which I enjoyed best. The label of 'gay' had begun to feel like it suited me most, and while I did continue to tell some people I was bisexual and I still kissed the occasional guy when I was drunk, I no longer felt the same pressure to explore the possibility of an attraction to the opposite sex. If it happened, it happened, but I wasn't fussed about it. That awful New Year's night with Matt really had been the nail in the coffin.

I did try to stay open to the idea that one day I could possibly fall in love with a guy, even though I didn't think I would. But I no longer gave heterosexuality my headspace. I was ready to embrace being gay and to move the hell on. Although part of me felt like I'd been on a journey of exploration and experimentation for a long time, another part of me felt like I was at the beginning of something new. I felt I could separate my past from my future and go back to my normal New Zealand life with not only a new identity but also a new attitude: no one can fuck with me now. Now, I understood what I wanted—and it wasn't a secret same-sex love affair, and it wasn't men, and it wasn't to be strung along by a girl who didn't respect me. I suddenly felt at peace with who I was as a person. I wanted to be open and proud of who I was, and I was ready to say 'fuck you' to anyone who couldn't get that. I had no fear about telling my friends I was gay—in fact, I was looking forward to it. I couldn't wait to get back to Dunedin to start my new life. For a time, I felt invincible.

Chapter 7

Out

The question 'What are you becoming?' is particularly stupid. For as someone becomes, what he is becoming changes as much as he does himself.

— *Dialogues II*, Gilles Deleuze

L ookin' at a girl on the street. I'm gay! Sneering at a guy eyeing me up at a bar. I'm gay! Wake up in the morning— wow, I'm gay! Talking to friends, thinking: *Hey, can you fucking believe I'm gay?* It was my own internal chant, a statement that once so frightened me but was now my constant companion, giving me comfort as I went through my daily life.

I felt . . . superior. Like I knew something no one else did. For a while, being gay felt like the most important part of who I was, and I dared anyone to challenge me about it. I thought about my sexuality with every interaction I had with another person, but in a positive way. It was like moving from the bedroom I'd grown up in to another room of the house. Mostly things stayed the same, except now I was looking out on the same view from a different window.

I arrived back in Dunedin from Colorado in early 2004 for my final year of university and immediately began telling my friends. It didn't take much for the news to spread—I only needed to tell ten people and within a couple of weeks everyone I had ever known seemed to be aware that I'd come out as a lesbian. Kind of. I hadn't got to the point where I could use the word 'lesbian' comfortably. It seemed too foreign, and I didn't like its implications—one of those being its connection to 'hot girl-on-girl action' flashing in neon from the banner of a porn site. In a way I did feel like a girl gone wild, like I was staging my own personal rebellion, but I wasn't about to enter a wet T-shirt contest or make out with women for the benefit of men anytime soon. There was also something about the word 'lesbian' that felt segregating to me. Perhaps because of my own insecurities, I saw the term as signifying someone who was somehow 'less than'. Or maybe it was the heteronormative culture of Otago University that made me feel that way. But there was also something about the way it rolled off the tongue that felt like biting into a piece of overripe fruit. The word 'lesbian' has a texture to it I'm not fond of. I've learned to be okay with it as a label applying to me, but I still don't love the word itself.

Being out, with my sexuality simmering so close to the surface of my consciousness, made me hyperaware of those around me. I watched with interest as some people's behaviour changed once they knew I was gay. I could feel eyes on me when I walked into house parties full of fellow ex-UniCol students, among whom the news had spread first. Everyone likes to talk about a lesbian they've unknowingly had in their midst and whether they would've ever picked it. Poor Nice Guy Robbie (who spread rose petals across my room in first year) was awkward when we bumped into each other, but I couldn't be bothered trying to explain things to him. I was over trying to justify myself to people, and I guessed he'd now figured out why I couldn't go through with sleeping with him. Mostly, I liked that people knew. I enjoyed their sideways glances or the mild tension when a girl who didn't know me well found herself alone in a cramped space with me. Sometimes I would wind them up: 'Sorry, look, I'll just lean behind you to grab this . . .' I revelled in their discomfort and felt it was a kind of payback for all the time I'd spent in a straight person's company feeling the same way. It was good for them, I thought. I quite enjoyed fucking with the people who couldn't see past my sexuality.

Overwhelmingly, though, my friends were supportive and amazing. They were happy for me, and in a way my being gay didn't mean too much to them. They already knew who I was—and this was just another part of me. Many people told me how much happier and more relaxed I seemed. It was true—I was more relaxed around other people because I was more comfortable with myself. But, in other ways, I was the opposite of relaxed. I felt a fire inside me, telling me to eat life. I wanted to get political, I wanted to explore everything about being gay and queer culture, and I wanted one-night stands. Or to have three girls on the go and not give a shit about it. I wanted to rub heteronormativity in people's faces. I was craving new experiences, feeling like I had a lot to catch up on. After all, most people have their first crushes on the opposite sex when they're just kids, their first sexual experiences when they're teenagers. I was only a few months away from being twenty and I was still pretty much, almost, a virgin. I had so much to learn and explore, and I was ready to dive in. And very soon, things began to happen.

As I settled back into my university routine, an unusual thing started to occur. A couple of girls from the outer ring of my social circle—girls I was friendly with but not quite friends with—started flirting with me. I was the first lesbian most of them had ever met knowingly, and I guess their curiosity extended to 'I wonder what it would be like to kiss a girl?' There was a particular way it would go down, too. First they would ask things like the familiar 'When did you know you were gay?' This would lead into a conversation that became increasingly intense and personal, until along would come an emotional confession on their behalf. I learned about people's eating disorders or depression, was shown hidden scars on wrists from self-harming. It was as though talking to someone who was so open and honest made girls feel comfortable sharing their own deepest, darkest secrets. 'We've both struggled,' they seemed to be saying to me. It didn't always turn into something sexual, but a couple of times it did. We would stop, they would look at me through the energy running between us, and then they would kiss me. Sharing our experiences and vulnerabilities seemed to turn each of us on.

Gay culture was still very new to me, and there was one place in particular that made me feel like Alice in Wonderland. FUNQ, pronounced 'funk', was the monthly queer night, which I'd visited once before with the girls from Blossom. I was interested to see how my perspective of the place would change now that I was out—now that I was one of them. But . . . I still didn't feel like one of them, though I desperately wanted to.

Down the rabbit hole at FUNQ, as I stepped into the underground bar and my eyes adjusted to the gloom, I would typically find this scene: lesbians, in packs, laying claim to the grotty couches in the corner, perched on chair backs and slouched over threadbare sofa arms, glaring at anyone who tried to broach their terrain. There would be two boys making out, and they always seemed to be standing under the sole overhead light in the murky joint. My eyes were drawn to the boys in the spotlight again and again, and though I told myself not to look, I couldn't help it. I'd never seen anything like it before. Two people of the same sex, going for it, in real life! It made anything seem possible. Towering over the crowd were the local drag queens, whom I would manoeuvre around with caution, never sure whether they were going to confront me or compliment me. Sometimes it was hard to tell the difference, as the words were always delivered in the same sassy tone. Drag queens will always symbolise my entry into queer culture and at the time they seemed fantastical. I couldn't believe that they were a part of my new world.

Had my straight friends walked into FUNQ, they perhaps would have seen and felt not freedom of expression and identity, as I did, but more the threat of an 'other'. I was certain that they would have judged, and left, and told all their other friends about the 'bunch of weirdos and losers'. Knowing this but also beginning to feel an association with the people who went to FUNQ was both an uncomfortable feeling and one that I revelled in. It was an amphibian itching as I grew into my new skin.

Even though I always felt somewhat out of place at FUNQ, acutely aware of the people looking me up and down in my skirt and dangly earrings in a way that seemed impossible to read as anything but dismissive, I also felt like I was on the right wavelength to read the energy in a bar for the first time. Everything seemed heightened. The hormones flying around were exciting rather than constantly hitting me in the face, which was how I usually felt in Dunedin's bars. I could see the community and the friendship and the sexual tension running through the room, and I wanted to be a part of it.

But it was hard to break through.

It was about my third visit to FUNQ when the bouncer stopped me on the way down the stairs. He glanced at my ID then handed it back reluctantly, looking at me suspiciously. I was of legal age by then, so I wasn't sure what the problem was.

'You do know what's going on down there, don't you?'

'Ah . . .' I paused, confused.

'It's a gay thing,' he said in a conspiratorial whisper, raising his eyebrows in a dramatic fashion. The message was clear—I didn't belong down there.

'Gays? Oh, thank god, I thought you were going to tell me there were straight people down there!' I said, grabbing my licence from him and trotting down the stairs.

No, I didn't. I mumbled, 'Oh, yeah, nah, that's all good' and sheepishly took my ID back. I clopped away down the stairs in my kitten heels, aware of his eyes following me. It was extremely confronting to be judged for my sexuality when it was so raw, and, although I wasn't 100 per cent a confirmed gay in his eyes, I was definitely guilty by association—and, by association, I felt shame.

By the time I got downstairs, my shame had become indignation. Who did that guy think he was! After my eyes adjusted to the gloom, I spotted my new friends, girls from Dunedin's lesbian soccer team.

'You won't believe what the bouncer just said to me!' I exclaimed. 'He was like, "Oh, you do know what's going on down there, don't you . . ." like, "Look out, there are gays down there".'

'Yeah, that's because you look too fucking straight,' replied one of the girls, and they all laughed.

I was a little hurt, but it wasn't my first or last taste of this kind of comment. It's ridiculous to think that a lesbian has to look a certain way, but I was the most femme out of all of those girls, and it made me feel self-conscious. Also: defiant. I continued dressing the way I wanted to when I went to FUNQ, even if I stuck out like a sore thumb. As my confidence in my identity grew, I quite enjoyed the looks. *You're judging me for looking straight? Well, I'm as fucking gay as a window, so fuck you for your assumptions.* I began to love the surprise on people's faces in all environments when they found out I was gay. And I still do. There's nothing better in life than having people realise you're something other than what you may appear to be.

I'd immersed myself in gay culture from the moment I got back to New Zealand that year, something made possible by having the internet at home for the first time. It's hard to overstate how exciting that was. The twelve 'personal use' terminals at the uni library—there to cater to the whole student population—had really been foiling my obsessive need to bathe in the waters of all things lesbian. Now I was free to unplug the extra-long cord from our flat's phone, pull it along the hallway to my room and connect it to my laptop. Of course, because it was dial-up, I had to check that my flatmates weren't expecting any calls first. I tied up that phone line for hours and hours downloading a little show from America I'd heard about called *The L Word*.

Our internet speed at that time was around 56 kbps. In comparison, the average internet speed in New Zealand today is more like 61,210 kbps. A file size of around 700 MB—the size of a one-hour episode of *The L Word*—would take over 27 hours to download. When you factor in the dial-up connection dropping out approximately every five minutes and taking about four minutes to reconnect, flatmates needing to use the phone to call their mums and other pesky interruptions like sleep, drinking time and, intermittently, a lecture . . . it was excruciatingly slow going.

The initial 35 seconds of *The L Word*—which took three days to download—were pretty much dead air. You didn't even see any lesbians. But the shot at 36 seconds blew my mind: Bette and Tina cuddled together in bed, asleep. I'd never seen such a thing. Two women cuddling! Simple domesticity! Not kissing to show off for boys or to practise for boys. Not a scene of experimentation when one character subsequently has a gay panic and needs to reassert their heterosexuality. These were mature women who had it together, I could tell in just those three seconds. Neither of them looked like they were going to be killed off or go back to men. Those few seconds of screen time gave me the motivation I needed to persevere. After a week of stops and starts and the agony of waiting, I had just over a minute and a half. This included the penultimate opening scene: Bette and Tina in their house, in their PJs, getting ready for work. Outstanding. Tina turns around with one of those pee sticks in her hand and says, 'I'm ovulating.'

Bette responds with 'Let's make a baby' and they kiss. With open mouths. Not just a peck, not just a hug. I couldn't tear my eyes away. I had never seen anything like two women, long-term partners, who lived together and engaged in something as simple as sharing a bathroom or dropping each other to work—and they had passion too. I suddenly saw how there could be revolution in the mundane. And although around the world I bet many queer women have reached for their girlfriend, made a kissy face and parodied the line 'Let's make a baby'—as I have—the fact remains: it's one of the most important lines in television history. Don't try to argue with me.

While this may have been the most extreme example of my

dogged determination to access lesbian content, it certainly wasn't the last. In years to come, I was always the person who knew about the obscure film made in a tiny country that had just one screening planned at 11 a.m. on Wednesday in a cinema a four-hour drive away—and went to that showing. I've watched countless hours of TV shows just to see lesbian characters, even if the pacing is so slow that you might catch just one hand hold or peck on the cheek for every four hours of content (shows such as *Out of the Blue* and *Coronation Street* have led me to this excruciating practice). I've spent far too much time watching telenovelas in a language I don't understand—such as *Los hombres de Paco* and *Tierra de lobos*. The people who also do this and then cut together scenes of lesbian characters for YouTube so that the rest of us have a shortcut, or add English subtitles, are—in my book—truly the unsung heroes of the world.

I didn't know that something called social media would soon arrive and that my passion for seeing hot ladies kissing would lead me to be a part of many powerful fandoms made up primarily of queer women. But I did know that, in seeing a representation of my identity in those first few minutes of *The L Word*, I felt valid and real. And I was addicted. I needed more.

But my feeling of invincibility wasn't to last. Because it was at this time that the Easter holidays came along, and I packed up for a visit home to my parents' house. I had no idea that they were about to find out about my sexuality and teach me the hard lesson that living as an out queer woman can have consequences.

Chapter 8
Aftermath

I stepped out into the autumn chill, pulling the heavy front door of my parents' house closed behind me. In the sudden quiet it was possible to believe that what had just happened had been a dream. That I could open the door and step back into the warmth and things would be just the way they'd been before. Before I was a disappointment, disgusting, a disgrace.

There are a lot of 'dis' words that are designed to hurt, when you think about it.

Instead, I turned away and trudged up the winding pathway towards the empty night-time road. My heart was thumping hard, and when I reached the top I had to stop to lean against a fencepost, feeling dizzy. Or perhaps I just felt as if stopping to brace against a post would be an appropriately dramatic reaction to have in a moment like this. That's when I texted Jack to come pick me up, opening with: 'Um, you'll never guess what just happened . . .'

This is a terrible phrase. It's completely uninformative and as a listener you never know the scale of what's going to follow that statement, just that you're supposed to be interested in whatever the person says next. And yet, this is the phrase I found myself using. Somehow it seemed easier to be kind of blasé and sardonic than to let myself truly feel all that had just gone down.

UM, YOULL NEVER GUESS WOT JST HAPPENED

MUM OVERHEARD ME SAYING I WAS INTO GIRLS
WHEN I WAS ON THE PHONE TO YOU, AND THEY WENT
PSYCHO AND KICKED ME OUT OF THE HOUSE AND
SAID THEY NEVER WANT TO SEE ME AGAIN SO I WAS
JUST WONDERING WHETHER YOU'D MIND COMING
TO PICK ME UP? SORRY, I KNOW IT'S A PAIN.

The time it took for Jack to drive from his side of the city to mine seemed to pass in seconds, and then I was in his car wondering how I'd lost 40 minutes. By then my shock was coalescing into a mixture of anger-fuelled adrenaline and disbelief, and as we bombed down the hill in his low-slung car I filled Jack in on the details. He seemed to be in nearly as much shock as I was. His relationship with my parents had always been warm and easy, and in fact there was usually a certain kind of joy in the air when he was around. He was like the son and brother we'd never had, and he was treated as such—coming on family holidays, being trusted to drive Dad's boat, getting teased about some of the fashion choices he'd made in the past (to be fair to Jack, we all wore super baggy jeans for a while back then). My parents' reaction was as disturbing to him—someone who had only received acceptance and generosity from them—as it was to me.

We reached the outskirts of my suburb and stopped at the side of the road overlooking the ocean to smoke a cigarette. Smoking was something we only ever did when we were drinking, and so—being dead sober—it seemed like an appropriate thing to do to punctuate this fucking bizarre event. Jack rolled mine without asking and handed it to me in silence. There was nothing to say. Neither of us had any idea of what was going to happen next beyond going back to pick up my suitcase tomorrow. The reality of the situation was sinking in, but as we got back in the car and drove towards Jack's parents' house we just kept repeating versions of 'I can't believe it' and 'What the fuck?' over and over. We had no answers, no resolutions or next steps.

The next morning when I woke up in Jack's bed, I felt better. It was odd. While there was still disbelief and hurt, it was as though someone had painted a clear varnish over the whole situation overnight. I could still see it there, but I couldn't feel its texture. It was probably long-term shock settling in. But for the meantime, it was easy enough to go out to the kitchen, make a coffee and joke around with Jack's parents the way I always had. He'd told them that I'd had some kind of fallout with Mum and Dad, but not what it was about. I didn't want to talk about it with them anyway, as much as I loved them. It's not that I was worried about coming out to them, it's just that I hadn't planned to come out to any adults at all. I was nineteen, an age when parents are only let in on small snippets of your life on a need-to-know basis. I hadn't planned for any of this.

By mid-morning the text message from my father came in as expected, giving me a time I could come by to pick up the rest of my things. That made it real again. He reiterated that I must come at the time I was told because I couldn't expect my mother to have to leave her own house for hours, waiting for me to come and go. We didn't have long to make the deadline, so Jack and I jumped in his car and cranked the music. It was a beautiful day, but as we came around the final long curve of road into the seaside suburb I'd grown up in, the familiar view of the ocean was already taking on a hue of nostalgia. I read somewhere that, in Greek, *nostos* means return and *algos* means suffering. So nostalgia is the suffering caused by an unappeased yearning to return. I knew without doubt that this fallout with my parents was real and devastatingly serious, and I had a sense that the rose tint of my youth, growing up in the safety of my family, would soon feel like the distant past. But I was feeling remarkably okay given the task we were about to do. This was in part due to Jack. He had an unflinching ability to be a smart-arse, even in tense situations. It was one of the things I loved most about him. With Jack playing silly buggers to lighten the mood, we were in high spirits when we reached my house—although I was a little worried when I couldn't see my suitcase anywhere at the side of the road as we pulled up. I hoped no one had stolen it.

With no suitcase to be found, we made our way down the path to the house and I cautiously opened the front door, which was unlocked. Now my pulse was racing. But there was no one home, as promised. The sunlight streamed through the windows and there was the familiar scent of the ocean and my mum's perfume in the air. The letters were still in the basket where letters went, the kitchen bench was wiped down and the fruit basket was full of glossy ripe fruit. Through the sliding glass doors I could see the ubiquitous clothes horse full of washing swaying lightly in the breeze. There were no remnants of the character assassination that had happened there just the night before.

But stepping closer to the kitchen bench, I saw a note in my mother's distinctive handwriting, although a more scrawled, erratic version, so I could see the emotion on the page before I read the words. The last line had been hastily tacked on the end—it was larger and written in black, though the rest of her words were penned in blue ink. These clues together—the untidy handwriting on stock-standard printer paper, written with mismatched writing implements—told me that whatever it said, it would be unpleasant. I was particularly afraid of that last line, the one not like the others. I leaned closer, and it said: *Don't insult me by leaving any shit to read. I'm not interested.*

I tried to ignore Mum's use of a swear word, but I knew what it meant. It meant extreme anger. Usually my mum is hard to rattle, handling everything with aplomb. That tacked-on sentence was a moment of pure emotion, which was rare.

I let the note fall back to the bench with an incredulous huff. She was assuming that I'd want to leave her a note trying to justify myself or apologise. That I had something to be ashamed of. But I wasn't ashamed. I'd found shame trying to hitch a ride in my back pocket many times in the past, but not anymore. Mum could kick me out and call me names, but she could not make me carry shame for who I was. I'd worked too hard to get here.

Jack and I worked our way through the house. Most of my things had been gathered up and put into my suitcase, which was sitting in my sister's room where I'd been sleeping. I imagined that it was Dad who'd convinced Mum not to leave it on the side of the road. It was a role that my dad would take up from here on in—the more rational party trying to slow down my mother's emotional erosion. But he was far from blameless. Without followers, the tyrant has no power. And Dad would be my mother's loyal minion too, defending her position for many years to come.

As I pulled my suitcase through the house, I spied the liquor cabinet.

'I think we might have to take a few bottles of dear Daddy's booze while we're here, Jacko,' I said. 'I think we deserve it.'

'It would be rude not to,' Jack agreed. I also stuffed some nice shampoo and conditioner, packets of chips and mini chocolate bars into my bag, in what felt like a parody of my normal scavenging behaviour when I left Mum and Dad's house to go back to uni.

I didn't feel much as we closed the door behind us, although I wished I could have said goodbye to our cat, who hadn't turned up in the time we'd been rummaging through the house despite me calling her. I was sad about the thought of not seeing her again.

'What do you reckon, should we have a wee dip in the spa before we go, Lilliput?' Jack joked as we lugged my stuff up the hill to his car.

'I could do with a wee soak, Jacko. Perhaps over this nice bottle of recently acquired sauvignon blanc,' I replied, and we both laughed.

My mother was hiding in the garage, listening to every word.

Chapter 9
Fallout

A pparently, finding out that your child is gay can send parents through a grieving process similar to the one experienced after a death. Shock, disbelief, anger, bargaining and finally, hopefully, acceptance. Or, in my case, a whole lot of those first four at once. But my parents weren't the only ones in shock—I'd truly been blindsided by what had happened. It's not like I'd expected a pleasant reaction once they found out. But the force of their reaction was stunning, and the unexpectedness of it happening made things worse. I wasn't ready. I wasn't ready for this! I hadn't planned when to tell my parents about my sexuality beyond 'no fucking time soon'. Maybe in, like, ten years, I'd thought, when I had a life completely independent of them. Now I'd had my choice taken away from me, and it was devastating.

They say that when someone close to you dies, grief can be pushed into the background as you deal with the practicalities of wrapping up affairs. Dying leaves a lot for a person's loved ones to do—organising funerals and paperwork and money stuff. In the first weeks after the fallout, I too went through the admin of saying goodbye. Based on what they'd told me so far, I'd expected the withdrawal of my parents' financial support to be a transactional certainty, a simple matter of cause and effect. I was gay, therefore they no longer had any obligation to support me. They seemed to think that I'd been playing them for fools all this time, laughing behind their backs as they'd funded my 'lesbian lifestyle'.

I spent the rest of the Easter holidays at Jack's house, which was the most comforting place I could possibly have landed. Still, I sometimes found myself with shaky limbs when I was in the shower, trying to gulp down waves of anxiety. I drifted around the house, enjoying it when I didn't need to speak to anyone. Or I went out with Jack and got very drunk, drunk enough to put my situation out of my mind. Finally, though, it was time to go back down to Dunedin for the remainder of my final year at university. The only time I'd heard from my parents in the ten days or so since I'd picked up my suitcase was when Dad had texted to tell me that Mum had been in the garage when Jack and I were at the house. And how they were disgusted at the way I had made light of the situation.

Then, the day after I'd arrived and unpacked my things into the second-hand chest of drawers that Katija had helped me haul up the stairs to our flat, I got a call from my father. He was ringing to deliver the verdict on whether they'd continue to financially support me.

I was completely financially dependent on my parents. They paid for my university fees and gave me a weekly allowance. I had a credit card for emergencies, a petrol card linked to my dad's business and a taxi charge card that they'd told me I could use rather than walk home alone late at night, drunk. I'd never really had to worry about paying for anything before. Now I was completely at their mercy. I felt sick when I saw DAD CELL flashing up on the screen of my phone.

Dad began the conversation by telling me that I should be grateful for what I was about to get. Mum wanted to cut me off completely, but he'd convinced her otherwise and they were going to continue paying my rent and giving me $120 a week towards food and bills. I had to pay for my uni fees from then on, and I was to cut up my credit card.

My first and lasting reaction was of great relief. I'd got off lightly. I could take out a loan for the rest of my university papers, and with that $120 a week I could survive. I wouldn't have the pressure of having to find a job to cover my living costs, something I'd realised I was going to have to start seriously worrying about. In a city where students made up a large part of the population, part-time or casual jobs during the university term were near impossible to find.

That it was fucked up to feel immense gratitude towards my parents for only partly cutting me off financially didn't escape me. But I knew that a lot of other young people, when they were kicked out of home, were really kicked out of home. I still had a place to live, a support system, regular money to keep me going. I was actually one of the lucky ones.

I realised that Dad hadn't mentioned the petrol card and I decided not to remind him. A small part of me hoped that he'd purposely let it slide, but I think that he'd probably just forgotten I had it as the bills went straight to his accountant. So I kept using it. When I was filling up I often thought *fuck you, fuck you, fuck you* as the petrol splashed into my tank. Oddly, I didn't use the card to buy coffee or lunch from the petrol station, although that certainly would have made life easier. But Dad told me once that it was only for business expenses: oil and petrol, that's it. So that's what I did. I didn't want to take the piss or anything. But I also didn't feel guilty for using it. I felt like I was owed this. I might not have their unconditional love anymore, but I had their money, and I was determined to pretend that was enough.

My coming out, which had started so well with my friends, had now been taken out of my control. There were more terms and restrictions that my parents had placed on me, mainly around who I was allowed to keep contact with in the family. In the letter Mum had left on the kitchen bench for me the day

I'd gone back to get my suitcase, I'd been expressly forbidden to reach out to my sister, Jen, who was away on a school trip in France. And I was warned to tell her nothing about what had happened when we eventually did speak. I was also told to stay away from my extended family. No one was to know, not my grandmother ('She's too old, she wouldn't understand'), not my cousins or aunties and uncles or our family friends. My mother's older sister was of particular concern to her.

'She loves a chance to see me taken down,' Mum had written.

I'd always known that Mum and her sister had a tumultuous, competitive relationship, but my own fall from grace was bringing out never-spoken-about feelings and family dynamics that I didn't even know existed. Why was one of the first things that came to her mind 'What will my sister think of me now?'

The first time I broke my parents' rules was a week or a couple of weeks later, when I got a call from Jen after she'd arrived home from her school trip. As soon as I heard the tone in her voice, I knew she knew something.

'How did you find out?' I asked her.

'They didn't tell me at first,' she said. 'But they were acting so fucking weird and kept saying all these really mean things about you, so it was obvious something had happened.'

'Yeah.'

I didn't really know what else to say. I wouldn't defend them and their reaction; I didn't feel the need to defend myself because I hadn't done anything wrong. I couldn't brush it off in the typical Kiwi way as something not as bad as it seemed—the 'she'll be right' mentality.

'Don't worry,' Jen said into the silence after a couple of seconds. 'I'll always be loyal to you.'

Somehow, it was the right thing to say. It told me that she knew things were bad and they might get worse, but no matter what happened she'd always be on my side. We'd grown close during our teenage years, despite the three-year age difference. I'd driven her to school every day. I'd tried my first puff of a cigarette with her—stolen from Dad's pack of Rothmans. I'd let her hang out with my friends when they were over and given her sips of my alcoholic drinks to try. She'd cried when I first left for university and thrown half her body through the open window of my car as I began to drive away, trying to give me a final hug in a way that pretended to be joking.

It was a great relief that Jen seemed to be okay with my sexuality, but underneath her jokes I could tell she knew how serious this was. She was the only other person in the world who knew my parents as well as I did. But, still, as I filled her in on the basics of what had happened, I didn't think she could really understand how it felt to have my character, my identity, my whole selfhood ripped to shreds by the people who had raised me from birth.

I realised how much anxiety I'd been holding as I waited to hear what her reaction would be. My parents' response had been one thing, and, as gutting as it was, I felt I could handle it because I'd already grown a life outside of them. But if I lost my little sister too, whatever was holding me together might have given way.

Before we hung up we said 'love you' to each other, which felt bigger than it ever had. Because it was. She was the only person left in my family to tell me that she loved me, and, more importantly, that she accepted me. I felt a weight lift off me and after I put the phone down I cried, really cried, for the first time since the night it all went down. Tears of hurt and anger. Tears because I was so fucking grateful I had her on my side.

I don't think either of us realised at that time how bad it was going to get for her at home. It still felt almost like a stupid joke, one of those parental overreactions that's unfair and irrational but ultimately you all forget about and move on. It was easier to take the piss out of Mum than to believe that her reaction would have serious or lasting consequences.

But the reality of this newly broken relationship soon started to make its effects known at home. My mother withdrew into herself. She spent hours at home crying, unable to stop. Or she would spit hate and throw angry fits. She wasn't sleeping. She was in the throes of grief, all because she had a gay daughter. But, though she blamed me, it was my sister who wore it.

A couple of weeks later Jen called to tell me that she couldn't take it at home with them anymore. She was crying, and I tried to keep the upset out of my own voice.

'They just keep saying so many nasty things about you and I'm trying to defend you but I can't handle it.' She broke into sobs.

'I'm so sorry, Jen,' I told her. 'I'm so sorry you have to deal with this.'

The repercussions were affecting her more than they were affecting me, in a way. Down in my university town it was easy to pretend it wasn't happening. She had to live with the fallout every day.

I felt like I'd let my sister down, properly, for the first time in my life. Not because I was gay, but because I hadn't protected her from this. Eventually, we just kind of stopped talking about it. It hurt too much and, though I felt terrible for my sister, there was nothing I could do. I was struggling myself, although I hid it well. My friends constantly asked me how I was, and I'd say, 'I'm fine!' in a surprised tone. Or I'd talk about my worry for my sister or even my worry for my parents. I worried about everyone except for myself.

YEAH, BUT HOW R U? I WANT TO NO ABOUT U, NOT THEM

It was a text message from Bridget, my old best friend who had been sidelined as my relationship with Coop grew. I'd barely talked to her since our first year of uni, when she'd found out about the true nature of my relationship with Coop. But even though we weren't really friends anymore, she still knew me better than most. She was the only person to call me out on my deflecting. It helped that she knew what my mother was like underneath the hostess persona she wore when guests were around, because Mum never warmed much to Bridget. Bridget was the one my parents accused me of having an 'unhealthy' relationship with; they never seemed to suspect Coop. Bridget was an innocent bystander who'd been tarred with the brush of my parents' prejudice before. So perhaps, out of any of my friends, she understood my parents' reaction the most.

I saved Bridget's text message and other text messages too. One from Lacey, who dropped the flirting for once and simply said she wished she were here so she could give me a hug. I got messages from my Aussie mates, whom I'd spent so much time with in Colorado—the first people I'd come out to. I heard from a couple of my old high-school friends, both First Ladies, who texted to say I'd always be welcome to stay with them at their parents' houses back home during the holidays. Both their parents had younger daughters the same age as my sister, who played in her school netball team. I knew from Jen that my mum and dad had been avoiding the other parents at netball games, standing on the opposite side of the court so that no one would talk to them. They seemed to think that all the netball parents from my high school would have heard the goss and be feeling sorry for them for having a lesbian daughter, that they'd be saying things like 'I'm glad it's not us'. They'd projected their own prejudices onto these other parents, even though I suspected they'd never admit they had any. Is 'I don't have a problem with gay people, I just wouldn't want my daughter to be one' prejudiced? I don't think they thought it was.

The thing is, I could understand why they had more shame around the high-school parents than anyone else. I'd also assumed that, out of anyone, it would be this crowd who would judge me the hardest. When I got text messages from my old schoolmates I was surprised, and I realised that I'd judged them unfairly. I'd assumed that they wouldn't be accepting of my sexuality, and their parents probably wouldn't either, because of their wealth and their conservative upbringing. When I'd first come out to my peers, my school friends were the only girls whose reactions I had been a little wary of. But their compassionate messages made me realise that I was the one showing prejudice. I decided that if I was going to ask people not to judge me on my sexuality alone, I'd better address some of my own prejudices too.

This made me look back at my family with greater clarity than I ever had before. I could see how critical we were of everyone who was different from us. If an overweight person walked past, one of us would point it out. Why? What was the point of that?

'What is that person wearing?'

'That person's unfortunate.'

'What a loser.'

That was the worst one. It wasn't just judging them on one thing; it was dismissing their whole self as unworthy of respect. *Loser.* It was a word that had been thrown about so often in my family that when I heard it now I physically cringed. I wondered why my parents were like that. Was it because they grew up without much money and once they'd done well for themselves they wanted distance from the less fortunate? I had a hard time reconciling that explanation with some of the things I loved most about my parents. Like how my mum chose to work at a low-decile school because she wanted to help the kids who needed it most—every time we went to visit her classroom we'd find our old books and toys.

'Hey, Mum,' we'd say. 'I can't believe you've given your kids my Polly Pocket. That was one of my favourites!'

'They need it more than you,' she'd reply.

Then there was my dad, who'd started his own company from scratch and, as far as I knew, was considered a very generous boss—throwing the best work parties, getting his storeman the Holden he'd always wanted as his company car, and always, always paying for meals out, drinks and activities. Or taking me, my sister and our friends on holiday and paying for everything. These were the ways my parents showed compassion. With practical help and, yes, with money.

But if this was true, then what did it mean that one of the first things they did when they found out about my sexuality was to threaten to cut me off financially? Was it because that's what they thought would convey the strongest message of disapproval? Was it because they wanted to do whatever would hurt me the most? It was incredibly sad to think about. Imagine thinking that your value to your daughter revolved around money. What I missed wasn't the financial security they gave me, the way money smoothed my path forward in life. It was much simpler than that. I missed the certainty of knowing that they would always be there. I just missed my mum and dad.

Chapter 10
Jimmychooshoes

It's hard enough having sex for the first time with anyone, but when you do it with a girl, you're just asking for it.

— *The Truth About Jane*

va, my future lover, was seventeen years old. She was a high-school senior in a city that straddled the border between Mexico and the US, and pretty soon she was going to fly to New Zealand to meet me, her future lover from the internet.

I started talking to Ava on the dating site Pink Cupid when

I was in my jubilant post-coming-out stage after arriving home from Colorado. Then, after the fallout with my parents, I really threw myself into the affair. I didn't talk much about what was happening with me and my family to Ava. Instead, I used our growing romance as a way to escape the hand I felt squeezing around my throat whenever I thought about my family and my future.

Ava's online handle was 'Jimmychooshoes', mine: 'PiefaceNZ'. She was intelligent and creative and seemed just a little bit nuts. Not in the absolute batshit-crazy way some people you met online were, but in an endearing 'wow, I have no idea what you're going to say next' way. She wrote me things like, 'Great time here, the weather has been like paradise. I now understand the sarcastic existentialist philosophers, I do—there is so much beauty in this matrix.'

Every email she sent was fascinating.

Ava and I spent a couple of weeks sending increasingly long messages before she broached the idea of talking on the phone. I was nervous, remembering those torturous evenings stuck on the line with Harry Gibbs, my first and hardly-even boyfriend, but I could sense this would be different. We actually had things in common, despite the miles and the two-year age difference between us. I thanked god for my classics, philosophy and gender papers because Ava seemed to have an unusually large knowledge about such things for her age. I even considered brushing up on my Nietzsche and Foucault before she called. Or perhaps researching Mexican politics just so I didn't sound like an absolute bottom-of-the-world hick.

But the day we'd arranged to talk came around before I knew it, and I had no time to do anything except take the landline phone and trail the cord from the lounge into Katija's room where I could have some privacy. Katija was the only person who knew about Ava at that time, and she was all for it. She was bloody excited, actually. I hadn't technically come out to my other three flatmates yet, but I'd been a big topic of gossip among ex-UniCol people for a while, so I figured they must have heard it through the grapevine.

It was a rare Dunedin day of blue skies, and the sun was streaming in through the windows as I sat on the floor with the phone's cord stretched to its limit. I was staring so hard at the handset that I jumped when it rang.

'Hello, Lil speaking.'

I heard crackling and static, then, finally: 'Hello?'

'Hi . . .' I said, struck by shyness.

There was another pause, then: 'Is this Lilly?'

'Yes, hi, this is Lilly.'

'Hi! It's Ava.'

'Hi, Ava.'

Things got better from there, despite a delay on the line and our nervous giggling. We muddled through in stops and starts, and I was immediately enamoured of her accent. However, my own Kiwi accent, full of blunt consonants and mangled vowels, proved very difficult for her to understand. It didn't matter. She found it cute, and I found her finding it cute flattering. To be honest, I could have been quacking down the phone line and it wouldn't have mattered. By the time we hung up a snowball had started rolling down the mountain, picking up speed and growing in size until it became an unstoppable force.

These phone calls became almost nightly occurrences once we figured out that the way to get around the delay was for Ava to call my cell phone. We ignored the fact that she'd be in deep shit if her father ever checked her phone bill, betting that he was too busy (and too rich) to pay attention to such things. Ava's dad was a pretty important guy in the Mexican government.

I don't know what we discussed on those long phone conversations because no one knows what teenagers talk about for hours on the phone, even teenagers. I do remember registering that Ava was a better talker than listener, but that was an inconsequential quibble at the time.

The first image of Ava that I remember seeing was inside a scrapbook she sent me. It was handmade, using pink craft paper, and Ava had filled it with photos and poetry. When I pulled the scrapbook out of the envelope, dried flowers fell out.

'What did you think?' she asked when I called her to say it had arrived.

'Well, I'm surprised that the flowers made it through customs,' was my first response. Yeah, so I wasn't perfect either. When it came to romance she was Rilke and I was Liz Lemon.

In the photos she looked young—really young—like she'd figured about 70 per cent of herself out. Like, she was smiling and silly in some photos, but you could still see glimpses of uncertainty in there, and the way she was dressed wasn't consistent. I was hypersensitive to this because I was in that phase too. I didn't really know which clothes expressed who

I was, because who I was felt so in flux. I still dressed in tight tops with low necklines or spaghetti straps when I went out at night. I wore heels and skirts and—like my peers—I refused to cover up my skin even though the average temperature across the university year sat somewhere between 0 and 15 degrees Celsius. I don't think I found a style that was 'me' until I was about 23, and there were some very awkward years in between. Photo evidence survives—me dressed in a posh Country Road skirt that had been mailed to me by my mother paired with Diesel street shoes and a hoodie, topped off with a ponytail and dangly earrings.

Ava was striking. Dark, deep brown eyes. Big nostrils and a distinctive mouth, one that I would come to know well.

I sent my own photos back and she exclaimed over them. I guess my blonde hair and pale English-heritage skin with freckles burned in by the harsh New Zealand sun was different to her. She told me I was cute and she seemed to think I was smart and well read, which of course is what I wanted to hear. Eventually, though, I realised that there was always something abstract in the way Ava described me in her observations. I'm not sure if they were actually true or just something she'd made up in her mind that I possessed. It's not like she was making me understand amazing things about myself that no one had ever noticed before; more that Ava's rich imagination didn't allow the reality of my actual personality to get in the way of her romantic projections.

I didn't know any of that yet because I was too swept up in the escapism of it all. For now, I was absolutely caught up in the mythology of Ava. She sent me Victoria's Secret G-strings for my birthday, which had me blushing as I tried to stuff them back into the package that I'd stupidly opened in the middle of a cafe. When I got home I tried them on, grimacing at my lily-white arse in the mirror, and I began wearing them even though I never got past the ongoing urge to pull my wedgie out.

After about three or four months of talking, our relationship started to become painful. It was agony to feel so close to someone but not be with them physically. At the same time, I needed increasing immersion in the world of 'us' to help me weather the ongoing silence from my parents—bigger and bigger distractions to keep out the things that caused me anguish. I needed her to be with me in person.

Then one day Ava told me she was going to fly to New Zealand. I couldn't believe it! I was so excited because I was finally going to see her, then I was terrified because I was going to see her. Shit. Everything was to be funded by her father, who seemed to know only that his daughter had made an overseas friend and wanted to do something exciting for her summer holidays. Perhaps he thought it was a good idea because of the recent kidnapping attempt he'd narrowly evaded. Maybe he thought it would be safer to send her over to the other side of the world by herself to stay with someone he didn't know than to risk her getting caught up in the currently dangerous political climate. That's right, Ava told me there was a kidnapping attempt on her father. She was so interesting! And now I was interesting too, because of my association with her.

And so, with Ava's father in the dark about funding an

international teenage lesbian rendezvous, we planned for her to arrive at the beginning of my semester break so we could take a road trip around the South Island of New Zealand.

It was happening. After years of angst and months of foreplay I was finally going to lose my virginity, properly, in the sense of two physical bodies coming together . . . because we'd been having a lot of phone sex already. I realised that I needed to have a Brazilian wax, because Ava and I had discussed such matters and according to her and the conversations I'd had with my straight friends, that's what sexually active women did. So a few days before she arrived, in between my exams, I booked myself into one of Dunedin's few beauty salons. I used a precious chunk of my small weekly stipend and prepared for pain. Holy shitting fuck-knuckle bastarding pain like I'd never experienced pain before. Not only did each rip of the wax strip cause the sensation of being flayed alive, but the nonchalant woman doing the ripping had placed the hot wax pot between my spread legs and every time I flinched I scorched my inner thighs. As I hobbled home afterwards, I was only slightly comforted by the thought that I would now look better in my Victoria's Secret G-strings. After a day or two, when the redness had gone down.

The day of Ava's descent upon New Zealand finally arrived. Getting back to my flat from my final exam, I flung open the door from the street to the stairwell and stomped upstairs, raising a cloud of dust and cigarette ash. We shared this stairwell with the flat next door, which meant that no one—for years, perhaps even decades—had believed themselves responsible for cleaning it.

One day in the future—thanks to a fit of hungover hysteria—I'd decide to clean it and would be blowing black crap out of my nose for hours afterwards.

As I slammed through the inner door to our flat and ran for my car keys, one of my flatmates called out, 'Ava's been calling from the airport, like, heaps. She says she's so nervous she wants to vomit?'

Just two days ago, I had figured I'd best tell my other flatmates that this friend of mine who was coming to stay was 'more than just a friend'. That's how I'd phrased it. The two who were more socially active had heard the gossip about my sexuality, as I'd expected, and they were cool with the announcement. My other flatmate, who still went to church every Sunday morning and had worn a ponytail and sensible shoes every day since she'd come out of the womb, had looked at me in shock and confusion.

'What? Bu-but, she's a girl, and . . . you're a girl . . . You're . . .'

'Gay.' I didn't think she knew where her sentence was going so I finished it for her. 'How have you not heard about this? Everyone from UniCol's been talking about it!'

'I don't know! I didn't hear!' She threw her hands in the air. I kinda enjoyed that reaction.

'Why do you think she's been talking to this Ava, like, every night on the phone?' Katija piped up from our baby-shit-coloured couch, where she was chomping through a bowl of pasta. 'Lil's totally dyke-ing out with her.'

'Argh!' My flatmate covered her ears, and I shook my head at Katija reproachfully for winding her up, something we both found irresistible in the face of such a naive character.

Even though the sound of that word, 'dyke', was jarring to me too, I actually liked that Katija called me this sometimes when she was being jubilant (or purposefully inflammatory). It told me that Katija was completely comfortable with me and my sexuality—and I needed that, because nearly everyone else in my life had been tiptoeing around me, not quite sure what to say, worried about offending me if they used the wrong terms. People said things like, 'Oh, it doesn't matter to me' or 'We still love you' or 'I don't care at all!' and I knew they meant well, but they didn't realise that those statements made me feel like they saw me as having some kind of affliction that they loved me in spite of.

It had been putting a barely discernible separation between me and many of my friends. But Katija had been with me in Colorado when I first began testing my sexuality out loud, so she understood the complexity of emotions that went hand-in-hand with coming out. She knew the pride and liberation I felt, as well as the toll it had taken. And she could see how sensitive I really was to the reactions of others, beneath all the bravado. Being by my side through the past eight months had made her the only person who understood that what I was looking for was to have my sexuality both acknowledged and celebrated, not dismissed as something that 'doesn't worry me, mate'.

With Ava already waiting for me at the airport, I drove like a maniac to get out there. I parked haphazardly then made my way into the terminal, scanning for someone who might be her. Now that the moment of meeting Ava had arrived, I almost didn't want it to happen. There was so much riding on it, so many expectations. The airport was surprisingly busy, although it was tiny so it didn't take many people to fill it.

When I did spot her, it was her purposeful walk towards me that made me realise who she was, not what she actually looked like. Because she didn't look like the picture I had in my head—at all. The person striding towards me, then slowing with uncertainty (probably due to the look of shock on my face) was . . . short. Shorter than me, even, which was uncommon. Her hair was a mess of wild curls, nothing like the straight hair from her photos. More frightening, she was very much a woman. She had womanly hips (I had none) and she was a solid C cup (I wore a B cup, but I was fooling no one). I immediately felt like I'd bitten off more than I could chew. I was just a girl! This seventeen-year-old was a woman! Thoughts crowded into my mind. *Is this really happening? Why did I think this was a good idea?* And worst: *I don't think I'm attracted to her. Shit.*

But it was too late, because we were hugging and saying hi, but we were also both shaking just a little. I might have committed myself to hosting someone off the internet for three weeks, but she was the one who'd got on a plane and put herself at my mercy.

I wasn't dealing with the situation very well. As we drove down the motorway towards the city, all I could do was take the piss out of her. It's what I did when I was super nervous—made self-deprecating remarks about myself or, in that instance, her.

'Wow, you're being kinda mean,' she joked, but I could see that she was actually freaking out a little.

'I'm really sorry, I know . . . I'm just in shock,' I replied.

'Uh, hello? Me too!' We both giggled and it relieved the tension a tiny bit. She grabbed my hand as it rested on the gear stick, and I smiled. This did not reflect what I was thinking, because I was still thinking, *Oh no, oh no, I'm not into her. I don't know if I can do this!*

Because we both knew what was coming. There had been too much foreplay, too much talking about it for us to not follow through with The Sex, even though it was suddenly a prospect I was freaking out about.

Then we were home, and I paused outside the inner door to my flat. I couldn't catch my breath—more than seemed normal after only walking up one flight of stairs. That's when she lunged for me. And we were actually doing it, we were kissing, and it was nothing I'd dreamed of and everything I'd been fearing for the past 45 minutes. I wasn't into her. Was it because I was sober? The last girl I'd kissed when I was sober must have been Coop, years ago. Who could hope to live up to her? Maybe that was it.

I smiled as we pulled apart. We both let out a relieved breath and laughed, glad we'd got that over with. For her, the kiss had solidified our connection. But I didn't know how she couldn't see the doubt in my eyes; I'd never had much of a poker face.

Then we were in my bedroom and I was stalling, pointing out the features of my room in detail and not looking her in the eye. When I turned around, Ava was taking her clothes off, she was reclining on my bed. Nothing was stopping this train, baby. I was faced with a near-naked female in a sexual environment for the first time. Up until then, lesbian sex had been merely fantasy. A sometimes pleasant, sometimes torturous dream of what could be. Now, faced with a woman's body in reality, I was utterly confused. I wasn't sure what I was supposed to be feeling. Wasn't I supposed to be caught up with a ravenous passion that worked itself out physically in some kind of biologically predetermined and fluid way? My main emotion seemed to be terror, with just a tiny suggestion of underlying attraction.

I was lost in my thoughts, wringing my hands, when she interrupted.

'Hey, get over here.'

And I did—I mean, what else could I do? I was committed. This is what everything was about, right? How could you turn down a Latina Casanova who'd been wooing you for months, who'd just flown eighteen hours to see you?

You bloody don't, do you? I was losing my virginity whether I had doubts about it or not.

I don't know how to describe my first time in detail, which I think is due largely to the time that's passed since then and partly to the state of shock it left me in. Afterwards, I acted normally but internally I withdrew, lost in trying to process so much new information. It had been weird. Exciting. Clumsy. Unsettling. Cool . . . but also disappointing. Her skin had felt wrong. Her breasts remained intimidating. I'd felt fine being naked with her but my body hadn't responded the way I'd thought it would. Being with a woman had felt right, I guess, but my physical and mental reaction hadn't. There was a disconnect between what I'd wanted to feel and what I'd thought I should feel—and how I actually felt. I wanted to please her but I also wanted it to be over. I was left very confused.

How does anyone not feel out of their depth in those early

explorations? Maybe we all do. I'm not sure whether the fact we were both new to sex was a good thing or a bad thing. (I didn't really believe Matt from Colorado counted and Ava had slept with her boyfriend, but neither of us had slept with a girl.) It was good because we could both learn and try out things together, but on the other hand oh my god, it's not like lesbian sex has a clearly defined road map. It might have been nice if one of us had had some practical experience. What was the order, who did what and when? And when was it over?

In this case, it was over when I couldn't bear to keep going. When I realised that I was going to be a failure at having sex in a 'normal', emotionally stable way like everyone else seemed to be able to. Because it turned out I was a crier. During that year, I would cry in the middle of sex or have to stop because I felt like crying well over 50 per cent of the time.

Nothing had prepared me for how emotional sex was going to be. When we learn about sex as young people we learn about the physicality of it, the importance of safe sex (usually heterosexual sex) and maybe we get lectured not to rush into it, to do it with someone who respects you. Why don't we talk about how much sex is an act of letting go? How much your mental and emotional state can play into your ability to feel physical pleasure or to trust your partner to create the sexual experience you want?

From that first time and ever since, I've had to battle with the feelings that sex raises in me. I find it hard to escape the pressure of 'getting somewhere'. For me, having an orgasm or even a fulfilling sexual experience requires shutting my mind off and focusing solely on the experience happening right at that moment. Sex is so much about relaxing and letting things happen—things that someone else is doing to you. This is hard. I've often found that the moment I loosen my tight hold on myself, unwanted emotions and thoughts rush in. In this first year of being out, these were very clearly thoughts of what had happened with my parents. And not just thoughts, but feelings of intense vulnerability and hurt. I felt the looming presence of my mother, judging me. What I was doing felt shameful and wrong—not wrong in the way that trying to have sex with a guy had, not wrong for me, but wrong in the eyes of someone else. I felt the weight of all her disapproval and disgust in those moments. Letting go meant allowing in all those feelings I'd crowded out, instead of permitting pleasure to take over like it was supposed to.

As a result of this, every time I had sex I felt this tide of upset rising. It was always a matter of whether the walls I'd built could hold it back. Most of the time they couldn't. And it was about control—it never happened when I was doing things to my partner, always when it was my turn to relax and receive touch. Maybe learning to manage this would be a matter of gaining techniques to relax and to turn my mind off. And, if possible, a matter of dealing with unprocessed feelings about past events. Healing. Gaining closure. But my big question—one that still remains well over a decade later—was this: how do you get closure when the main perpetrator has never acknowledged what happened? How do you close the door on something that—in their eyes—never occurred? Why do you have to be the one with the responsibility to forgive and forget, when what happened was not your responsibility in the first place?

Moving forward past these feelings, for me, was also about changing the structure and texture of the ways I had sex. It was things like figuring out which sexual acts I enjoyed, and being more vocal about what I did and didn't like. It was coming to understand that it was the gentle, intimate sexual moments that affected me the most, but also to learn that I couldn't always go into the act in a dominating way—because I'd find that I couldn't always maintain the bravado I went in with. It was learning that I need to know from my partner that I'm desired, and that this starts before the sexual act. Sex for me has always been so tied up in power and control and respect and shame. It is as much emotional as it is physical. I can't separate the two.

Before I had sex and in the first years of having sex, I didn't think much about needing or wanting to learn what someone liked and didn't like when having sex. I guess I just thought that everyone liked all the main things you do in bed, and you were either good at a sexual act or not. If someone didn't get off on you doing a particular thing to them, it was because you weren't good at it and you had to get better. Not because of other factors, like maybe they didn't like you going down on them until they trusted you, or they liked another thing but only when they were in a certain mood, or they never liked another thing at any time. All I'd been conditioned to consider was whether I was 'good at sex' or not.

Having sex with Ava was the very beginning of my journey to understanding all this stuff. Many years later, I'm still learning. Poor Ava, though. It wasn't her fault at all. What was I going to say to her? 'Hey, Ava, sorry for freaking out all the time, but when you touch me in certain ways for too long I just end up thinking about my mother and how much she hurt me, soz, lol.' I didn't have the tools to understand that or to communicate it. How could I tell Ava that having sex sometimes made me think, *Is this what it was all for? Losing my family? For this?*

My sexual relationship with Ava highlighted what a brittle state I was in after the breakdown of my relationship with my parents, but there were other factors related to Ava's visit that piled on pressure. Like having someone fly around the world for you. And the pressure to love that person, in person, when you've been telling them you love them over the phone. (Were we lying? Or did we do the best we could with the information we had?) It was also a new test for me to exist in the world as a queer person in such a visible way, with Ava by my side as my partner. At that time, in 2004, it felt like queer people's acceptance in society was tolerated or treated with ambivalence rather than celebrated. We were still nine years away from gaining the legal right to marry in New Zealand.

I remember on that first night, after we'd got dressed and I'd introduced Ava to my flatmates, we went out for what was my first-ever romantic dinner, complete with wine and candlelight. We held hands across the table, giddy at the newness of it, but when the waitress came over we hastily pulled away from each other. We had an inbuilt wariness about showing affection in public, and it didn't take being gay-bashed or harassed to learn that lesson—it was innate. We're all exposed to societal attitudes from an early age. Learning that those attitudes and expectations apply to us usually comes later. I think that even now, many gay people in most countries would still think about where they were or who was around before they reached for their partner's hand. Just as a girl learns not to walk alone through a park at night, to text her friends that she's home safe or to feel potential danger when approached by a man on the street, even in broad daylight. LGBTQ+ people cannot exist in the everyday unthinkingly.

In the end, the real problem was that Ava and I were such different people. If magnets are held the right way, they're drawn together with a snap and they hold tight. But when one is flipped, no matter how you try to bring the magnets together, they will slip and slide and bounce away. That was Ava and me. When we came together it was a clash of bodies. Our hugs banged cheek against cheek, always finding the bone. And, like that inverted magnet, my reaction was to try to spring away.

But there were nice moments, important moments, between us during Ava's visit to New Zealand. I took her to the old UniCol haunt, Gardies. With great pleasure, she lit up a Cuban cigar, something that was hard for her to get at home because of the USA's embargo on Cuban goods. And, like moths to a flame, boys with their own cigars—cheap knock-offs—flocked to her, exclaiming over her exoticism. 'That's my girlfriend,' she would say, pointing to me, and her cool credits transferred to me. It felt really good to be a girl's girlfriend. Ava puffed on her cigar in her best impression of a Mafioso and drank for free for the rest of the night.

Ava and I left Dunedin for a road trip around the South Island, stopping first in my hometown. We didn't go anywhere near my parents' domain out in the suburbs, instead staying on the twelfth floor of a fancy hotel in the city centre. Paid for by Ava's father—everything was paid for by Ava's father.

One evening we ordered room service and, being naked, I jumped into the bathroom to hide when the porter brought it into the room. After a minute or so, I assumed that the room-service guy had gone and flung open the door of the bathroom. I bounded into the room butt-naked only to find the porter still at the door, holding out the bill for Ava to sign. Everyone froze, then I screamed and scuttled away. Ava and I laughed about that a lot. The look on his face was a kind of stunned befuddlement. The scenario of Ava and me wasn't computing for him.

We met my sister at a bar one night and I introduced her to Ava, but I didn't tell Jen who Ava really was to me. Just a friend I'd met somewhere along the way who had come to visit. It was a mistake not to be honest, and when Jen did find out, months later, she was hurt. 'Why didn't you tell me?' she asked. 'I would have been fine.'

I think that mistake contributed in a small way to the loss of my close relationship with Jen, which had begun to slowly unfurl when she'd been left behind at home in the wreckage of my coming out. It was too hard to explain to Jen why I was scared about being honest. Telling her would have been the first time I'd come out to a family member on my own terms. And I wasn't 100 per cent confident that Jen was as okay with my sexuality as she'd said because she hadn't asked me any questions about it. Not how long I'd known, if I was dating anyone, what it meant. No details, no discussions. Maybe she was fed up with the topic, having to live with my parents bitching about me constantly. Or maybe she didn't want to think too deeply about me liking girls. Either way, I didn't want to 'rub it in her face'—that phrase that's attached to queer people so often. It was clear to me that Jen wasn't going to be the sisterly confidant you see in the movies, one who'd chat with you regularly over the phone, gossiping and offering dating advice. And that was okay. She had enough to deal with. I could handle this myself—I had to get used to standing on my own two feet.

Ava and I made our way to Queenstown. The leg between Geraldine and Twizel is one of my favourite New Zealand road trips when I have a foreign visitor by my side. I always squirm in my seat as I wait to breach the rise just before Tekapo, because I know my guest will exclaim in wonder when they catch a glimpse of the glacier-fed lake with its unusually turquoise water. We arrived in Queenstown at night-time, and in the morning I told Ava to fling open the curtains of our five-star hotel room. She reacted the way I wanted her to at the sight of the dramatic mountain peaks surrounding us and the quaint village buildings clustered around the lakefront. A gondola struggled up a steeply wooded hill to where paragliders were flinging themselves off, one by one. Ava took in the vista naked while I watched from the bed and laughed. For a moment I could imagine that we were a couple in love. That, after filling her eyes, she'd jump back into bed and roll on top of me, and we'd giggle together and kiss, which would turn into a passionate and mutually rewarding love-making session that would leave us breathless and sated. We'd order room service and talk into the night, satisfied and content in our little bubble.

But this was the real world. And in the real world, the sexual activity that happened on that super king bed with its downy pillows was the two of us lying on our backs with a foot of space between us, touching ourselves and racing to see who could orgasm first. I'd been creating scenarios like this to try to trick Ava into thinking we were still having sex, while in fact we were interacting little. This gamifying of sexual acts was the adult equivalent of telling a kid to play 'who can be silent the longest'. I wasn't sure how long it would fool her, how long before she realised that I was avoiding having her touch me in a sexual way. I feared that I was dysfunctional; I knew that we just didn't work together.

Before our road trip, back in Dunedin, Ava had driven me to annoyance, even near-rage, on a number of occasions. First there was the time we'd been walking shoulder to shoulder in Dunedin's central city and she'd grabbed me and manhandled me to walk on the other side of her, the side farthest from the road.

'What are you doing?' I'd exclaimed.

She'd said she was protecting me. 'Pimps always walk on the street side of their hoes to protect them from drive-bys.'

'I am *not* your hoe,' I'd told her. What grated on me wasn't that she was describing me as a prostitute, but that she was constantly trying to play the role of protector and provider.

Then there was the evening that I'd had to wrench a $200 bottle of champagne out of her hands at the alcohol store. 'It's for you and me, babe, for you and me!' she'd cried. The next day she'd wanted to buy me a DVD player, which was a luxury item back then.

Why did I really care? Was it a misplaced sense of guilt that we were spending so much of her father's money? If that were the case, why feel guilty about a $200 bottle of champagne but not a $200 hotel room or $200 dinner or $200 bungy jump or any of the other costs we were racking up daily?

It wasn't just the presents and that she was paying for everything. Ava also wrote me poems and romantic notes constantly. I had neither the financial means nor the emotional drive to reciprocate, and so our relationship felt lopsided. I did buy her one present: a pair of warm pyjamas to sleep in because she was always complaining about the cold. Perhaps I was trying to insulate myself against her by wrapping her in flannel.

I increasingly felt like I couldn't live up to who she'd thought I was before we met in person. I don't think she noticed, though. It seemed like she was making everything fit the narrative she wanted from this experience. I had to admire that, but it was annoying. She called me a philosopher; I was like 'Huh?' She said I understood darkness. I really didn't. She described me as someone who reads poetry—I'm not sure where she got that idea. She showed me some of her art, pencil drawings of naked male bodies. I didn't get it. She thought me more evolved than I was. In reality, I was devolving into the worst parts of myself the longer I was with her.

I became that person who's always saying no.

'No, I don't want to go to another bar with this group of lecherous guys who've been hitting on us for the last half hour.'

'No, thanks, I don't want you to buy me those possum-fur nipple warmers.'

'Do you really want to stop the car so you can run up a hill chasing sheep?'

I was a stick-in-the-mud. Or perhaps I was trying to put a stick in the mud so that I could cling to it in desperation as she tried to drag me closer to the image of me she'd created. Someone who was spontaneous and carefree, not considered and critical as I was. The tipping point for me to finally end things came when we reached Wanaka, the last stop on our road trip before we made our way back to Dunedin. After a day of sightseeing we were in bed having sex, when I realised that the sounds coming from her as her head lolled against my shoulder were not whimpers of pleasure but snores. She'd fallen asleep.

Oh, thank god, I thought. *Thank bloody god she's asleep.*

And that's how I knew I had to call it. I had to end it, for her sake but mainly for mine. I can't remember if I waited until we were back in Dunedin to have the talk or if I waited for the moment she woke up.

She didn't take it well. I couldn't understand how she hadn't seen it coming.

'What did you think was going to happen?' I said. 'You're still in high school, you live in *America*. It's just not practical.'

'But I love you!' Her upset had been awful to deal with but it was overwhelmed by my own emotional distress, which I'd— rather admirably, I thought—kept to myself for three weeks. If I didn't have a moment to myself, if I had to pretend for one more day, I would explode.

'It's just not going to work.' I was resolute, chilly even.

'Do you want me to change my flight to go home early?' she asked, expecting me to say no.

'It's probably for the best,' I agreed gently.

The day before her flight, three dozen red roses turned up at the door of my flat.

'Why did you get me these?' I said. She had selfishly hoarded all romantic pathways during our time together—dinners, poems, effusive praise about everything that made me amazing, flowers—and now she also seemed to think that roses might change my mind.

'Ava...' I sighed.

Ava's belief in us was so absolute that even when I hugged her goodbye at the airport and gave her a gentle push towards the plane, I still don't think she really believed it was the end.

When we met up in the future, years from then, I wondered whether her image of me had shifted. One evening in 2015 we'd arranged to meet for dinner in the city I was living in. When we literally ran into each other rounding a corner she recovered first, grabbing me in a hug that pushed the air out of my lungs. We sat at the bar of a trendy Asian-fusion restaurant, and I was reminded of her intensity. Her eyes pinned me like a bug to a board when I talked, making me shift on my seat and lick my lips too much. I felt very conscious of what I was doing with my hands. I didn't know if she still looked at me sexually, but I knew she was looking. Her eyes followed me as I tried to inconspicuously grasp a strand of hair that had stuck to my lip gloss.

What does she think of me? Who does she think I am? I kept wondering. *Surely she's realised how different we are by now?* When I talked to her, I felt like all my observations landed the wrong way, like *Tetris* pieces I couldn't line up properly in time. Ava wasn't a critical person or hard to talk to; I just didn't know who she was seeing when she looked at me. I was fairly certain it still wasn't me.

Despite this, I enjoyed the first 45 minutes of dinner with her. Ava was living in New Zealand by then, in a different city from me, and she told me a story about her recent break-up.

'It's my second heartbreak,' she said, and I looked at her with sudden clarity. I knew what she was going to say next. 'You were the first.'

I immediately felt bad about how heartlessly I'd called things off between us. I'd been so over it that I hadn't really thought about how she'd felt. After two glasses of wine and seeing her heartbreak over her ex-girlfriend, I felt warmly towards her. But then the conversation shifted.

'You know Nine-eleven is just this great conspiracy, right?' she said. She was gearing up for a rant, but she interrupted herself first. 'Oh, hey, do you want dessert?'

Ah, yes, I thought. I recognised the crucial tipping point. It was time for us to part again, while I still had a warm glow about being in her company. So, for the second time in our relationship, I cut our time together short.

'Let's just get the cheque, shall we?'

Chapter 11
The Purple Passions

**A woman needs a man like
a fish needs a bicycle.**
— Irina Dunn

I'm standing in my room, curling my toes over threadbare carpet that's some shade of poo, and I'm looking at my bed. I'm remembering something that my first-ever lesbian friend told me: 'Lesbians always have navy duvets.'

So I'm looking at my duvet. It's navy. Well, it's kind of blue with a darker blue stripe, not exactly . . . faaarck, it's navy, alright?

Lesbian things had happened on top of and underneath that lesbian duvet. There was also a blue vibrator I'd purchased with Ava tucked under the bed covered by that navy duvet. And that vibrator—close enough to navy to fit into the category—had also been a participant in decidedly, thoroughly lesbian activities. It was reason enough to pause.

I looked at my desk, which was still dominated by Ava's last-ditch-effort-to-win-me-back roses. I'd thought about throwing them away, because that would've been tidy and symbolic, but I knew that I wouldn't. I'd keep sinking my nose into them, breathing in their beautiful scent until the petals started to drop, covering my desk in red like pools of blood at a crime scene. Maybe that was symbolic enough.

Ava had also left behind a painting she was making for me. When she'd told me she was a painter I'd expected something refined and amazing, not cartoonish, clumsy drawings that didn't seem to relate to each other. *A child could do that*, I'd thought. It was also half finished, which was just, like, *so* her. It was very annoying. Even now, after she'd been shipped back to the States, she still had the ability to annoy me. But, much like the roses, I couldn't throw the painting away just yet. I wanted to keep physical reminders of her, because, despite everything, I was aware that knowing her had changed me. Being with Ava had helped to solidify my identity as a gay woman. Before, I'd just had an innocent navy duvet. Now I had a non-innocent gay navy duvet and an almost-navy vibrator too. I shoved the painting to the back of my closet.

At the end of that year, my parents would come to Dunedin to witness my university graduation and help me pack up the last of my things, and my mother would find Ava's painting. I wasn't in the room at the time, and I never saw that painting again. Dad told me later that she'd broken down in tears when she'd come across it.

'Some painting,' Dad said. 'Some lesbian painting. It was very uncomfortable.'

So sorry to make things awkward with my super lesbian painting of a bird, a flower and a fucking moon, parents.

After Ava had gone, reality began threatening. But I devised a plan to distract myself from the shittier aspects of my life. I pushed aside the hurt of my parents sticking to their promise to cut me from their affections, and instead focused my attention on infiltrating the local lesbian community. I conducted research in the field—lurking in corners at the monthly queer night at the uni bar—and I soon figured out a way in: the lesbian soccer team.

The name was as gay as the players: the Purple Passions. But I'd attended a coming-out group called Blossom, so this kind of cringeworthy name was nothing unexpected. I was willing to look past it. I also had to deal with the fact that they all seemed to think they were way cooler than they clearly were. But the Purple Passions were the key to the queer kingdom in Dunedin and getting in the door—or, in this case, on the field—was essential.

I arrived for my first game on a Saturday morning and some-one gave me a team shirt in resplendent purple satin. As I pulled it over my head I heard a voice say, 'Lil?'

I yanked the shirt down and pawed at my hair to get it out of my face so I could see who was talking to me. Standing there was a younger girl from my high school, who I'd played soccer with for years. Before I could speak, she blurted, 'What are you doing playing for *this* team?'

'This team', aka the most notorious team in the league, aka the lesbo bitches, aka the social pariahs of Otago University.

'Um, oh,' I stuttered. 'I'm just filling in for someone.'

'Righhhht,' she said, unsatisfied with my response. She walked back to her teammates and said something that caused a few to turn and look at me. I smoothed my shirt uncomfortably before joining my teammates. As much as I could deny it verbally, I'd associated myself with them. And that reputation would stick, just like the BO of other women had stuck to my soccer shirt.

I began playing with the team every Saturday morning, and every game was a new experience. Almost weekly, the boys who cut across the playing fields on their way home after rugby games sought out our telltale purple and shouted things like 'Lesbians!' and 'Carpet munchers!' as they walked the sideline.

'They do know that they're carpet munchers too, right?' I joked to a teammate one day.

'They wish,' she retorted.

Other experiences were less easy to brush off. One morning we arrived at our match and began warming up, but by kick-off the other team—physical education students from the local polytech—hadn't turned up. We found out later that they'd forfeited the game because they didn't want to play against lesbians. When the game pool brought us back around to playing them again, we were surprised to see them turn up. They brought with them an aggression we could sense from the other end of the field, and once again there was a girl from my high school on their team—Bridie. She and her mates kept looking at us from the sideline and laughing, making a show of covering themselves up as they got changed into their gear. I caught Bridie looking over, and she shook her head at me sadly. *That's cheeky*, I thought, considering she'd been in theatre sports at school, which was pretty bloody low on the social totem pole. Particularly compared with me, deputy head girl. And I'd always been nice to her! I guess I'd lost my social capital by being in this team.

As we lined up for the match to begin, I walked past her on my way to the right wing.

'Hi,' I said brightly.

'Hi,' she said back, smirking at me and making a show of looking at my purple top. Once I passed her, she turned to her teammate and said, 'Fucking lesbians' under her breath.

I stopped and turned to glare at her, but she studiously avoided my eyes until I continued walking. Which was a shame, because I have a *great* death glare I inherited from my mother. I believe that people could literally wither to the ground.

The whistle blew, and the tone of the match was immediately set when their centre forward charged ours with a bellow. They played aggressively but were also avoidant, their behaviour expressions of both hatred and fear. Some were overly rough, barging our players and taking advantage of a referee who wasn't equipped to deal with the situation. Others leaned back as they used their feet, pantomiming that they didn't want any part of their bodies to touch us. We were fuelled by this, determined to win but also to play fair—to take the high road. To teach them a lesson but to retain the title of the victimised party.

That is, until Bridie went too far. One of our players was dribbling the ball and Bridie shoved her, causing her to trip and fall. It wasn't a shoulder barge that could be passed off as an attempt to get the ball—it was an assault, and the ref finally called a penalty. But it was too little, too late, and our mood shifted to one of outrage and vengeance. We were going to hammer them. They thought they were tough? We would be more than tough. We would be fucking ruthless. We were the oppressed, staging a revolt in the face of their revulsion.

The second half began and there was aggression in the air. Then Bridie got a breakaway. She was dribbling up the field and I found myself sprinting back to our defensive half, screaming, 'Get her!' with a rage that surprised me. I was so focused on Bridie that I didn't see one of my own players coming in at her from the side, jumping into a slide. Her momentum took Bridie's feet right out from under her and she smashed to the ground in a crash of bones and flesh. Everyone winced collectively. Her team members ran over as Bridie lay on the ground, screaming at us for being fucking bitches. I stood there with my hands on my hips and laughed heartily like a lumberjack. Then I felt bad. This kind of retaliation wasn't what the 'bigger person' does. But then I thought, *Fuck it*. Sometimes you just want to enjoy a homophobe getting hurt.

We beat them by two goals. When the final whistle blew, their team turned quickly and headed for the sideline, avoiding any attempt to shake hands.

I made a point of walking past Bridie as I left. 'Hey, Bridie,' I said casually. She looked up from where she was icing her ankle, her face grubby from where she'd hit the dirt. 'I guess that'll teach you to mess with "fucking lesbians", huh?'

It was a weak comeback, but I walked off feeling pretty damn good.

———

'Fuck you!'

'Get out of it you bloody clam digger!'

'Fucking dykes!'

'Oh, fuck off, ref!'

Just the everyday on-field patter of Jade, our lesbian centre forward. 'Charming' was not a word you'd align with Jade. You might choose 'crass' or 'confronting'. Maybe even 'a bit of a cunt'. But she had caught my attention. In the years ahead a number of my favourite queer characters would have elements of Jade: Naomi Campbell from *Skins*, Gail Peck from *Rookie Blue*. I liked people with confidence and sharp edges, and that was Jade. I'd watched her charging around the soccer field for a few weeks now, screaming at everyone, cracking jokes and making lewd gestures.

One day we were warming up before a match when I heard her shout, 'Oh, fucking arsehole, fuck this, fucking bloody bastard . . .' I looked across to see her kneeling on the wet grass. She stood up abruptly, mud slathered on her knees above her purple woollen socks. 'Can someone untie my *fucking* shoelace for me?!'

'I'll help.' I saw my opening, leaping to her and kneeling at her feet. She looked at me suspiciously as if she'd never noticed me before. She told me that later: 'I'd never even noticed you before.' I'd been playing with her for four weeks.

But as I retied her shoelace for her and stood up, a current passed between us. Which I totally knew would happen. Tying someone's shoelace for them is in a specific genre of acts, alongside dotting an eyelash off someone's face, putting sunscreen on someone's back or slipping an errant clothing tag back inside a T-shirt. These strangely intimate yet 'permissible between people who don't even know each other well' actions can change the atmosphere between people in a flash.

'Thanks,' she said slowly, still looking at me warily with eyes I now noticed were different shades of green. I'd wanted a girlfriend with eyes of different shades ever since I'd seen Kate Bosworth in the Oscar-worthy movie *Blue Crush* a few years earlier. This was a good start.

After the match, two of my Blossom friends who were also in the team invited me to go for bagels and coffee at a cafe, one of a handful of queer-friendly businesses in Dunedin. Queer-friendly businesses are one of those things like Platform 9¾—they've always been there but most people don't register them, not until they become relevant to them. Now I notice every little piece of rainbow out in the world, even almost-rainbows. Yellow-red-and-green flags catch my eye every time. Innocuous rainbows on children's tops demand a second look. I note every rainbow-flag sticker on the windows of businesses. There weren't many back then in New Zealand, but they quietly grow in number every year.

It was the first time I'd been to this more intimate get-together and it was warming, like I'd taken another step towards the core of the community. There was something comforting about hanging out with fellow lesbians, even when we had nothing much else in common. We didn't need much—just knowing that these women liked women was enough for now. I went home to my five straight female flatmates and I felt like I had a special secret fizzing inside me. It wasn't like the stressful secret I'd hidden from my flatmates the year before, when I was living in the Haunted House and sneaking off to Blossom every Wednesday. This one felt good. If I'd been on *Oprah* I'm pretty sure she would've told me it was because I was 'living my truth'.

A couple of hours later Jade texted me asking if I wanted to meet her tonight at a pub to play pool. *I am so 'in'*, I thought to myself. By the end of the week we were officially dating.

Dating Jade felt like what I'd always imagined 'normal' might be like. She slotted into my life easily, and I enjoyed learning about her habits and foibles. Her humour was dry, bordering on acerbic, but she was a show pony too, so it often contained an element of performance that I enjoyed. I liked people who could be silly. Jade was prickly but sensitive, defensive but soft. I appreciated her contradictions because I acknowledged them in myself too.

I was pretty sure that the end of the university year, coming up in three months or so, would be the finish line for me and Jade. I knew that before we even got together. But that didn't concern me in any way; in fact the near-certainty of this was kind of comforting. So much else up ahead in my life was hazy and undefined. I knew that I was moving to New Zealand's largest city, Auckland, the following year, because I'd been accepted to advertising school . . . and that's about all I knew. I didn't even know where I was going to live for the summer months before that started, let alone if I'd ever have a relationship with my parents again.

Jade might not have been my forever person, but she was exactly what I needed at that moment. She wasn't the person who helped me heal, but she did help me to forget. And that's all I wanted. I didn't want to 'deal' with things; I didn't even know what dealing with things would look like. I wanted to push aside all the sadness and hurt and get back to the post-coming-out sense of power and freedom that was still roaring through my veins like cocaine. I was on a coming-out high, and Jade was the perfect person to help me rage and revel.

Jade smoked very strong Port Royal Kentucky Bourbon roll-your-own cigarettes, which seemed pretty badass to me. I liked to watch her put them together—she did so with such proficiency.

'Why do you always wait until your coffee arrives before rolling your ciggy, then leave your coffee there getting cold while you smoke?' I asked her one morning as we sat shivering outside a cafe, trying to pretend that just because it was sunny it was warm.

Jade shrugged. 'I like it like that.'

'But it's not an efficient process!' I exclaimed.

'Shut up, O'Brien,' she said, calling me by my last name as she tended to do.

Jade always teased me about being an upper-crust private-school girl. She was self-proclaimed 'white trash' from a notorious neighbourhood in our nation's capital city. 'You're not white trash,' I said, but one evening as we got ready to go out she put on knee-high white lace-up boots, a miniskirt and a singlet with an American flag on it and I wasn't so sure anymore. I think she almost wanted to be seen as white trash. Another night we went to an actual white-trash themed party wearing too much bright eye shadow, skimpy outfits and fishnet gloves up to our wrists. Years later, I saw her on Facebook wearing those same kind of gloves—and not for dress-up purposes.

We were out at a student pub one night, about a month and a half into our relationship, when she writhed around like a stripper on the pub tabletop dressed in a skimpy outfit—including the white boots. All the guys around the table reacted as you'd expect 18- to 21-year-old drunk straight males to react, and I was so embarrassed to be associated with her that I yelled at her and we broke up. She slept in her car outside my flat despite me telling her to go home and came grovelling the next day, but I was still mad. I went out that night and kissed a straight girl I'd gone to UniCol with, and this time it was me with a group of guys standing around me cheering. But the difference was, I told myself, that I hadn't wanted the attention and Jade had. Either way, that kind of male attention was gross.

We made up a couple of days after that and went back to spending too much time together. On a rare night I went out without Jade, one of my friends said, 'Don't get me wrong, we like Jade but it's really nice to see you on your own.'

I was stoked! Now I was like all my other friends over the years who had started a new relationship and ditched their friends as a consequence. But there were a few reminders that maybe people didn't see my relationship in quite the same way they saw heterosexual ones. After Emma had met Jade a couple of times I'd asked her, 'So, what do you think of Jade?'

'Meh.' She'd shrugged, dunking her Big Mac into a slop of ketchup. It was 4 p.m. and she hadn't got out of bed that day but she had managed to convince someone to get her McDonald's. So that was two impressive things.

I was so shocked by her unthinking response that I didn't reply for a few seconds, gathering my thoughts.

'Wow, that's what you're going to say?' I finally said. 'You could at least pretend to like her! I mean, you wouldn't say that about one of our other friend's boyfriends. Think of all the shit that Kev did to Bella and we always said he was great to her face!'

'Huh.' Emma paused and, to her credit, said, 'I'd never thought about that. I'm sorry. You're totally right.'

It was easily forgiven but it was a reminder that I was different.

One day Jade and I trekked through town to the sex shop— the same one where Ava and I had bought the blue vibrator. Now I was stepping up to the next level with a strap-on. This being the only sex shop in town—and hardly one that catered to women—there was only one option. I peered up at it hanging from a tangle of straps near the ceiling and wrinkled my nose.

'I really hope it's not used,' I said to Jade.

'Probably,' she replied.

We asked the shopkeeper—a man in his fifties with a tangle

of grey hair falling down his back—to get it down for us. I was super embarrassed, even as I realised the best approach to being embarrassed in a sex shop was to pretend you were completely unembarrassed.

We studied it for a few seconds, pretending we knew what we were looking for and had any kind of choice, then paid for it and got it home. We sat on my bed (still the navy duvet) to decipher this thing. First there was the dildo part itself, which was actually a double dildo—one for each person. Then there were the straps, which were thin and made from shiny black material with a metal buckle. It reminded me of patent leather children's shoes, which made it worse. To top it off, there was a metre-long pink cord running from the dildo to a remote control that turned the vibrate function on and off.

'My sister used to have a toy dog that walked and barked that had a remote control like this,' I said.

'You're fucking sick,' Jade replied.

'This is ridiculous,' I said, and we laughed. Laughing made it better.

'Who's going first?'

Things did not go well. The straps dug into my hips and cut into the soft skin of my inner thighs, and I had to hold my arm out straight from my body to stop the remote-control cord getting tangled.

'Ow . . . OW,' Jade said as she lay on her back and I tried getting on top of her.

'What?'

'It's the wrong angle!'

'Hold on.' I pulled back and studied the angle of the fleshy thing sticking up in front of me. 'Try doggy style.'

Jade rolled over.

'Ow,' I said. 'Ow!'

'I feel like it's going to come out my butt!' said Jade.

We both got the giggles.

Eventually we found a position that kind of worked. But not really. Exhausted, we gave up and I stripped the horrible thing off with relief. It left red marks from the straps all over my body.

'What a disaster,' I said. We lay there for a while before Jade got up to use the bathroom. I was still lying there when she came back and said, 'We have a problem.'

'What?' I said, sitting up.

She pulled her pants down and showed me a very angry-looking vagina.

'Jesus.'

I pulled my own pants off. I too had the beginnings of a rash in just the place you don't want a rash. I prodded it with a finger. 'Ow!'

'Fucking cheap piece of shit!' Jade laughed, picking up the strap-on and throwing it against the wall. It flopped down onto the bedspread, remote control trailing behind.

'Wait, I have an idea.' I yanked open the top drawer of my bedside table and pulled out my pocket knife.

'Oh my god, you are such a lesbian.' Jade laughed.

I retrieved the strap-on and, using the pliers and the knife, unsheathed the dildos of their outer layer of latex. It peeled off surprisingly easily. Then I closed the knife, opened the saw function and dragged the teeth through the flesh until the two dildos separated.

'That was oddly satisfying,' I said, flopping the liberated phallus around.

And then we had a new, streamlined strap-on that no longer gave us a nasty rash and didn't require us to create the angles of an isosceles triangle to have sex. It was the first serious purchase we'd made together.

———

Jade was lacing up those awful knee-high boots again. But they 'went with' her new white dress from Lippy and I could tell she felt good in what she was wearing, so I bit my tongue. We didn't know it yet but by the end of the night that dress was going to be covered in another person's blood.

We were in my hometown. It was only the second time I'd been back since shit went down and I felt quite disorientated. It wasn't the same place I grew up. Or it was the same place, but I was different. The weirdest thing was, we were staying at my parents' house. Yeah. They weren't there, but I was there with my female lover. Let's back up.

My parents and I—well, my dad and I, as my mum still wasn't speaking to me—had entered the beginning of a phase defined as 'hesitantly talking when absolutely necessary to communicate essentials, but certainly not talking about *it*'. I'd texted Dad a few weeks before asking if he and Mum would be in the house this weekend and if I could come to stay as I was in town. After a day of what I'd assumed to be deliberation he'd replied that, given they'd be up at our family bach with my sister, I could stay in the empty house if I needed to. Taking my girlfriend to stay there made me feel a little nervous, but happy in a vengeful kind of way. They didn't know she was coming with me, of course. And they certainly weren't told the reason I was in town. Jade and I, along with pretty much the entire lesbian population of Dunedin, were in town for the lesbian ball—the queer women's event of the year for the whole South Island.

I found the spare key under a log of firewood on the stoop and opened the front door. My first concern was to see whether my mother had put clean sheets on my sister's bed for me. Actually, that's a lie. My first concern was to check that they weren't waiting inside to ambush me. But the house was empty.

Once I was in and had reassured Jade, who seemed hesitant to step over the threshold into the house, I went to check the sheets on my sister's bed, where I was supposed to be sleeping. The state of those sheets was going to tell me a lot. If Mum had left dirty sheets on the bed that would mean she was very, very angry with me and was sending me a real 'fuck you'. If the bed had been stripped but there were no clean sheets in sight, she was very angry with me and was sending me a strong 'you're on your own' message. If the bed had been stripped and there were clean sheets waiting on the bed for me to make it myself, she was less angry and probably still loved me but also wanted me to know things had changed for the worse and I should get used to that. But if she had put clean sheets on the bed, I would know that she still loved me and there was hope.

There were clean sheets on the bed.

But instead of bringing our stuff into Jen's room I steered Jade into Mum and Dad's room and we had sex in their bed, because y'know, fuck them, right? (But I washed those sheets and put clean sheets back on their bed carefully before we left because I was terrified of my mother and her sixth sense for all things untoward.)

That night—after we'd put on our dresses and make-up, Jade had painstakingly laced up those goddamn white boots, and we'd caught an expensive taxi across town (thanks to Dad's taxi charge card that he'd forgotten I had)—Jade and I walked, nay, strutted into the lesbian ball. We thought we were hot shit. And we were respectively 23 and twenty years old . . . we *were* hot shit.

We quickly found our group of Purple Passions and other related lesbos, and I surveyed the truly abysmal group of people at the event.

'I've never seen so many unfortunate-looking people in one place,' I said to Jade out the side of my mouth.

She greatly enjoyed this because it was the kind of comment she would usually make, except she'd be meaner.

'But seriously, though, everyone is really old and butch.' I looked out across the sea of khaki blazers and Hilary-Swank-in-*Boys-Don't-Cry* haircuts. People were standing around clutching pints of beer, shuffling from foot to foot underneath bare fluorescent light bulbs.

I felt heady with power. In this rowing club full of far too much corduroy, we were the alpha hotties. Young, femme, hot, trendy . . . okay, there was still the matter of Jade's white boots, but in this environment they could've passed for Louboutins.

I headed to the bar and ordered us glasses of wine, which I watched the bartender pour from a cask sitting on the tin bench. At least they were filled right to the brim.

A couple of hours in and the volume inside was rising, as it tends to do when people actively work towards intoxication. Jade and I went outside to smoke cigarettes, shivering against the winter drizzle with a rotating cast of other smokers.

When we pushed back through the swinging glass doors to head inside, there was palpable tension in our posse.

'What's going on?' I asked one of the girls.

'Some shit's going down between Jacquie and Tanya,' she muttered, rolling her eyes.

'Ah!' I said knowingly. 'Lesbian drama.' We all knew about that.

I looked at Jacquie, who was sitting on a ratty couch by herself. The pint she was holding, too large for her hands, made her look even younger than she was. Jacquie played on the soccer team with us. She was fast but she always walked with hunched shoulders, as though waiting for a blow to come. From what Jade had told me about her, she'd had a lot of heavy stuff to deal with in her life. Of course, Jade used to date her. By dating someone in the soccer team, I'd become part of the incestuous-lesbian-friendship-group trope.

Suddenly things turned crazy. I was the only one who saw her coming, catching movement out of the corner of my eye. It was Tanya, her dreadlocks swinging as she ran towards Jacquie. There was a fleshy smack as she tackled her, her momentum tipping the couch over. They both landed on the floor in a heap, screaming. There was a ruckus as Tanya stood up and people grabbed her to hold her back, while Jacquie's friends, including Jade, moved to help her on the floor. I just stood there. I'd never seen this kind of behaviour before and it had rendered me paralysed. Tanya shrugged off the people holding her and walked outside, fumbling her tobacco pouch from her back pocket. Jacquie stood up from behind the couch, twisting her strapless dress back on straight. She seemed weirdly unshaken, like this was a normal thing for someone to experience. I watched as she, too, shrugged the others off and headed the same way Tanya had gone.

'Jade, what the fuck? I don't think you should let her go out there,' I said as Jade plopped down next to me on the couch with an exhalation of air.

'She'll be okay,' Jade said, reaching for her drink on the sticky folding table.

'What? Her girlfriend just threw her over the back of a couch. I mean—' I struggled for words. 'What the fuck, Jade.'

'Yeah, well, she's a fucking psycho, isn't she?' Jade said angrily.

I didn't understand. Jade seemed to accept this as part and parcel of Jacquie and Tanya's relationship. Some people were still standing around talking about what had happened but many had gone back to their drinks or drifted back into the main room and the dance floor. No one went to find Jacquie and check on her in case she and Tanya were getting into it again.

The ball went on for another hour, but it had been ruined for me. I watched the door until I saw Jacquie come back in, but there was no sign of Tanya. When they turned the music off and all the fluorescent lights flickered on with that distinctive *tink, tink, tink* noise, we groaned, tipped back our drinks and slowly shuffled out the swinging doors. Being concerned with appearance over warmth in the manner of many young people, neither Jade nor I had brought coats. We stood around rubbing our arms, our breath pluming white into the drizzle, while everyone tried to figure out if someone was having an after-party or if it was home time.

Then I heard screaming.

Jade and I pushed through the crowd. Everyone was just standing there, craning their necks to look at the two people scuffling on the ground. Tanya was on top of Jacquie on the wet concrete, punching her in the face. Jade let out a yell and rushed forward but it took me a beat longer because I was expecting someone else—at least a few people—to come forward and help too. But no one moved, except to try to get a better view of the action.

Jade was struggling with Tanya on the ground when I grabbed Jacquie—who was now trying to hit Tanya back—under the arms and yanked. But gravity and the fact that she was hanging on to Tanya's suit lapels worked against me. We struggled, and finally someone else seemed to be helping, but the wrestling and yelling continued.

'Fuck this,' I said, letting go of Jacquie and stepping back. 'Fuck this shit.'

I walked away without looking back. They hadn't locked the doors to the rowing club yet so I went inside to the bathroom and flicked the lights on. I grabbed the sides of the sink and looked at myself in the mirror, but I wasn't really looking. I was thinking about the sight of two women smacking the shit out of each other. And I was thinking about all those people who had stood there and let it happen. The scene was looping in my head. Finally I let out a big breath and I knew that something had shifted in me. I didn't want to be part of this community anymore. If this was what it meant? No. It wasn't a reflection of me, who I wanted to be, who I wanted to spend my time with, how I wanted to relate to others. I'd tried so hard to get 'in' with this crowd despite feeling at odds with these women time and time again. I was done.

But Jade was still out there, so I wet some toilet paper and used it to wipe the mud off my high heels, brushed the grit off my knees then checked my dress for rips. It looked intact. I pulled open the door to the bathroom and headed back outside.

The crowd had dispersed and there was no sign of Tanya or Jacquie. Where had everyone gone so fast?

'Hey,' I said to someone smoking at the edge of the parking lot. 'What happened? Where are the girls who were in the fight?'

'I think they got taken to hospital.'

Shit. But where was Jade? I weaved between the small pockets of people who were left, looking for Jade, for anyone from our crew. I say 'our crew', but I'd mentally cancelled our affiliation. They weren't my friends.

There was no sign of Jade anywhere. I walked around the corner of the building and finally heard something from the bushes—the sound of someone hyperventilating.

'Jade?' I called, before spying a white dress in the darkness and running forward. 'Fuck.'

Jade was standing in the dirt, holding her hands up in front of her like a surgeon who'd just scrubbed in. Or perhaps more like a surgeon who'd just stuck her hands in a body, because blood had rolled down from Jade's wrists to her elbows. Her chest was heaving as she struggled to breathe, and her white dress was covered in splashes of blood.

'What the fuck happened? Are you okay?' I grabbed her but she couldn't speak; she was having a panic attack. 'Are you hurt?' I questioned, ducking down to try to see her eyes.

She managed to shake her head and I rubbed her back, feeling the goosebumps on her exposed skin.

'Hey, it's okay, it's okay,' I said in what I hoped was a soothing tone. I didn't know what else to do. After a few minutes she'd caught her breath, but she was still shaking from the cold, adrenaline and shock.

'What happened?'

'I had Tanya's head,' she choked out. 'I had her by the dreadlocks, but then I slipped and dropped her head on the concrete.'

'Shit!' This was obviously not a good response; now Jade was crying.

'What if she's dead or has a head injury!' Jade said in panic. 'There was so much blood!'

'Hey, I'm sure she's fine. It's not your fault. It was an accident,' I said, gripping her firmly. 'We'll get hold of someone, don't worry. We'll find out.'

I tugged on Jade's shoulders and led her out of the garden, getting her to stop and wipe her bloody hands on the wet grass. By now everyone had left and the suburban streets were deserted; it was nearly 1 a.m.

'Let me try and get a taxi.'

It rang and rang, and no one picked up. I tried the other two cab companies in the city and got busy signals.

'Shit,' I said, hung up, then dialled again. This was a familiar routine. The average time to get a taxi on the weekends was probably an hour: 30 minutes or so of trying to get through and the rest of the time waiting for the car to turn up. If you didn't hear it tooting, it would be gone in less than a minute and the routine would start again. Sometimes if too many people called from one address and didn't come out to get their taxis, the company just stopped sending them. Uber was still ten years away.

'Where's your friend's house?' I asked Jade. 'We have to get out of the cold.'

Jade called a friend of hers who lived nearby, and after getting directions we trudged along, heads bowed against the drizzle. Jade was limping from the blisters her white boots had given her, whereas I'd ditched my heels and had them hanging from my index finger. I was shaking now too; I was angry and upset and worried about Jade. We took a couple of wrong turns and I started to worry that we'd never find the house. But after twenty minutes we finally saw a house with the lights on and heard the sounds of women laughing inside. We banged on the door.

Someone let us in, and when I stepped inside the relief was so great that I had to blink back sudden tears. But then I remembered how mad I was at all these people.

'Oh my god, what happened to you?' someone asked Jade, and the six or seven people sitting around the living room looked up at us. One of them leaned over and said something out the side of her mouth to another, who grinned. I hated them all. They were all culpable in my eyes.

While Jade's friend led her away to find her a sweatshirt I brusquely asked someone where the home phone was. It was our best chance of getting through to a taxi company as we all knew they trusted calls coming from landlines more than cell phones—there was a lower risk of someone not being where they said they'd be.

Finally I got through, then I sat with Jade in the kitchen ignoring everyone else until we heard the honk of the cab outside. No one had offered me anything warm to wear, and when I ran my index finger down the fine hairs on my arm it came away damp.

When we got home to my parents' house Jade was still shaking and I thought she must be borderline hypothermic. I put her straight in the shower with her dress still on, stopping only to unwind the long laces of her boots, cursing those damn things once again as I tugged and tugged to get them off. I got in the shower with her and helped her get the blood-stained dress off, washed her hair and then just held her.

After a good while, her shaking subsided. I'd never seen her this vulnerable before, her usual sharp edges washed away. She looked at me as though no one had ever looked after her like this before. Maybe they hadn't.

The evening had brought Jade and me closer together, but at

the same time it had shown me the side of our community that was ugly, violent and uncaring. It had stripped away any warm glow of acceptance and belonging I'd felt, which was devastating. After that night I walked away from those women, and because the soccer season was over that was easy to do. I stepped back into my old friendship group, tugging Jade with me. But the sense of loss stayed with me for a long time.

Chapter 12
Busted

Maybe it's a daughter's job to piss off her mother.
— *Diary*, Chuck Palahniuk

I n late November of 2004, Jade and I said our farewells in my empty bedroom. The poo-brown carpet was even more startling without furniture to hide it, but staring at its worn patches and miscellaneous stains made me feel nostalgic. It had been a good room. A lot had happened here . . . two girlfriends—two! Would you call Ava a girlfriend?

Maybe not. Maybe you'd call her something better than that, like my internet lover from across the seas who fled to New Zealand to escape political turmoil only to have me break her heart and put her on the next plane back to America. That had a more adventurous ring to it. I felt like I'd come across as cooler to people if I told the story that way.

Jade helped me carry my final bits and pieces out to my navy Subaru Legacy. Yes, navy. Both Jade and I cried more than I'd expected as we hugged goodbye, clinging to the familiar feeling of each other. It felt good to mark the end of three years of university with some hyperbolic emotion. Then Jade pulled back and cracked a joke, which was comforting in its expectedness, and finally I got in the car and drove away, winding north through the hills. I put on my copy of the CD I'd made for Coop after she'd broken off our 'not natural' relationship. It was appropriate in that it was still the most emotionally over-the-top mix I had.

Around halfway through my journey, my sadness had morphed into something else: fear. As if a break-up wasn't enough for one day, I was on the way home. Or to whatever my parents' house was to me now. I hadn't quite figured out why I was going there, apart from it being habit. I didn't want to but I felt like I had to be there, as though not going home would've been some kind of betrayal even though I'd had to ask permission from Dad. A large part of the decision was practical—I needed somewhere to store all my stuff for nearly three months before I moved to Auckland for advertising school, and your parents' house was supposed to be where you did things like annoyingly dump all your stuff when you'd finished university at twenty years old. I didn't intend to stay there the whole summer, but for some reason moving to Auckland straight away never crossed my mind either. Home was just where you went when you finished university, to reset and prepare for the next stage in your life.

When I'd negotiated with Dad where I'd stay for the summer after university finished, I'd made the ridiculous suggestion that I should take a trip to Australia—funded by them—in order to fill in three weeks of the summer I had to get through before moving to the North Island. I'd reasoned with Dad that this way I'd be out of their hair by Christmas: I would come home from uni for a week, go to Australia for a few weeks, hop back to New Zealand for my graduation in December then head to Queenstown to get a job and live there for the rest of the holidays. In early February I'd briefly swing past their house again to get all my gear, then I'd be gone to Auckland for good. I figured that they'd rather pay for me to be away in Australia than have me in their house or staying with friends where I'd no doubt reveal all kinds of family secrets.

My bargaining had worked. Dad had given me his credit card number to book the flights.

But, even though I'd only be staying with them for a week, my body knew that something was wrong with this scenario, and it told me for the rest of the drive. I stopped every half hour, sure that I needed to go to the bathroom, but when I got into the McDonald's toilets or KFC loos there was nothing. Just stomach cramps and odd moments when it was hard to breathe. *Why am I going home?* Then: *Why shouldn't I go home?*

It's my *home too, isn't it? Who are they to take it away from me?*

I was so confused by what I was doing, but I drove closer and closer until finally I was pulling in next to our garage. I got out of my car and stood looking down at the house below. It felt like a scene in a Stephen King novel: everything looked normal but I suspected something sinister was waiting inside.

My arrival was anticlimactic. I opened the front door with a too-bright 'Hi!' lathered on candy-pink. They called back, 'Hi,' but Mum's greeting sounded weird to me. It was the kind of 'hi' you say when someone has just popped down to the shops for some milk and has only been gone ten minutes. It was too breezy. It didn't match the distance between us—the fact that this was the first time I'd seen Mum since she'd told me to get the hell out of this very house and never come back.

I believe Dad was genuinely pleased to see me. His 'hi' was authentic, but his usual term of endearment for me, Dot, dried on the tip of his tongue. 'Hi, D—' The rest of the word dissolved.

I poked my head into the lounge where they were sitting, not quite ready to commit my whole body. Mum was looking all too interested in the *NZ House & Garden* in her lap and barely glanced up, keeping up the act. I'm sure Dad had made her sit down and 'relax' before my arrival; had she been left to her own devices I would have walked in to find her up to her elbows with dishes in the kitchen sink or hanging out the washing with an underlying air of mania.

I'd planned my arrival for near dinnertime in order to cut down the length of an evening's natural talking period, but there was no carefully curated meal of fillet steak or roast lamb for us tonight. There were takeaways, which I offered to drive and pick up way too eagerly. I left long before they'd be ready—anything to make the minutes until bedtime run down—and drove around the village I grew up in. I passed the library, where Mum used to take my sister and me after school every week. There was the fish-and-chip shop—the one that did the best deep-fried doughnuts—and the surf store, where Mum bought me my first surfboard, and the first coffee shop our town got, where Mum would drink her flat white and I would have an iced chocolate with cream and chocolate flakes on top. And there was the car park overlooking the beach where Jack and I stopped to smoke cigarettes after that evening seven months ago, the night my parents told me I was unnatural and sick and most of all wrong. Not enough time had passed to allow me to filter out recent memories from the good ones of my childhood. It was like taking a drink of water on a hot day and feeling something unexpectedly textured pass your lips and bounce off the back of your tongue on the way down. These new memories were the blowfly swimming in my favourite beverage.

What did families finding themselves in a tense dynamic do before television? We ate our takeaways in front of the TV, which we never did, or at least we never had before. But now none of us wanted to sit at the dining table and look each other in the eye. The TV stayed on the whole night and we pretended too hard to be interested in every second of it.

My sister was away again for some school thing so I was sleeping in her bed—in the room with the too-thin walls that had betrayed me. Before I could scuttle away for an early night, my phone beeped. It was Jade in a furious mood. She was supposed to be driving up and staying the night in town tomorrow before flying home to Wellington the next day, but her bed had fallen through. She reckoned she was going to sleep in the airport before her morning flight.

DONT B STUPID, U CANT SLEEP AT TH AIRPORT!

ITS FINE DONT WORRY BOUT IT. WHATEVA.

When Jade was upset her aggression fired off in all directions, striking targets at random.

Then I had a reckless idea: Jade should just stay the night here.

It was ridiculous. Or was it? Although having her here would add a certain level of danger, it might also help me. I had to weigh up the risk versus the reward. The risk lay in whether Jade and I could keep up the charade that we were just friends and that she'd never been to the house before. The pay-off would be that my parents would need to be on their best behaviour in order to ensure that everything seemed normal, creating an emotional buffer between me and them. But the stakes were high.

I was hit with a burst of courage.

U CANT DO THT. JST STAY HERE.

I sat waiting for her response, my pulse pounding at my own daring.

RU FUCKN CRAZY? U WANT ME 2 STAY IN UR
HOUSE W UR HOMOPHOBE PARENTS? ITS WEIRD
ENOUGH THAT UR EVEN STAYIN THERE.

It *was* weird. Again I asked myself why I was here. My parents
were definitely not motivated by forgiveness. I suspected they'd
let me stay because it was what they thought good parents should
do, not because they actually wanted me there. Maybe they just
didn't want me staying with someone else, like Jack, because of
how that would sound to anyone who asked. But, then, part of
me felt like they did want me here. They just didn't want the 'me'
that I was now to be the 'me' that was here.

I'LL JST TELL THEM UR MY FRIEND FRM THE
SOCCER TEAM AND UR BED FELL THRU. THEY WONT
WANT U TO SLEEP AT THE AIRPORT EITHER.

OH YEAH, LIKE UR FRIEND FRM THE SOCCER
TEAM ISNT GOIN TO SET OFF ALARM BELLS.

WHO CARES? THEY CANT PROVE ANYTHING.
THEY WONT LIKE THE THOUGHT OF YOU
HAVN TO SLEEP THERE LIKE A BUM.

I was pretty sure that my parents were going to say yes, because
that was the kind of parents they were—they'd always gone
out of their way for my sister and me, and for our friends. They
were people who helped other people, and I thought that would

include giving a bed to a young woman who needed somewhere to stay for the night.

U REALISE THS IS DEEPLY FUCKED UP

I knew.

I looked up from where I was sitting on the couch. 'Hey,' I started. 'Is there any chance my friend from the soccer team could crash here tomorrow night? Her bed fell through and she reckons she's going to sleep at the airport before her flight in the morning.'

I couldn't believe my audacity. It was invigorating. Even though they wouldn't know what I'd done, I thought I'd feel better for getting something over them.

'Oh no, she can't sleep in the airport,' Mum tutted, in just the way I'd predicted.

'What, she's going to sleep with all her luggage in the terminal? She'll get robbed.' Dad was always the practical worrier. Every time I left home to drive back to uni he would remind me to check my oil and petrol before I got on the road, and to always drive on the highway with my lights on. 'So you'll be more—'

'—visible to other drivers,' I would finish his sentence.

'Yeah,' I replied to Mum and Dad. 'I mean, she's pretty adamant she's going to do it, but I think it's silly. She won't be any trouble.'

'No, she can't do that,' Mum said again. 'Tell her she should come here.'

And that was final. My (ex) girlfriend was going to meet my parents tomorrow.

Jade arrived late the next day, wisely staying away until relatively late just as I'd done the night before. I figured the longer she was here, the higher the odds one of us would do or say something that gave the game away. Mum was such a naturally suspicious person; she was likely to be the one who'd pick that we were more than just friends. I was taking a massive punt that this was such an outrageous move that she wouldn't see it for what it was, see Jade for who she was. That she wouldn't expect me to have the balls to do this after everything that had happened.

'Mum, this is Jade,' I said as Jade followed me inside the house hesitantly.

'Hi, Jade, nice to meet you.' Mum's welcome sounded so much more normal than the one she'd given me the day before.

'Hi,' Jade said, and we all stood semi-awkwardly for a second. 'Thanks so much for letting me crash tonight. I hope I'm not inconveniencing you.'

'Hi, Jade!' Dad entered the room. He introduced himself and shook her hand. 'Don't worry about it at all, we're happy to have you,' he said. 'You're in the soccer team with Lil, are you?'

'Ah, yep, yeah we play soccer together,' Jade said. She wasn't very good at this, and I flashed her a warning with my eyes. I'd already briefed her that my parents loved gregarious and polite young people, which was not Jade's natural default. It had been Coop's forte, which is why my parents always loved her.

'Jade, I've put you down in the dungeon—that's what we call the room downstairs—I hope you'll be okay there. It's a bit rough and ready and the washing machine is in there, but the bed's comfortable.' Mum always took command by talking logistics. It was a reassuring quality that I'd unconsciously adopted in my adulthood.

'Oh, yeah, that's fine,' Jade said. 'It's a lot better than an uncomfortable seat at the airport, that's for sure. Thank you so much.'

Once we'd got the niceties out of the way and Jade and I stepped outside onto the balcony to look at the view, Jade brought up the sleeping arrangements in an exaggerated whisper. 'I'm sleeping in the dungeon?'

'Yeah.' I smiled wryly. 'I mean, they don't trust me *that* much.'

The evening went off without a hitch and I patted myself on the back for making such a good decision. Things felt almost normal with Jade there to break the awkward tension. Although Jade was crap at being the perfectly polite guest she did have a dry sense of humour, which went down well with my dad. He liked people who were a little cheeky.

In an alternative universe where my parents were accepting, this was what it might have been like to introduce my girlfriend to them. It made me sad to think I'd probably never have that situation for real.

The next morning Jade came upstairs and sat in the lounge. Mum and I were in the kitchen.

'Jade, would you like a cup of tea?' Mum called out to her. It was so, so weird to hear her say that, in this version of reality we were living in. Without thinking, I replied, 'Jade doesn't drink tea, only coffee.' At the same time, Jade called from the lounge, 'No, thank you, I only drink coffee.'

My stomach dropped and I had to force myself to continue doing what I was doing without looking at Mum to see her reaction. It seemed very obvious to me that people who were just 'friends from soccer' wouldn't know each other's morning refreshment habits.

Mum, to her credit, carried on as normal. 'Oh, I can make you a coffee if you like?'

I took Jade's coffee into the lounge for her and Jade widened her eyes at me and mouthed, 'What the *fuck*?!'

I covered my face with my hands and shook my head at her. It had been a close call.

We saw Jade off without a hitch, and my dad commented on how nice she was. 'Yeah, she's cool,' I said nonchalantly. I thought I'd got away with it. I had less than a week to go before I left for Adelaide for a few weeks to visit the Aussie friends I'd made in Colorado. Maybe this wasn't such a bad idea.

———

A couple of nights later I went out on the piss with Jack and arrived home after 2 a.m. with the room spinning. I tried not to wake Mum and Dad as I pulled my things out of my pockets—keys, cell phone, digital camera—and dumped them on the kitchen bench before stumbling to bed.

The next morning I woke up and walked into the kitchen looking dishevelled. Mum was waiting for me.

'You lied.'

'What?' I said.

The familiar fear came rushing back. This felt like déjà vu.

'You lied to me about that girl and you, didn't you?'

'What girl?' I played dumb. Maybe if I played dumb she'd let it go.

'That girl who came to stay—she's a lesbian, isn't she?'

'What? No. What are you talking about?'

'I can't believe you'd take advantage of us like that. You have betrayed me *again*.'

'Mum.' I tried to stay calm. 'What are you talking about? Jade and I are just friends.' I didn't know how she'd figured it out.

'What's this about, then?' she said triumphantly, brandishing my digital camera at me.

On the screen was a close-up picture of Jade sleeping in a bed. The sheets were distinctive, patterned with coloured squares. They were the sheets that Mum had bought for me when I left for university.

Oh, fuck.

'Huh, what? No.' I managed an indignant tone. 'I just took that because she crashed in my bed one night and was so hungover, it was really funny.'

Mum didn't believe me for a second. But I could see her tossing up whether she was willing to pretend she believed me in order to avoid further confrontation. Whether she would just stuff this down, lock it inside her mental black box.

'Somehow you seem to think everything is okay between us.' Her voice now had a deadly calm to it. That was always the worst. 'And that you can bring some girl into our house and we'll just get over it. But we are not okay. I am *not* okay. You don't even know what you've put me through. I can't sleep, I can't concentrate—I can't even read a book.'

'Mum—'

'The doctor put me on anti-anxiety medicine, and I'm a wreck.' The volume of her voice was escalating, the pitch ascending. 'You have no idea how hard this is on me. And now you do this?'

'Mum, look, I'm sorry for all that's happened to you, but that's not my fault. I can't help that you feel this way.'

Mum shook her head and walked away, hands on hips. It's a posture that I too adopt when I'm furious.

I needed to get out of there. What had I been thinking? I could feel the upset growing so I went into survival mode. I couldn't stay there. But where else could I go? I thought of my cousin Becca. I knew she was house-sitting just down the road. She didn't know anything about the situation with my family, but she was the type of person who would either take things at face value or know not to ask. She was discreet and kind. I texted her and asked if I could come and crash with her for a few nights. I only needed to get through a few days before I could get on that plane.

While I waited for Becca's response, I quickly packed my things. I had to at least take everything I needed for my trip to Australia, if not for when I moved to Auckland for good, but I didn't have time to sort through the boxes of my belongings stored in the dungeon. I checked that I had my passport and all my toiletries from the bathroom at least.

Mum was in her bedroom with the door closed; Dad was out, luckily. He would've only escalated things.

'Mum.' I tapped on her door. There was no response.

'Look, I think it's best if I go and stay somewhere else for a while.' I tried not to cry. 'I'm sorry if I upset you. I didn't mean to.' There was still no response.

'I'm going to Australia on Thursday, so I guess I'll see you . . . when I see you.' I didn't know when I'd see her again. My university graduation was coming up in December, but given this backwards slide in our relationship I doubted she'd come to that.

'Um, okay, bye.'

While I was grabbing my gear and putting it outside, stacking it at the front door as fast as I could in case Mum decided to lock me out, I got a text back from my cousin. She told me that of course I could come to stay. It was a massive relief, even though I knew I'd have to keep things close to my chest. After all, my parents had told me not to tell our extended family about any of this, and I was too scared to defy them. They'd already be mad that I was staying with Becca at all. There was no way to win in this situation.

When I got to the house, Becca was full of concern for me. I told her that things weren't good with my parents but didn't go into any further detail, and she said she understood. As the oldest cousin in our family and the one who often used to babysit my sister and me, she had a close relationship with my parents. She knew what they could be like and didn't ask any more questions. I could tell it was on her mind though, and over the next few days she prodded gently, but I stayed quiet.

You might've thought it would be a relief to no longer be

staying with my parents, but there were new pitfalls to navigate staying with Becca. I had to go back into the closet. All the newfound honesty and openness in my personality was packed away. I felt like the earlier quiet, shy version of myself that I had tried so hard to shed.

Dad texted me that day, something angry about what I'd done to the family and to my mother, but I ignored him. I didn't tell him where I was staying but I knew they'd find out because, to make it more complicated, Becca's house-sitting gig happened to be at the home of Mum's best friend. I knew that would make things worse, but I didn't have the emotional energy to deal with reaching out to other friends and having to explain the situation. My decision doesn't really make sense to me now. Staying with Becca was likely to get me in trouble in so many ways—because I'd defied my parents and reached out to a family member. Because Mum's friend would find out and ask Mum all kinds of questions. Because my parents had no control over what I might be telling Becca. While I was here, not under their roof, they couldn't control the spin.

So, yeah. The situation very much fitted the clichéd phrase 'out of the frying pan and into the fire'.

I spent the next few days in isolation, unable to handle friends and trying to avoid Becca too. I stayed in bed all day reading books or took long walks up into the hills that framed my hometown. I felt like I was carrying a heavy weight with me.

Finally it was the morning I was due to leave for Adelaide to visit Jules, who I'd worked with at the Lion's Den in Vail, and the other Aussies, and I couldn't wait to get away.

My phone beeped and I had a minor heart attack, as I did every time I received a message or phone call these days. It was Dad.

WHAT TIME IS YOUR FLIGHT? I'LL
MEET YOU AT THE AIRPORT.

Fuck, why couldn't they just leave me alone? I was drowning and just before I could grab a lifeline, Dad wanted to dunk me under again.

DONT WORRY I DONT NEED YOU TO MEET ME

It was worth a shot. I stared at my phone.

I WANT TO SAY GOODBYE TO YOU BEFORE
YOU LEAVE. WHAT TIME?

I sighed and gave him the flight details. Maybe this was his olive branch.

I spotted Dad as I finished checking in my bags. He was in his business suit and he looked the same as he'd always looked: short and cute in a teddy-bear way. We looked alike, with the same blue-grey eyes.

'Hi,' I said.

'Hi, all checked in? Have you left plenty of time to get to the gate?' This was so Dad.

'Yeah, I've got half an hour.'

'Okay, I'll walk you there.'

We walked in silence through the airport. I didn't know what to say.

'You know how lucky you are that you're getting to go to Australia, don't you?'

Here we go.

'We could have cancelled your ticket. Most parents would in this situation.'

We sat down in the airport cafe and Dad hushed at me to lower my voice when I exploded at him. 'Well, why didn't you bloody cancel it? I'd rather not go if you're going to hang it over me. Why did you even let me book it in the first place?'

'Well, we shouldn't have,' he said. 'I don't understand why you want to go there in the first place. Those girls are all lesbians as well, I'm sure.'

'What are you even talking about? They have boyfriends, they're, like, the straightest people in the worl—What does it even matter!'

'Well, you've never made normal friendships,' Dad said bitterly. 'Always writing those poems. Trying to buy people's love with gifts.'

I fell silent. That one really hurt.

Dad sighed when he saw the tears that I was frantically trying to blink away. 'You don't know how hard it's been. On your mother. On me. And your sister.'

I was too upset and angry to respond. All I could do was scream the words in my head: *What about how hard it's been on* me?

It wasn't even the direct interactions with them that had hurt the most. I'd been rocked by two unpleasant scenarios in the past week alone.

The first one: I realised as I was packing my bags for Australia that I was desperate for some new undies. My credit card was gone, cut up under direction from Dad. And I had no disposable income for myself—I was still relying on the $120 a week that Dad had continued sending to my account. Then I had a brainwave: Mum's Farmers charge card. Farmers was central to my childhood. It was where Mum had bought our PJs and nighties and where we'd picked out new handkerchiefs and socks for Dad. It was where Mum went to get the latest trendy piece of crap that kids absolutely had to have in the 1990s, like a Furby or a chatter ring. It was where she would take my sister and me to see what bits and pieces we could find to make the perfect costumes for dress-up parties—costumes that would always feature hand-sewn additions to make them unique. The other kids were always jealous of the costumes my sister and I had, thanks to my mother.

Farmers had a bit of everything. It was the answer to my grundies problem.

It was good to go to town for a purpose. I'd been spending too much time in isolation, and being out among other people that I didn't have to interact with was good. At Farmers I picked out five pairs of underwear, nothing too expensive, and took them to the counter where a woman with silver hair combed back to show her pearl earrings said, 'Hello, dear,' and began taking all the hangers off.

I handed over the Farmers card and she swiped it then

frowned, reaching for her glasses, which hung on a gold chain around her neck, to look more closely.

'Hmm, there seems to be a problem with your card. Let me try again.'

She swiped it again then leaned close to the screen. 'Is this your card?'

'Yes—well, it's my mum's account but that's my card. Uh, like, she gave it to me to use?' My skin was starting to prickle.

'Okay,' she said. 'But I'm just going to have to ring accounts to see what this means.'

See what *what* means? I craned my neck but couldn't see her screen.

'Mm-hmm, yes, yes . . . I see. Okay, thank you.' She hung up and looked at me. 'I'm sorry but this card has been frozen.'

'Oh,' I said, and a sick feeling of shame rushed up to my ears.

'Yes, it was reported stolen?' she said.

I'm not sure if I was imagining it, but I felt like the kindness in her eyes had been replaced with steel. 'Stolen?'

'Yes, dear, stolen.'

'Oh, ah, that's weird. I'll have to talk to my mum about that—'

I went to reach for the card, but she pulled it back ever so slightly. 'Why don't I get rid of this for you. It's no good to anyone now.'

'Right, sure. Okay, um, well, I'll just leave this here, then,' I said, gesturing to the plain cotton underwear piled up on the counter. A line of people shifted impatiently behind me.

'Yes, don't worry. I'll take care of it.'

I turned away and headed for the escalators with my head

down. My cheeks were burning with embarrassment and I had to sit in my car in the parking building for a few minutes before I could pull myself together enough to drive.

This was a massive reality check about the situation I was in with my parents. I realised then that this wasn't something that was going to blow over, which was a fantasy I'd found it easier to believe when I was living four hours away in my own little university bubble. It was now clear that I couldn't wriggle my way back in just by turning up and being on my best behaviour, being the version of me that they wanted to see so that they remembered they loved me.

This was really, truly serious—quite possibly lasting—and I knew it now because dressing my sister and me, taking us shopping, making sure we always had nice clothes, had always been one of Mum's favourite 'mum' things to do. The fact that she'd cut off all means for me to buy clothes and had done it by reporting my card stolen? It was devastating. She'd made me feel like a criminal.

The second incident happened a few days after Undiesgate. I went to see our family doctor, who'd been treating me since I was about five years old. It was for something routine, like a flu shot. It took just a few minutes, then I stood up to leave.

'Why don't you sit down for a minute?' the doctor said.

'Okay . . .' I said, sliding back into one of the chairs nearby.

He came out from behind his desk and sat in the chair next to me. 'So, how are you, Lilly?' he said, leaning in towards me. I could see the sun damage on his bald pate.

'I'm fine,' I said.

'You're moving to Auckland soon, aren't you?'

This is when I should have got suspicious. How could he know I was moving to Auckland? I hadn't been to see him for over a year.

'Yeah, I'm going to advertising school.'

'Oh, great, that's very exciting. Are you looking forward to it?'

'Yeah, I can't wait to get there, actually,' I said honestly.

'You're not feeling anxious?' he asked.

'No . . . I mean, I'm a little nervous, starting something new, you know?'

'Right, yes, of course. And you haven't been feeling sad recently?'

I was starting to get confused by this conversation and pulled a face.

'You've been struggling a bit, haven't you?'

'Ahh, no?' I said, feeling suddenly alarmed.

He sensed he'd pushed me too far and changed tack. 'How are your friends? Did you make some good ones down at university? Were they good people?'

'Um, yeah?'

'Right,' he said, crossing his legs. 'Do you think they've been good influences on you?'

I felt a little sick as I realised what was going on, though I was disbelieving. 'Yeah, look, I've gotta go,' I said, jumping from the chair and scurrying for the door. 'Bye.' I walked quickly down the hall before I could hear his response.

Stopping to pay at reception was agonising. I kept looking back to the door of his room, waiting for him to come after me.

I made it to my car and quickly drove away, not feeling safe until I'd turned onto the road. What the fuck was that? Seriously, what the fuck was that?

I knew exactly what it was. That was my fucking mother, speaking through my doctor. That was my mother making my doctor ask the questions she didn't have the guts to ask me herself. That was my mother trying to find a reason for my sexuality, and that reason being either mental illness or bad influences.

That was something that felt very, very unethical. But I'll bet I'm not the only queer person who has faced something similar, or much worse.

After that, I was even more desperate to get away from this shit. Now I had this final hurdle: facing my dad and whatever else he felt he needed to tell me before I got on my flight to Australia.

I sat across the wobbly airport table from him, begging in my head for them to hurry up and call my flight for boarding.

Dad was getting more wound up now. 'This has been the year from hell. You just don't understand the damage you've done, you selfish girl.'

I stared at the tabletop. My chest felt so tight.

'You nearly broke up our marriage, you know.'

That was the last straw. It was such a stupid and unfair thing to say that it gave me a burst of strength. I scoffed at him, grabbed my carry-on bag and left. That's what I remember happening, but, to tell the truth, it might not have been that statement that made me walk away. He did say that, but maybe I stayed. Maybe I only walked away when they called for boarding. Maybe I didn't have the strength to leave until he released me. It's hard, looking back, to remember the truth. Because I want to believe I stood up for myself, but I always fear that I didn't do it as much as I should have.

Chapter 13

What Mums Do

**Mother's love is bliss, is peace, it need not
be acquired, it need not be deserved.**

— The Art of Loving, Erich Fromm

When I'd told various friends the story of my coming out, they were always shocked by the 'get out of this house and never come back' bit. But that was never the worst part of the story for me—just the most dramatic. The phase I was in now was the worst part, when the first sharp shocks of pain had given way to a bone-deep ache, and the initial hesitant steps my parents and I had taken back towards each other only served to show us how big the divide between us really was.

It took three flights to get to Adelaide. Plenty of time to think about everything. I was hurt, sure. But I was also so *angry*. How dare Dad put that kind of thing on me, telling me I'd nearly broken up his marriage with Mum. Just by being me? I couldn't get over how ridiculous they were being, and it was pushing me further and further away.

During the flight to Australia I ran through all the fucked-up things they'd done and said to me, as though keeping the tally accurate might help me stay in this feeling of indignation rather than getting upset. When I was sitting on my final flight from Melbourne to Adelaide, my thoughts turned to the friends I was about to see again, the Aussies I'd met while living in Colorado at the same time last year.

Have you ever had friends that you love so much you're constantly scared they don't—or couldn't possibly—love you as much in return? But you don't want to be the overenthusiastic creeper friend who crowds their space, so you're hyperaware of being super cool and chill about hanging out with them even though inside you're screaming with excitement every time you get the chance?

That's pretty much how I felt about my Aussie friends. A lot of my feelings had come about because they were among the first people I'd ever told about my sexuality. Their wholehearted support (and teasing) really helped to normalise something that I hadn't been sure I had the strength to claim as part of my identity. I'd last seen them about four months earlier when they'd arrived in New Zealand for a ski trip and the five of us had squeezed into a motel room in Queenstown. Jules had insisted that three of us could sleep in one bed, which included her, me and Jo but not Kellie because she refused to sleep with clothes on and was relegated to a top bunk. These girls truly didn't have any concerns about being naked or nuzzled near a lesbian. I needed that kind of unfettered acceptance right now.

The Aussie girls clicked on pretty quickly that I wasn't myself when I arrived in Adelaide. There was a part of me that was absent, hiding away somewhere and trying to recover from the past eight months. I crashed at Jules's mum and dad's house in the Adelaide Hills, staying in Jules's older sister's room. Rachel had also been with us in Colorado and I had a total crush on her. She no longer lived at home, and Jules and her younger sister, Alicia, had taken over her wardrobe and dresser space. I couldn't believe the mess: clothes spilling out of drawers and cupboards, bulldozed into mounds to make a pathway to the bed. Jules literally had to get down on her hands and knees and paw through a pile on the ground to find something to wear. I'd heard about these kinds of girls but had never experienced it before. I kind of liked it, though; it was so different from the way everything in my family home had its rightful place.

I spent a lot of time in this room, staying in bed while Jules was at work and reading the Harry Potter series for the first time, getting through a new book every day or two. When I felt guilty about wasting away the sunny days I walked down the winding road to the servo at the bottom of the hill, gum-tree leaves crackling underfoot.

Once loaded up with sugary treats I would walk slowly back up the hill, sweltering in the heat I could see shimmering up from the tar-seal road. One day Jules took me for a walk with her mum up to the very top of the Adelaide Hills. I'd always thought that Jules was the unhealthiest person I'd ever known; she'd been fall-down drunk every single day for the three and a half months we were in Colorado. But now she powered ahead, slim and tanned, handling the incline with ease—as did her mum—while I had to stop, panting, every ten minutes. I'd been smoking a lot, drinking too much and not looking after myself. We made it to the top and took in the view. Adelaide's streets had a similar grid-like structure to my home city, and it gave me a sense of familiarity. But when it came to family dynamics, being in Adelaide surrounded by Jules's family felt nothing like the damaged relationships I had left behind at home.

On a Saturday, Jules's dad, Don—a man of few words but a big heart—decided he was going to take Jules and me on a pub crawl through the Adelaide Hills region. We started at their local tavern down the hill, where the bartenders knew Jules and Don as friends and helped us map out the route over a Coopers sparkling ale. We hit twelve pubs in four or five hours, drinking a schooner of beer at each. I met a couple who turned out to be the third cousins of my father. We took a picture outside a pub with a windmill. In the photo I'm wearing a hoodie and baggy jeans and carrying, jarringly, a mint-green handbag. It's like I was a shapeshifter who'd glitched and got stuck between two different forms. I think Jules had encouraged me to buy the handbag from Witchery, which I would describe as the store for a woman who wants to stick within strict boundaries of a feminine norm. That my personal style was so mixed up was hardly surprising given the state of flux I was in. I was so malleable, being hammered into new shapes by my experiences and not sure of what my ultimate form would be.

By the time the pub crawl ended, Jules was still able to function whereas I was as drunk as I'd ever been in my life. Somehow Jules managed to get me to a Turkish restaurant in town where all her friends were having dinner, including people that sober me would have been desperate to make a good impression on. I threw up in the toilets and—near tears—begged someone to let me go home. I wanted to crawl into a cave made from Jules's and Alicia's discarded clothes.

Near the end of my trip, I dragged myself into the lounge late one morning, hungover as fuck. I thanked god that Jules was at work and the house was empty. Feeling acidic and feral after drinking nearly every night, I was curled up reading when Jules's mum, Judy, and Don arrived home.

'Hi, Lilly!' her mum said brightly. In the time I'd been there I'd come to love Judy in the same fierce way that I loved her daughter. She was one of those lioness mums who would jump into the fray if anyone tried to mess with her cubs . . . but at the same time she was chill as fuck. She had long blonde hair like all her daughters and big eyes that only Jules had inherited. She wore suede jackets with tassels on them and although she came across as a little ditzy, I sensed that she actually missed nothing.

'Hi,' I said. I felt so guilty, crashing at their place. But I needed this so much right now that I had to get over the part of me that hated to ask other people for help.

'How're you doing?' Judy buzzed around the house while Don sloped behind her, silent and laidback as always.

'I'm good, thanks,' I said. I knew they were aware of my situation because Jules had the kind of relationship with her mum where they shared everything, but they hadn't pressed me to talk in the time I'd been there. They were the kind of parents who knew how to give people space while supporting from a distance. However, about fifteen minutes later Judy came and stood in front of me.

'Don and I are going out to lunch. Do you want to come with us?' she enthused.

'Oh, no, I'm fine thanks,' I said. 'I'm pretty hungover.' I just wanted to be left alone.

'Okay, sure,' she said casually.

Ten minutes later I was in the car with her and Don wondering what had just happened.

We walked into a historic building that had been converted into a restaurant, ascended the creaky stairs and settled at a table made of heavy wood that you were probably not allowed to chop down anymore. I was nervous. Being hungover made me anxious and antisocial, and sitting down to a formal lunch with my friend's parents would've been hard at the best of times.

'Okay, let's get a bottle of red, what do you think?' Judy said, looking at me.

'Oh no, I'm okay, I'm not going to drink today, thanks,' I said.

'I've been drinking so much since I got here. People say Kiwis are big drinkers, but you guys really take it to a whole new level.'

It was true. I'd never before met people who'd merged the Italian practice of having a drink with every meal with the Aussie culture of binge drinking.

Judy ordered a bottle of wine anyway and five minutes later I found myself sipping from the full glass in front of me.

I was anxious because I couldn't afford to pay for this and didn't want to assume they would, but Judy came to my rescue. 'Get whatever you like, Lilly, it's our treat,' she said when the waitress arrived to take our order.

'No, Judy, you guys have given me so much already. It's too much.'

'Don't be silly.' Judy beamed and waved me away.

We were eating our main course and I had a nice buzz on from my second glass of beautiful South Australian wine when Judy gently opened the conversation about my parents, as I suspected had been her plan all along.

I gave a brief recap, presenting the facts fairly dispassionately. Telling the story quickly and with some emotional distance from the events was a coping mechanism, but it was also because I felt slightly embarrassed each time I gave someone the rundown. I didn't want them to know how much I wanted to tell this story, how telling it had an analgesic effect. It wasn't even really a want so much as a need. I needed to hear that it wasn't my fault. I needed to hear that my parents' reaction was over the top and that I didn't do anything wrong. I needed people's enraged or sympathetic responses to tell me that I was justified in finding this so hard. But I also felt a little guilty each time I told the story, because it felt like I was dobbing in my parents. As much as I wanted people on my side, I also didn't want them to write my parents off as horrible people. That's why I always couched my story with, 'They're great parents, it's just this one thing.' Sometimes people thought I was trying to justify their behaviour, but I wasn't. It's just that I couldn't bear to see all the ways they'd been fantastic parents count for nothing in the eyes of others. I wanted other people to know they'd behaved badly, but to also know they'd been good too. Most of my friends didn't understand these complicated feelings.

Maybe, deep down, the reason I always defended my parents was because I still held on to the hope that one day in the future all the great friends I had and continued to meet would get the chance to meet my mum and dad. Some parents talk about what they lose when their child comes out—the chance to attend their wedding, to have grandkids (both not true, obviously). But what I was beginning to understand was all that I'd lost from my coming out. Sharing Christmas with both my partner and my family. My parents getting along with my friends and understanding more about who I was because of the friends I kept and how I related to them. Or even my parents simply knowing who my friends were. Knowing what my life was like. Who I was as a person. When I thought about it like that, I reckoned I'd lost a lot more than them.

Judy was the first parent-adult I'd talked to directly about all of this. I knew that some of my friends had told their parents about me and they tended to react with outrage. A few of my friends' parents had even offered to write my parents a letter or speak to them.

'No, no, no,' I always said firmly when one of my friends told me their mum wanted to do this (it was always a mum, not a dad). I knew it would make it worse. My parents hated the thought of other people knowing, and someone confronting them in any way would have sent them into a tailspin. Sometimes, years later, when I was being hard on myself, I would tell myself I *should* have sent all those people to confront them. And I *should* have ignored Mum and Dad's warnings and told my extended family what was going on and let them stick up for me too. Why did I keep protecting my mum and dad and bending to them time and time again? The answer was simple: I was just too scared. It was a fear I'd never felt before, and I carried it for a long time.

Judy got all this like others hadn't.

'Tell me about your mum,' Judy said.

No one had asked me that before. They only ever asked specifics, like 'Is your mum religious or something?'

Judy's question put me at ease. It was nice to just talk about my mum's personality, including the good bits, without having to defend her behaviour.

So I talked about Mum, and about my dad's relationship to my mum and the way our family functioned, for twenty minutes. As I talked I felt the pressure coming off me. Partly because I'd been given the space and time to paint a three-dimensional picture of my parents and also because I could tell that Judy wasn't going to leap into the attack.

Then the focus turned to me. How was I feeling? How was I coping? What were my plans? Was I looking after myself? Did I need help?

I felt tears threatening. Most of the friends that I'd told this story to reacted instinctively with anger and threats against my parents. To them, it made absolutely no sense, and they wanted to jump to my aid. But Judy wasn't doing that. She was a mum too, and she understood the relationship between a mother and a child in a different way. So she just gave me a chance to talk, supported me and tried to understand. I guessed this must be what going to a counsellor was like, something I'd been too proud to do because it would have meant asking my parents for the money to pay for it. I didn't want to admit to them that they'd affected me so badly that I would need to ask for help. We didn't do that in my family; we didn't ask for help.

Then I started to think that Judy wasn't being a counsellor, she was being . . . a mum. And I got all mushy inside because it made me realise just how much I missed *my* mum. In the coming years, many of the mother figures I came across would end up occupying an important place in my heart, even if our interactions were fleeting. Nothing has the ability to make me as upset and deliriously happy at the same time as when someone mothers me. And it's not only the older women who give me hugs or tell me to dress more warmly or tell me how great I am that get to me. My favourite-ever flatmate was a girl only a year older than me who once scolded me for walking around with my hands in my pockets. I would have let her boss me around like that every day if she'd been willing.

After lunch I was feeling light-headed but also more light-hearted than I'd been in weeks, and I sat bonelessly in the back seat of Judy and Don's car as they drove me along the curling, gum-tree-lined roads to their local pub. We pushed open the heavy wooden door and Judy and Don were greeted by a number of people. Alicia untied her apron and joined us at a long table when her shift ended, and Jules and Rachel arrived a little later to their own chorus of greetings. I sipped on my fourth or fifth wine of the day and watched them interact, laughing at their antics. They were so at ease with one another, and I thought about my own family and wondered whether we'd ever been like this. I'm sure we were never quite this free. But watching Judy reach over to stroke her middle daughter's hair as she talked or seeing Alicia tease Rachel about something made me happy. Positive representation of a family was exactly what I'd needed. It warmed me, and it gave me hope even as it brought me to a painful realisation. I could have a family like this, but it would never come from the family of my childhood. It was something that I'd have to go out into the world and create for myself.

Chapter 14

Lesbian Paraphernalia

'You're very–how do you say?–
strong,' she said. 'Very strong.'

**I shook my head. I wasn't strong. I was just
organized into little sections inside. The
sections didn't touch each other, necessarily.
I hadn't seen some of them for a long time.**
– *The Gin Closet*, Leslie Jamison

I crashed with Jack when I got back to New Zealand, sleeping under his Ninja Turtle duvet for a few nights until it was time to drive to Dunedin for my university graduation.
   I'd opted to have my official graduation ceremony in December rather than in February with all my mates, and I wasn't sure if that was the right decision. But I'd be living

in Auckland by then and I couldn't imagine coming back. Looking back. I wanted to be only looking forward by then. But graduating in December meant a whole weekend with my family.

I was scared about being around my family, but, still, I keened for them. I particularly missed my little sister, who still wrote me funny letters pretending she was a character from our favourite TV show, *Kath & Kim*, and whom I hadn't seen in months. Why were they coming to my graduation? I didn't ask them to and I certainly didn't expect them to. This was the last hurdle before they were rid of me forever, so why were they making it such a big deal?

I suspected it was because Grandma—whose spare bedroom with its flammable pink bedspreads my sister and I had spent many nights in growing up—wanted to come. She didn't know anything about what had happened, so Mum and Dad had to play along. But maybe the truth was more complicated. Maybe they came because it was one of those big life milestones for your child that you look forward to as a parent, and they thought it could be their last chance to experience one with me. There wouldn't be a wedding, they were probably thinking. There wouldn't be the birth of their first grandchild. So they'd better take this last chance to celebrate a family achievement. I could imagine Dad delivering this reasoning to Mum. Convincing her that even though I didn't deserve it, they should be there.

When I arrived in Dunedin I felt like I'd made a mistake. The streets, usually filled with the energy of crowds of students wrapped up in ski jackets and scarves against the ubiquitous southerly wind, were empty. I saw only a few tottering elderly shoppers and families who were finally safe to stray further into North Dunedin—usually the domain of rowdy students. This was the version of Dunedin that existed when we weren't there. It felt alien, and it added to the feeling of unease that never left me the whole weekend.

My parents had rented three motel rooms—one for me, one for themselves and one for Grandma and Jen. Mine was across the courtyard from the others and I wondered if that was on purpose. I was suspicious of everything. Mum and Dad were suspicious of everything. Grandma was in the dark. Jenny was stuck in the middle. Welcome to a relaxing weekend away.

After the ceremony we suffered through a celebratory dinner, then Grandma went to bed and Mum and Dad settled in to watch TV at the motel. I took my little sister to my old flat, which was now empty of everything except the ads torn from men's magazines that I'd plastered across one of the lounge walls. We sat on the dirty carpet with a bottle of vanilla Absolut that I'd bought from duty-free, got drunk and took selfies (which, in this pre-smartphone era, were not called selfies yet). It was a shiny few hours of happiness amid a miserable weekend. Hanging out with my sister like this, getting drunk and bonding as near-adults, was something I'd always looked forward to as I'd waited for her to reach the later years of being a teenager. The possibility of this happening had begun to slip away over the past nine months as the tensions in our family worked against us. That's why this night was so important to me.

When we were sufficiently sozzled, I took my sister to a famous student haunt called The Bowler as part of my big-sister introductory workshop on the student lifestyle—Jenny was coming down to start university in Dunedin in just a few months. We took our two-for-one drinks across the sticky carpet to a booth. As I was talking I put a cigarette in my mouth and lit it.

'No!' My sister slapped the cigarette out of my mouth and we stared at each other in shock as smoke drifted up from where the cigarette now lay on the floor.

'What the fuck?' I said.

'It's illegal!' Jenny exclaimed.

'What?' I was so confused.

The last time I'd been in here, just a couple of months ago, the air had been thick with smoke, as always. But in the weeks that I'd been out of the country, smoking indoors had become illegal. And boy did that pub suddenly stink to high hell of BO and old booze without the smell of nicotine to hide it. I wished other aspects of my life could change so fast. I'd never been so desperate for anywhere but where I was.

The next morning Jen and I were both predictably hungover, but we made it through brunch with my parents and Grandma before we got into our cars to leave the city. I was driving to Queenstown to find a job that would get me through the rest of summer before I moved to Auckland, and they were headed home. I was reminded that technically, at that moment, I didn't have a home. It didn't feel as freeing as it should when you're twenty years old, have the privilege of relative financial security and there's a new phase of your life coming just around the corner. In fact, that weekend felt like my lowest point since I'd been outed to my family.

When I visited my parents' house two years later, I came across my official graduation picture from that weekend on a shelf above the fireplace. I was genuinely taken aback that they'd displayed a picture of me from a time when things between us were so bad. But, I guess, even back then I knew that my parents remained proud of me. Having pride in your child's accomplishments is a useful tool. They could keep that for when their friends and neighbours asked about me. They could tell them I had a university degree or that I was at a prestigious advertising school or that I was one of the few people from my class to be offered an internship or that I was the first to get a paid job in advertising after school. They could list my accomplishments and they could attach pride to those things. That way, they could keep up appearances to outsiders and they didn't have to think about whether they actually *liked* their daughter. They didn't have to know me. They only needed to know my markers of success. They could even tell me they were proud of me, which is something that did continue through those post-apocalyptic years. Maybe that helped them to pretend that everything was okay between us.

The photo I remember from that weekend tells a different story. It shows the five of us—Mum, Dad, Jenny, Grandma and me—lined up in front of the Town Hall. I have a stupid grin on my face because I had affected a kind of manic extroversion to get me through the weekend. The others look normal, except for Mum. I'd put my arm around her and the camera captured her response. She has her arms clamped against her sides as if she's about to throw a military salute. As though she can't bear my touch.

Queenstown—known as 'the adventure capital of New Zealand'—is a town for tourists and thrill-seekers and anyone with Peter Pan syndrome. I hoped it would distract me from reality while offering me a chance to find short-term work in a place where people constantly came and went. When I arrived in Queenstown I put a smile on my face to greet some friends who I'd be staying with until I could get a job and sort out a place to live for the next couple of months. I hated this. I hated asking my friend if I could stay at her parents' flash house, even though we weren't very close and she already had two other people staying. I hated that needing to take financial responsibility for myself had become real.

I wasn't in a good place emotionally. Those days in Dunedin for graduation had really taken it out of me and made me realise that perhaps things were going to get worse in our family before they got better. If they ever got better. So now I was in survival mode. The glitter of Auckland was still two painful months and a Cook Strait ferry crossing away.

I'd got pretty good at playing the role of someone who was okay. I spent my first three days in Queenstown partying with the girls. I had my first-ever one-night stand with an English chick I met at a backpackers' bar. The next morning I walked home past my friend Kay, who was working at the jet boats on the lake. I yelled out a greeting to her. 'Walk of shame, mate!' I said, hoisting the high heels I'd hooked over my fingers into the air in a kind of salute.

'Bloody good on you, mate!' she'd yelled back while handing life jackets to tourists.

But when no one was watching, I was a different person. I carried copies of my CV around with me, but when I looked at job ads in the windows of cafes and restaurants and thought about going in, my anxiety skyrocketed and I ended up scurrying away, shaking. While my roommates went off to work, I stayed in my bunk bed reading books and cherishing every hour I could find to be by myself, away from the pressure of having to pretend. I wasn't a good houseguest, just like I hadn't been a good houseguest at Jules's in Australia. Usually I was a great houseguest—pulling out the vacuum cleaner, cooking meals and wiping the kitchen bench. But not this time. I didn't get out of bed until I knew someone else would be home soon—I didn't want them to see me with my defences down.

I was flailing, if quietly. And the pressure was building and building. I couldn't impose on the girls much longer without contributing, but I couldn't get myself together to find a job.

Finally I gave in and picked up the landline phone. I dialled my parents' home phone number, praying that it would be Dad who picked up and not Mum. He did, and I managed to get the first few sentences out:

'Hi, Dad, it's Lil—'

'—Yeah, look. I really didn't want to have to ask you this, but . . . I can't do this. I can't find a job and—'

That was when the upset started choking me up.

'—I can't cope, Dad, I can't cope.'

I dissolved into a snotty, crying mess. I could hear my dad saying my name over the phone but I could only gasp for air between sobs.

I don't think he'd ever heard me lose it like that. Not when I broke my leg in two places at eight years old. Not when I'd had debilitating headaches nearly every day for a year after being hit by a car at ten years old. I had cried like this before—after Coop had broken things off with me and in private moments in the past seven months—but he'd never seen it. I was the stubborn, stoic one in our family. Dad had his rages, Mum had her martyr-like tantrums and Jenny had always been the drama queen of the family, but I was the silent sufferer.

'Can I come home, Dad? Please, I just need to come home,' I pleaded.

I think I really frightened him. He told me that he would talk to Mum and to give him a couple of days. He didn't say no straight away.

Two days later Dad texted to say I could come home, which left me with mixed emotions. Relief, but dread. I would be heading back in just a couple of days. I texted Dad before I left Queenstown to let him know around what time to expect me, hyperaware that I was on very thin ice and any misstep—such as turning up unexpectedly—could change the game.

He texted back.

> OKAY THANKS FOR LETTING ME KNOW. KEY IS
> UNDER THE DOORMAT. WE'RE AT THE BACH.

I frowned and replied.

> OKAY. HOW LONG WILL YOU BE THERE FOR?
> IS JENNY AT HOME?

> NO, WE'RE ALL HERE. DON'T KNOW WHEN WE'LL COME
> BACK. MAYBE BEFORE YOU LEAVE FOR AUCKLAND.

I realised that my whole family had relocated to our holiday home. Had they always intended to be at the bach at this time? Or, in between me begging to come home and now, had they packed their things in order to be gone when I arrived? Dad hadn't mentioned anything about this when I'd talked to him, which made me think it was the latter.

I kept picking up my phone and peering at the screen as though his message could give me more clues. I thought I could no longer be shocked by my parents' decisions, but I felt hurt at the idea that they were actively avoiding me. I'd just assumed that the go-ahead to come home had been their capitulation, that they would allow me back in and deal with having me there. Even after all the hurtful words and behaviour, I still thought that. It was another reality check.

Then a feeling of relief seeped in. I overlaid my hurt with the revelation that I was going to have the run of the house to myself for the remainder of the time before I moved to Auckland. And that was the feeling I chose to focus on. I realised how lucky I was. My privilege meant that, even at my lowest point, I'd landed in a pretty sweet place.

When I got home to my parents' house, I stepped out the sliding door onto the balcony and took in the sound and smell of the ocean below, something that had been a constant throughout my childhood. I watched the waves and thought of all my memories to do with this beach, like the time Mum was swimming all the way out around the head of the peninsula when the town shark alarm had gone off. The rest of us had watched frantically through binoculars, sure we'd seen a dark shape and a fin, and imagined the worst. When we'd finally seen her coming up the garden path, wrapped in a towel, we'd breathlessly asked her if she'd heard the alarm. Mum had laughed and said not to worry, it was probably only a bronze whaler—harmless. And I remember thinking how brave and capable she was, and that I wanted to be that way too.

The rest of the summer holidays passed. Mostly I hid away at home by myself with interludes of going to town to get drunk with Jack. I really needed that time to do nothing much and put myself back together. I thought of how close that new life in Auckland was getting.

One thing was hugely important in helping me get through this period: lesbians, more lesbians that I could imagine. Lesbians talking. Lesbians laughing. Lesbians loving, breathing, fighting. Lesbians fucking, crying, drinking, writing, winning, losing cheatingkissingthinkingdreaming . . . That's right. I got my hands on seasons one and two of *The L Word* and life suddenly made sense, even if that theme song did not.

Looking back now, I can't believe how ballsy it was to order those DVDs to arrive at my parents' house. Anything from the States would have taken a good three weeks to ship, so did I order them after I left Queenstown when I knew I'd be there to scoop them out of the mail? Or did I order them earlier and allow for the fact that my parents might or might not have opened the package despite my name being on it? I'm not sure, but it was a sign that I was prioritising my own happiness, even if that happiness came with risk.

If someone asked me to name a moment of great excitement in my life, getting those DVDs is one of the first things my mind would go to. And when I get excited about something, I analyse and plan it to death. So the first thing I did after taking the plastic wrap off the outside of the box set, which was covered in femme women striking sensual poses, was to pull out each DVD and see how many episodes there were. I calculated how many total hours it would take me to watch from start to finish. Then I created a timeline to work out how long I could stretch it out, rationing those precious episodes like a person lost in the wilderness would ration water.

Two seasons, thirteen episodes each. The runtime of each episode was approximately 52.48 minutes, which was a total of 1364.48 minutes, which was nearly 23 glorious hours to get lost in the world of women who loved other women. At that moment, I couldn't think of anything much closer to heaven.

Of course, I failed miserably at the ration plan I'd set out. It was impossible to limit myself to two episodes a day (one in the morning, one in the evening, with enforced outside time in between). The first season went by much too fast and I vowed to slow my roll for season two, already projecting myself into a dark future where there would be no more *The L Word*. Sometimes I would find myself clasping my cheeks, cupping the smile on my face. I left the background music from the DVD menu on when I took breaks to make lunch, its sultry beat beckoning me back to the TV. Just one more. Just half of one more, then I'd stop. I talked to the women on the screen and projected myself into their world. At first it was enough to imagine myself one table over at The Planet, eavesdropping on their conversations, hiding a smile in my latte (non-fat with extra shot). But then I wanted to be one of them or parts of all of them. I was Bette. I was Alice. I was once a bit of a Dana and I wasn't Shane at all although I wanted to be. I wanted her confidence, her magnetism. I took the feeling the show gave me to bed each night and held it close.

According to Brené Brown, the social researcher who became famous for a 2010 TED talk about the power of vulnerability, shame is a property of perceived scarcity and the opposite of scarcity is the belief that we are 'enough'. Brown says that with a sense of being enough, we can take off our protective armour. I kept the armour I'd taken off over this month close at hand, ready for the day my family came home. And it was back on when they walked in the door.

When their voices filled the small house it was no longer my sanctuary. I retreated downstairs into the dungeon under the house with its single bed and the bags and boxes of all my stuff. I was sitting down there one afternoon, thinking about how it was time to begin sorting and packing for my new life in Auckland, when Mum came in. It was a tiny space and she filled it with menace. She ignored me and began sorting through the laundry, so I pretended to be busy too. I was looking at a book in my hands when she said, in a tone that was oddly flat, 'I went through your things.'

'What?' I said.

'I went through your things and I found all your lesbian paraphernalia,' she spat.

'What are you talking about?'

'I found those love letters from that girl, and a—a dildo!'

(This phrasing may be incorrect because I really cannot imagine my mother ever saying the word 'dildo'. But you get the idea.)

Briefly I thought that she was talking about Coop's letters from all those years ago, although I'd hidden them deep in our storage garage. Then I realised she was talking about Ava, which meant she'd found a pretty comprehensive stash of dirty talk and Shakespearean sonnets.

'Oh,' I said.

I was surprised to find that my primary feeling was one of overwhelming sadness for my mother. And a deep, hollow pity. I wasn't even angry that she'd rummaged through my boxes and bags or that she'd rather judge me on my possessions than try to understand me by talking to me.

'Why do you keep doing this to yourself, Mum?' I said quietly, smiling sadly up at her. 'It's not helping anyone. You're just hurting yourself.'

She didn't like this response. I think she wanted me to be ashamed. Or to feel sorry for her. I'm not sure. I had no idea what was going on in her mind. But I did know that the past nine months had probably been some of the toughest in her life.

I don't remember what she said next or if she just left. I don't remember exactly if we had any further unpleasant conversations before I left for Auckland—but I believe we did. I have a memory of standing in the lounge, being yelled at, and trying to defend myself against someone who wouldn't listen to reason. To this day, when I'm trying to articulate my position to someone who can't or won't see my point of view, or who remains irrational in the face of logic, I'm often brought to tears. It doesn't matter if it's a customer-service person or a fight with someone I love. Being misunderstood or disbelieved is one of the things that I remain most sensitive to.

Finally the day came to leave for Auckland. My dad offered to help me carry things up the steep path to my car, but I told him I had it. And that probably hurt because packing the car before family holidays was always Dad's big thing, even if he kind of sucked at it. I knew I was pushing him away, but what did he expect? This was what they wanted, after all.

The four of us stood just outside the front door to say

goodbye, and this goodbye felt a lot bigger than the one three years ago when I left our family home for the first time ever to go to university. This time there was no guarantee of texts and phone calls, of care packages and visits home in the holidays with Mum cooking my favourite meals and getting all the stains out of my clothes. My sister squeezed me too tightly, and I laughed and pretended to pull her off me like we always did. But she held on for longer, and I could feel that this time maybe she really didn't want to let me go. I gave Dad a brief hug and he patted me on the back. Then I looked over to Mum, who was standing off to the side.

My parents have never really been huge huggers. It was only in the past few years, since I'd first moved away from home, that we'd implemented the ritual at all for hellos and goodbyes. I wished we'd done it more. I wished we'd known not to be afraid to show how much we loved each other in this way, before it became even scarier.

'Bye,' Mum said.

'Bye, Mum,' I said. Then, in an impulsive moment, I took two steps over to her and gave her a hug. I did it in part because I felt like I'd regret it if I didn't—not being the bigger person and reaching out. But I also did it as an act of aggression. I hugged her because I wanted to shake her and say, 'Don't you get it, Mum? I'm leaving! I'm leaving and I don't know when I'll see you again. This is the final string being cut. I'm leaving you and all this behind.'

When I touched her, she stiffened. It was like wrapping my arms around a shop mannequin—soft clothing and hair but just hardness underneath. And I almost came undone. I wasn't sure what was keeping me upright as I choked out a final bye, grabbed my bag and set off up the path. I didn't see my sister crying or the sadness in my dad's eyes, and I didn't look back at Mum. I couldn't look at her.

I made it to the top of the path and got in my car. It sat low on its suspension, heavy with the weight of all the possessions coming with me to start what I kept calling 'a new life' rather than a new chapter of my life, a subconscious nod to my desire to start completely anew.

I might have had all my material possessions with me, but I had been hoping to leave my emotional baggage behind. I wasn't starting so well. I felt the old sadness cloaking me, wrapping around my shoulders in a way that my mother's arms would not.

Chapter 15
Go Your Own Way

T he next day I was standing on the top deck of the ferry that crosses between New Zealand's North and South Islands, watching the wake of the boat churn up the water into a foam. I pulled my hoodie over my head to stop my hair from whipping around and leaned against the railing to watch the South Island coastline grow smaller in the distance. My earphones were in my ears, a rollie cigarette ready to light. I usually never smoked unless I was a few drinks in, and I knew that its sweet death taste would make me feel slightly sick. But I still did it, persevering against the wind. It felt critical that I punctuated this transition from one island to another, one part of my life to another, with a symbolic cigarette.

I'd already had a lot of time to think and to shake things off during the long drive, but it was only as I stood there that I finally felt a weight blow off me. I felt like I could stand up straighter and look to a horizon line that was further away than just getting to the end of the semester, the end of university, the end of summer. Even to the end of a single evening around my parents. I no longer had to measure the days.

I realised that in the past nine months I'd been in a state of shock—one that came from being thrown out of the closet and all the things that followed. No one should ever be 'outed'. I hadn't considered that I'd been outed because I'd been so in control of my coming-out process up to that night when the walls were too thin. I'd thought I had this coming-out thing down. I'd tested the waters by coming out in Colorado so that I could take it back if I needed to when I returned to my 'real life' in New Zealand. Clever thinking. I'd educated myself in the safe environment of Blossom, my coming-out group. Smart. I'd come out to friends once I was ready, emotionally, to handle any reaction from them. Genius. But my family finding out? That hadn't been part of the plan. It hadn't been in the short-term plan and it wasn't in the long-term plan either. They weren't supposed to be part of my coming-out timeline until some future undefined state of adulthood. I didn't know exactly what that would look like except that I'd be older and self-sufficient, and I'd care a lot less what they thought about how I lived my life.

By the time I was outed to my parents, putting my head in the sand and denying it wasn't an option—I had too much forward momentum. So instead I'd just had to cope. The paradox is that, at the same time as having been thrust into the open of being out to my family, I was also being shoved into a box. Told not to talk to this person or tell that person. Having to pretend that nothing bad had happened when I was around my parents. Falseness and niceties and small talk. I'd had to put on a mask, to play along, and it was everything I'd been trying to leave behind by coming out in the first place. That push and pull of being outed but silenced had created a terrible tension. No wonder my feelings towards my parents were so confused. I was simultaneously drawn to them and never wanted to see them again. I hated them but defended them to others constantly. And I think that their feelings were just as unruly, making them want to punish and exile me while sticking to the rituals of family. Graduation. Cooking dinner. Preparing me a bed with clean sheets.

I'd been carrying my things out to the car the day before when my sister had handed me two shopping bags full of wrapped presents.

'What's this?' I'd said.

'They're your Christmas presents from Mum,' she'd replied, shrugging in a way that meant she was angry and a little upset. 'She's been tossing up whether to give them to you or not since

December—she kept saying you didn't deserve them. But you know what she's like . . .'

I did know. Mum would have had some of these presents for months—possibly even since before the fallout. She was the kind of person who, if she spied something she knew one of us would like, would buy it and save it away for a birthday or Christmas. She was probably the best present-giver in the whole world. And I realised then that even though I'd barely spoken ten words to Mum through all these months, and none of them particularly nice, she'd been thinking of me. Despite herself.

I'd looked at Jenny, smiling sadly, and her bottom lip had started to quiver. She'd pushed the presents into my hands and turned away. Somehow it was when we were being kind to one another in our family that things felt worse. It was like throwing a bucket of water on a burning building then watching it continue to go up in flames anyway.

But now, standing on the ferry listening to my iPod, I could forget. A new song started, and I felt my body react to the guitar strum.

When the chorus of 'Go Your Own Way' hit with a crash of drums, undeniably rousing, I blinked back unexpected tears and snuck a glance at the people crowding the decks around me to see if anyone was looking at this crazy girl, crying in public with her hood up and a rollie cigarette dangling out her mouth.

But no one was looking. I was alone in my moment brought on by the greatness of Fleetwood Mac. I sang the words softly to myself, feeling my emotions swarm then settle into a new resolve. The lyrics were validating that I couldn't change what

I felt, who I was. I just had to forge ahead. And at some deep level I knew everything would be okay, even if okay was defined by being happy with who I was in otherwise less-than-ideal circumstances. Finding this resolve hopefully meant that the bad things to come might not leave such a deep imprint. Maybe they would impact upon me but not always leave a scar. I thought that even if things with my parents never got better, that would be okay too. Not ideal, but okay. I would be alright. I would keep going forward into a future that was mine to define.

Chapter 16

Ad
Wankers

**Find out who you are and
do it on purpose.**

— Dolly Parton

I stood next to my creative partner, Christian, and stared
up at the gigantic word written in a cursive black type:
Ballingers.

Made of steel and fixed to a 30-foot-high wall, you
couldn't help but notice it from the street. It was suitably
striking. Appropriately ad-wankery.

'I have to admit, it's pretty impressive,' I said.

It was a month since I'd finished advertising school, and almost a year since I'd made my new home in Auckland. Christian and I had an interview at Ballinger Group for a junior creative team position. Everyone in my graduating class was going for this job, but for some reason I was weirdly blasé about our potential for breaking into the industry. I'm not sure whether it was the confidence of youth or that it didn't seem that scary compared to what I'd been through the past couple of years, but I knew that something would work out. Looking back now, though, this confidence seems misguided. There were a number of pressure factors. Firstly, if we couldn't get a paid job in the next two months, Christian's student visa would expire and he'd have to go back to Austria. Secondly, my parents were definitely not going to keep paying me a living allowance for much longer. I mean, I'd really stretched this beyond the point of sense: I hardly even spoke to them. Sometimes I suspected that Mum was on the line, listening, during a rare conversation with Dad, but we never spoke directly. I felt guilty about continuing to take their money, but not guilty enough to make my life harder by stopping it. Maybe that's why I was blasé about getting a job; maybe the stakes weren't high enough because I still, at 21 years old, had never truly had to stand on my own two feet.

'It will be a lot of bloody hard work for shit pay—and that's if you can even get a job,' my copywriting tutor at ad school had told us a lot over the past ten months. She was quick to flare up when we misbehaved or took our impending high-flying advertising careers for granted. It didn't help that most people in our class were a bunch of cocky shits, and extroverts to boot. I wasn't the same, but those months at advertising school had definitely brought me further out of my shell. I felt really, truly comfortable with myself and my friends for the first time. I'd been out with everyone from the start, which was another new experience, and I was also noticing a weird phenomenon that I'm sure many gay women come across: becoming a sort of lesbian mascot for your guy friends. Our class was primarily male, and they all loved having a chick they could talk about hot ladies with. If a female creative from the industry walked into our classroom to give us a mentoring session, the boys would swivel in their seats to look at me, waiting for my 'hot or not' judgement. I would either nod or grimace and shake my head as though they had terrible taste. I felt like the lesbian godfather. This kind of behaviour makes me cringe now, but at the time I was still going through the sexual awakening that most people had started years before. I'd also never had the kind of formative bonding that a group of straight teenage girls have, checking out hot boys, talking about the latest crush, dissecting what his text message really meant. Now I had twelve boys to giggle and joke with, and, to be honest, I loved it. I finally understood what everyone else had been going on about for the past half-decade.

Our class was made up of only twenty people, and we formed a pretty close bond grown through constant proximity, shared stress and the vulnerability that putting forward creative ideas and getting them shot down brings. Often our days blurred into nights as we worked towards deadlines, and we'd draw straws to see who had to run down the road to pick up the Domino's pizzas for dinner. As the year went on, sheets of paper covered in scrawled drawings or scripts piled up on our desks and on the floor. When we were given assignments to come up with concepts for one brand or another, we had to show proof that we'd come up with 100 ideas before settling on our best two or three, which would then be pinned to the walls of the classroom for review. Our tutor would put his face close to each mock-up, and when he didn't think it was good he would yank it from the wall and throw it over his shoulder. By the end, the floor at his feet would be littered with dozens of ideas, and on the wall would be sometimes only one or two. Occasionally we would have a 'website idea' to go with the other parts of the campaign. That's pretty much as far as we got with online ideas, except for the occasional web banner. Digital was still a newborn back then in 2005. It came into our world yelling and demanding attention, and none of us knew what to do with it in a commercial sense. But we did spend a lot of time online personally, mainly checking our emails. Our version of what might be today's Instagram post, Snapchat or Facebook status update was to write long, essay-length emails. Particularly group emails. I mean, if you were going to take an hour to write an email, you might as well send it to as many people as possible.

We all had Myspace pages though, which was our first taste of social media besides a short-lived site called Bebo. Then, one day, someone walked past a guy in our class and noticed he was on a website called NZDating. After we'd all gathered around and given him shit about it, I piped up. 'Guys, I actually have an NZDating profile too . . .'

'Me too,' someone else replied.

'Yeah, I do too . . .'

And so on.

By the end of that day, anyone who hadn't been on the site now had a profile—written for them by one of the copywriters in the class. It was a fun day, and we were excited by this new way of meeting people. Particularly me. For anyone with some kind of interest or identity outside of the mainstream, the internet was probably really important in their life. Perhaps even a lifeline for some. For me, it was how I would begin to grow something that every lesbian could benefit from: a queer posse. The first lesbian friend I made on NZDating was Nadia, who drew my attention because she was a brilliant writer who didn't, couldn't, take things too seriously. Every sentence she typed made me laugh or shake my head in disbelief. When we arranged to meet in person, I told her I'd be wearing whatever I was wearing (probably a girly skirt and tight top), and she'd answered that she'd be wearing a red coat and picking her nose.

'You weren't picking your nose!' I said about ten minutes into our first face-to-face conversation.

'I chickened out,' she said sheepishly. I liked that she had bravado but vulnerability too. We went out, got really drunk together and ended up at Auckland's only real gay bar, Family, talking about how depressing and disgusting it was. Nadia liked to talk about how depressing and disgusting things were, including how depressed she was and how disgusting she felt she was. I loved her immediately. She was the dark side of my psyche come to life.

The second girl from NZDating I arranged to meet was Lydie, and this time it was with the potential of maybe being into each other. You know, in a sexy way.

My suspicions about Lydie's suitability as a love interest were piqued when she suggested that we meet for our date at the White House, a strip club downtown. Granted, it was the classiest strip club in town, but . . . it was a strip club. My suspicions were further aroused when she told me that she used to date one (or more?) of the girls who worked there. But I could tell she was a funny character, and she gave me a hard time, which I liked.

Lydie turned up to our date 45 minutes late, having left me at the strip club alone feeling very intimidated. It was perhaps only the second time I had visited a strip club and I wasn't sure how to act. Nonchalant? Well, that would just be rude—these girls were working hard. Should I look? Enjoy? I was too ashamed. I was there *alone*. The only people who go to strip clubs alone are the type of guys in the background of any movie featuring a strip club. Trucker hat, puffer vest, facial hair and a general air of unwashedness. I slunk upstairs away from the strippers to the balcony, blinking in surprise when I saw it was still light outside. In the minutes I'd been inside I'd already lost all sense of time.

When she found me, Lydie apologised for being late and told me she'd already had six bourbons with 'her boys'. It was only 7 p.m. I could tell immediately that she was ridiculous and not dating material at all, but I liked her. Much like Nadia, she was forthright and honest.

'You're a lot less arrogant in person,' Lydie told me in our second minute of chatting.

Then: 'We have to stay out until five a.m. because I've missed the last bus back out to Howick, and that's when the first one runs.' She was hyperactive and slurring a little.

'I am *not* staying out until five a.m.,' I replied.

I was hungover from partying with my advertising mates the night before and could already sense that I wouldn't be able to drink my way past that. Instead I took her home with me around eleven, arguing with her as we pulled up outside my flat.

'I'm paying for the taxi, stop being stupid,' I said. 'You've paid for everything tonight!'

'No, no, I'm paying. I've got to pay for my girl!' she slurred.

'I am not your girl, you dickhead.' I laughed, batting her arms away as she tried to give the taxi driver money. If I had been her girl I probably wouldn't have been too impressed with her flirting with the strippers all night.

'Lydie, drop the chivalry act, would you!' I said, and finally pushed her hand aside to give the cabby some cash. 'Get out, you idiot.'

After we clattered inside I bundled her into my UniCol hoodie and into bed, and agreed to a cuddle.

'Can I kiss you?' she said in the darkness.

'No, thanks,' I said, and within minutes she had passed out. I patted her fondly, then snuggled into her back. Lesbians make friends with each other quickly, I was learning that.

The next morning Lydie caught the bus home to Howick, still wearing my hoodie and with my DVDs of *The L Word* seasons one and two tucked under her arm. I didn't see any of those items again for five years despite repeatedly asking her to give them the hell back.

———

When we weren't at school, most of my advertising class got drunk together, probably because we were insufferable to all other people. All we talked about was ads, ads, ads. So on a Friday night we'd pour out of school and walk a few doors down to Deschlers Bar to talk about advertising while watching all the rich Aucklanders trying to parallel park their Maserati convertibles and BMWs on the narrow street outside. We'd heckle them as they inched backwards, cheering if they managed to get into the parking spot or cheering louder if they got too intimidated and gave up, gunning their engines as they sped away. We couldn't really afford to drink in bars, but having a drink—even one—in a posh bar was like testing out the glamorous careers we were bound to have in just a few months. Then we'd schlep to my flat via the booze shop and get properly pissed. I shared a tiny villa perched on the side of a hill in Kingsland with three other flatmates, and it was there, surrounded by my new friends, that I turned 21. The theme was 'rock stars', which fitted the level of ego among us. I dressed as Blondie. We sang karaoke. We felt like we ruled the world.

By the end of that year of advertising school, the reality of how few of us would actually make it in the industry had begun to hit. That's why the interview Christian and I had at Ballingers was so important.

It went pretty well, Christian and I thought. We knew we had a fairly good portfolio of work compared with most others from our class, and we also knew that at least one person from each of the other teams was an egomaniac who'd probably make a bad impression. And we were correct. In fact, one of the teams managed to get into an argument with the creative director interviewing them, which made us titter gleefully. But by January—a month after our interview—we still hadn't heard if we'd got the job. During this waiting period, however, we had sent cleverly written, funny emails to hassle the creative director, which I think made him like us more.

Then, just a few days before Christian's student visa ran out, we were told the job was ours. Life seemed to be working out.

Chapter 17

The

Letter

'Hey, Lil! A letter came for you. Exciting,' chirped my flatmate Pottsie one day.

It was April 2005, only a few months since I'd arrived in Auckland and started advertising school. I was still adjusting to everything that a new city and direction brings, but I already felt like I'd left so much negative stuff behind. Sure, I'd had one or two incidents when I'd got drunk around a straight girl I had a crush on and cried because I knew I could never be with her and was reminded of how hard being gay was sometimes. But, y'know. Aside from that and the normal dramatics of being twenty, I was doing pretty good.

Pottsie handed over an envelope made from a thick, textured paper stock, and my stomach dropped as I recognised my mother's handwriting on the front.

'Thanks,' I stuttered, then went swiftly to my room, closed the door and sat at my desk. I pulled out a letter written on the same deep-crimson-coloured paper that the envelope was made from. It was no coincidence that Mum had picked this colour stock, perhaps from the stationery shop down the road in the village or maybe even from a fancier store in the city. Maybe she had made a special trip, or maybe she'd combined the purchase with other errands for efficiency. She was an efficient person.

The red. That red paper, the colour of blood, of love and of pain. It was a purposeful choice, I was sure of it.

'Lilly,' the letter began. 'It's now coming up one year since we first found out about your sexual preferences. It has been the saddest time of my life.'

I took a deep breath and put the letter down. She'd caught me completely by surprise. Had she marked down the date our family turned to shit?

I picked the letter back up and devoured its contents with a sick hunger. It was the most I'd heard from my mother in a long time. News of my family was passed to me through my dad or my sister now, and I sent news back that way too, like some strange World War I-era communications system.

The first time I read it, tears began to roll down my cheeks and my breathing became ragged as I tried to control myself. As I finished the letter, I burst into heaving sobs and cried helplessly for long minutes. Then I pulled myself back together, wiped my face and blew my nose, and read it again. This time, as I read my anger grew, and when I was finished I threw the letter on the desk and started bouncing off the walls of my room, eventually snatching it up again and ricocheting out into the lounge where Pottsie was working.

'It's a fucking letter from my mother!' I exclaimed. 'I just, I just can't even believe what she wrote! Do you want to read it?'

I shoved it at her, and she froze like a possum caught in the headlights of a car, staring at my blotchy face.

'Um, no, that's okay,' she said awkwardly.

Pottsie and I were once on the verge of being friends, that is until she told me and my other flatmate that she and her boyfriend only ate arugula and could we stop buying the much cheaper iceberg lettuce when we did the flat shopping (on our small weekly food budget). This wasn't the only thing, but it had been the final passive-aggressive nail in the coffin. So it was a bit much that I was trying to make her read a very personal letter from my mother.

'Yeah,' I said, 'you're right.' And I swept back into my room, closed the door and sat down at my desk with purpose. I pulled out some sheets of paper and started to write. It was the first opportunity I'd had to say all the things that had been gathering, swarming for the last year, and I wasn't about to waste it. This is what I wrote, edited for length.

Dear Mum,

First of all, part of me is glad you wrote, because I hope it is a sign that you are going to get on with your life and stop feeling so miserable. But at the same time, your letter brought back all the old feelings in me that I've felt many a time over the last year.

In reply to your letter: I can see how you feel I have hardened towards you, but how could I need you the same with all the horrible things you've said to me, the blame you've forced upon me and your ambivalence towards me. I have tried and tried to treat you the same and to be the unchanged happy girl around you, but then you seem to think I'm flaunting my happiness in your face. In reality I just want you to see me and think, 'Well, at least she's happy now.' And I am happy now, god, almost every month someone says to me that it is so good to see the old zany Lilly back, or that I seem so much happier and sure of myself.

I am sick of trying to prove to you that I'm a funny, confident, well-liked and respected person. Parents should not need hard proof of these things, they should believe it of their children. I shouldn't need to do these things to 'prove' it to you. And perhaps because of this lack of faith in me, perhaps because for a while you would no longer listen to my stories or my test results or even my opinion, that's why I have stopped needing you to validate me, my lifestyle and my achievements.

Whether you like it or not, my friends are the ones who have been there for me, because instead of judging me they've said, 'We're so glad you're happy, and that's all that matters to us! You'll always have our support.' I would give anything to be accepted by you again rather than just tolerated.

You have so much to cherish in me and in my life, yet you choose to focus on the negatives and the things you're going to miss out on—like a wedding. How can you devalue your child just because she's not going to give you a wedding! Is that all I was to you, a chance for you to have a wedding so you could say, 'Look, my child is normal and has succeeded in life'?! Perhaps it is a generational thing, but a wedding is not a symbol of success. How narrow-minded it is of you to think that without one you do not have a family.

You tell me I have disrespected and betrayed and lied to you. Well, I would have loved to have been open with you, but I knew I couldn't because you were too fragile and emotional and I didn't want to cause you more pain. Although you won't believe this, I have tried to protect you from being hurt, and I have stood up for you in the face of other people's anger towards the way you've dealt with this. Even though you probably think I've tried to turn people against you, I have done the opposite.

And that comes back to the fact that you will always be my mother, no matter what you do. Because I only have one of you and you are so important to me and I do not want to lose you. But I will never forget the way you have made

me feel over the last year. Your letter brought it all back
and I sobbed the way I used to before I moved up here. I
have had to be the strong one, the mature one, the adult,
and I shouldn't have to be. I shouldered the weight of your
blame, the rash, harsh statements against my personality
and the things I cherish and believe in. And not once have
you seemingly stopped to think, 'Hold on, she must have
had a hard time with all this too.' This would have been a
hard period of my life, struggling with who I am and the
choice I have made to come out, even without all the extra
shit you heaped upon me. I'm sorry that you have suffered
attacks and have had to go on medication and have become
a 'social recluse', as you put it. But there is only so much
responsibility I can take for that—the rest is your reaction
and I cannot be held accountable. If I let myself, I would be
an absolute mess. But I am stronger than that, and part of
that strength comes from the upbringing you have given me.

As it is, I have suffered because of you and your reaction,
not my sexuality. You don't have a monopoly on suffering,
Mum. I'm hurting too, it just shows in a different way when
I am around you—and that is the 'hardness' you talk about.
But whenever you or Dad say something even mildly nice
to me the hard shield I've grown cracks, and I struggle
not to cry. Because I miss you. Sometimes all I want is my
mum and dad back. I would give back every present or trip
overseas you've given me if only I could have my mum and
dad back. You can list all the material things you like, but
the true measure of parents is not through tangible goods,

it is through the love and care and acceptance they show towards their children. And if you love me the way you say you do, then you would stop behaving the way you do.

Here is where I give you the answers you have asked for. Yes, at this point I am pretty sure that I am gay. I've been through and experienced a lot to get here, and it is not something I decided overnight. I realise that there will be some things in life made harder by my choice. I realise that not all people will accept me for my sexuality, and that I will probably face prejudice and maybe even cruelty because of it. But I have the strength of my convictions and I would rather face the negative reactions and judgements of others than live an even unhappier life because I am not being true to myself. I cannot live a lie, I cannot resist what my feelings tell me. As much as I love how awesome guys can be, every time I've been with them there is something not quite right. And this is not just a physical thing. As time has passed I've come to realise that I just do not connect with them the same way I do with girls, on that relationship level. I know that will be hard for you to hear. But I cannot help who I love. How can I possibly know if I've never had a proper relationship with a guy, you might say? I just know. That's like saying 'How do you know you're not gay if you've never had a same-sex relationship?' Who knows, maybe one day a guy could come along and sweep me off my feet. But you cannot cling to that hope.

Don't worry, I won't tell the family about me or the troubles we've had as you've requested. But you have to be prepared that one day they may find out. And if one day one of them asks me, I will not deny it. Because, unlike you, I am not ashamed of who I am.

I am still your 'cute little courageous girl'. You just don't see me anymore.

I hope one day you will look at me in that way again. Until then, I love both you and Dad very much, and I miss you and want you to be happy. I cannot change who I am, but you can learn to change how you feel about me.

Your Dotty always,

Lilly

The letter was the last time my mother and I had any communication about the topic for fifteen years and counting.

Chapter 18
Mad
(Wo)men

Thou art to me a delicious torment.
– Ralph Waldo Emerson

'Lil, turn around, I need to look at your arse.'

'Um, no,' I said to the male account executive who'd just walked up to me. 'Why do you "need" to look at my arse?'

'We need to find a female bum to shoot for a concept storyboard, but we want, like, a really good one.'

The suit—this was what we called the people in an ad agency whose job it was to deal with the clients—was holding a notepad. His pen was poised and he was ready to write down comments about my arse.

'Go find Veronika,' I said, looking back at my sketchpad.

'Oo! Good idea,' the suit exclaimed, and he walked swiftly away down the long corridor, the old wooden floorboards emitting a series of creaks and squeals.

'This industry is so fucked up,' I muttered.

I was leaning against the back of the bright green couch in the creative department, waiting for Christian so we could go brainstorm ideas for throat-lozenge mailers.

Christian and I had been working as a junior creative team at Ballingers for a few months, and there was a lot to love about advertising when you were 22 years old. The always accessible booze fridge. The Friday night piss-ups and the company holiday house up the coast, free for staff use. Prolific swearing and a lack of censorship. And the rambunctious behaviour that this environment allowed—like the time the whole creative department did bicycle time trials from one end of the agency to the other while working late one night, until someone crashed into a large potted plant and sent dirt and terracotta flying. Laughter often echoed around the high ceilings of the renovated textile mill that Ballingers was located in, and it was an environment that crackled with energy.

By 3 p.m. on Fridays the only people without a beer or a glass of wine on their desks were those who had gone to lunch and got too drunk to come back. Before it hit 5 p.m. we'd stop pretending to do any work and a rotating cast would gather outside the photography studio to smoke and drink, with people making runs back inside to grab more bottles of wine out of the fridge. If it was someone's leaving party we'd schlep up the road to a popular yet overpriced Italian restaurant and bar, where we'd consume the bar tab at speed. The days of paying for alcohol were over, just like we'd dreamed of back in advertising school when we could only afford that one precious pint on a Friday.

It was on one of these Fridays, after getting thoroughly liquored-up at the Italian restaurant with my workmates, that I found myself at ladies' night in a gay bar somewhere kissing Veronika, one of the account execs who I worked with on Unilever. Hovering in the background of this scene were two male execs from work, who had followed Veronika here like a pair of dogged personal bodyguards. They were still wearing their suits, which made them stick out nearly as much as their gender did. Many of the girls in the bar had been shooting pissed-off looks at them for infiltrating our space. I hadn't. In my drunkenness I was far less subtle.

'Can you guys please bugger off?' I'd asked them repeatedly.

But they seemed to be worried that I was leading Veronika astray. The presence of these two zealots was irritating and seemed a bit weird too, but in the coming weeks I realised that Veronika always had men near her ready to serve and protect. I reckon it was something to do with her fantastic giggle, which I felt she employed with strategy. It was a giggle that made you want to be the one who made her giggle. It was a power giggle. I watched her around her male colleagues, the way she deployed it, sometimes pairing it with a fleeting touch to their arms. There must have been more to how she cultivated this flotilla of males, but I never saw it. It was hidden from the eyes of other women.

From my spot on the dance floor I could see Bodyguard #1 imploring her to ditch me, but Veronika just tilted her head back and laughed. I liked that she didn't give a shit, like I didn't give a shit. Alcohol had made me unconcerned about any of this—whether she left or stayed, and whether it would have any consequences for the workplace. In advertising the line between work behaviour and off-duty behaviour long ago disappeared up someone's nose in the agency bathroom.

I noticed that there was another girl dancing close to me and giving me eyes. Or did I dance up to her? She was cute, so I kissed her. Then I pulled away, thinking, *Shit, I probably shouldn't have done that*, but when I snuck a look at Veronika she just met my eye with a wry smile. Her two bodyguards were not so cool with this. It was clear from their stabbing points in my direction and their imploring gestures that they thought I was bad news, and I liked that they thought that.

Veronika came home with me that night, probably because those two guys told her not to. We fooled around but didn't have sex.

'You have an amazing arse,' I told her the next morning, watching the short boxer shorts I'd loaned her ride up as she leaned over my desk to look at my photos on the wall.

Veronika got back into bed. 'Your arms are really dry,' she told me, pinching at the skin of my forearm. 'See, if you pinch the skin and it wrinkles, it means your arms are dry.'

'You really know how to make a girl feel special' is what I would have said if I wasn't hiding my arms under the covers and blushing. Who knew you were supposed to moisturise your bloody forearms?

I saw Veronika around at work most days. She carried a large designer handbag everywhere, and I would've loved to know what was in it. Definitely some weird things, I'd bet. As the months rolled on from our first kiss, I still couldn't get a clear picture of who Veronika was and what her motivations were. I knew she was ambitious and good at her job, which was a turn-on. But that's about it. If you'd asked me about the facts of her life or background, I couldn't have told you. Did she have siblings? No idea! A mother? Probably? Where did she even live? I stayed at what I thought was her house one night, only to find out in the morning that it wasn't really where she lived, and that maybe she was looking after it for her father, who lived overseas somewhere? The details were always hazy.

A couple of months after that night we first kissed, someone at work mentioned that she'd once been in a popular punk band with four boys.

'Like, they were kinda famous, in crust punk circles or something,' the suit said.

Crust punk circles? Firstly, what the fuck was 'crust punk'? And secondly, how would New Zealand have enough crust punk enthusiasts to complete even one circle?

One day when Veronika and I were walking back to the agency from a meeting—her carrying a purple alligator-skin handbag that matched her Christian Louboutin heels—I asked her about it. She just giggled and shrugged before walking away towards her part of the agency with a sway in her step that told me she knew I was watching. Damn. Turns out I was as susceptible to that giggle as every other fool. After that, I dismissed the crust-punk-band thing as just one of the weird false rumours that Veronika seemed to evoke. There was no way it could be true. She wore pencil skirts and looked like she brushed her hair with 100 strokes before bed each night, for god's sake.

Then one Friday night Veronika and I were walking along Karangahape Road—a grimy and wonderful street lined with op shops and strip clubs, grungy bars and great, cheap food from other cultures—when she pulled me towards a dark doorway. I followed her down a pitch-black set of stairs, confused. As we pushed through a door, I was confronted by a wall of noise. We rounded a corner and emerged into a windowless cellar, where a pummelling beat drove into my chest and the distorted screaming of a guitar made me want to cover my ears. On a low-slung stage a young guy with filthy-looking dreadlocks, torn black jeans and a studded leather vest was making unearthly sounds into a microphone. While I was looking around wide-eyed and trying not to wince at all the BO, some of the guys in the audience recognised Veronika, nudging each other and smiling. They all wore black and had the same air of unwashedness, with tattoos crawling up their arms and necks, and clothes covered in rips and patches. I looked at one guy's foot-high mohawk in mild admiration as he waited for his turn to hug Veronika. A few of the punk dudes then tried to coerce her towards the stage, gesturing and tugging at her arm gently while the blistering noise went on around us, but to my disappointment she denied them, pushing at their shoulders and laughing in a teasing, flirting way. I watched on in amusement. It seemed the men in no subculture were immune to Veronika. I couldn't help but be impressed by all of this, which of course is what she wanted. When we finally emerged back onto the street, she declined to explain much further.

'I used to know those guys,' was all she said.

Although Veronika had me captivated, I did recognise that it would be to my benefit to feign nonchalance. I didn't want to be like one of those sycophantic males she kept around. So instead I bossed her into making me coffees all the time at work, and ensured that I peppered all my comments to her with slightly mean teasing. But I was fooling nobody, and she totally had the upper hand. Sometimes she would treat me like just another colleague, sometimes like a friend—the type of friend you go out drinking with but not the type of friend whose heart you know. But, then, sometimes she stood too close in a way that meant something or sat on my lap at work. And always there was a disapproving straight male hovering nearby, watching.

After a period of keeping me on a low boil, Veronika invited me out to a mansion she was house-sitting one weekend. She had led me to believe it would be just us, but when I got there I found an 'old friend' of hers settled in for the night. It was a guy who had obviously been infatuated with her for so long that he thought he was her closest confidant, but I immediately understood that he was her comfortable footstool. I didn't hide my disdain for him very well over the course of the evening and felt superior to think that I'd never become like him. After all, I was sure that I'd be the one sleeping in her bed that night. But then I got too drunk, and when I woke up in bed the next morning I was indeed next to Veronika, but on the other side of her was this guy. My suspicion that they'd had sex next to me while I was passed out grew as his smirk did. I left as soon as I could drag my hungover arse out of bed, but he had to be asked to leave by Veronika. That was the difference between us, I told myself. I still had my self-respect. Didn't I?

The first time I saw Alena, Christian and I were standing outside the agency so he could smoke a cigarette before work. I was shuffling my feet around impatiently and not talking much because it was only our second day at Ballingers and Christian was going to make us late.

We heard Alena's motorbike before we saw her pull into the car park. She dismounted and took her helmet off, and her wavy black hair tumbled down her back.

'It's like a Pirelli calendar,' Christian whispered, and I frowned at him because he was always making sexist comments like that, ones that he would defend venomously as not being sexist at all. He didn't understand that you could enjoy looking at a beautiful woman without imagining her with barely any clothes on. Or, if you did, that maybe you shouldn't say it out loud.

'When you see an attractive woman, what do you look at first?' I asked him one day.

'Hmm, her arse, her boobs—no, probably her boobs then her arse.'

'Oh god,' I muttered, shaking my head.

'Why? What do you look at?' he defended.

'Her face!' I said. 'Then maybe the way she holds herself, her posture, the way she moves through the world . . .'

Christian pissed himself like this was the funniest thing he'd ever heard. 'But you do like a good arse,' he said when he'd recovered.

'Well, yeah,' I responded. 'Hello, Veronika?'

We laughed. Sometimes being a lesbian and a feminist is tricky.

A few weeks after we first saw Alena, we were excited to hear that we'd been assigned a brief for the account she looked after. Our desks were parked right in the centre of the open entranceway to the creative department and they shook every time someone walked past, but the benefit was that you could see everyone coming down the hallway. We both watched as Alena walked the length of the agency to brief us, saying hello to most of the people whose desks she passed.

'Hello!' she said to us as she got close. She had an awesome Czech accent on top of everything else. I noticed the way her warm brown eyes crinkled at the edges when she smiled, which Christian no doubt didn't notice because he was probably looking at her arse or boobs.

'You must be the new creative team. I've been hearing a lot of great things about you two!' she said, waggling her finger at us.

She was lovely, and by the end of our briefing I'd fallen in love with her just a little. I fall in love with most new female friends when I make them, just a little or sometimes more than a little. And then when I learn their flaws one of two things tends to happen: I end up loving them more for those flaws or I realise that I've got ahead of myself and I don't like them as much as I've led them (and myself) to believe—then I have to dial back the friendship.

By the end of the project and some wines shared after work in the parking lot, Alena had become my friend. She made me pasta at her house and asked how I was every day and waited to hear the answer. I liked that underneath her niceness she had fire—when she got pissed off her speech took on a staccato pace and she gestured wildly. She said 'motherfucker' a lot. And, of course, there was that sleek black motorbike she rode to work every day. What was not to love?

We got drunk together and hung out on the weekends and after work. And as we became emotionally closer, the flirting crept in. I looked at her lips a lot. She always had shiny pink lips, and I started trying to catch her in the act of reapplying gloss, which she must have done a lot, but I was never successful. When she wore singlets my eyes lingered on the curves of her shoulder blades, appreciating her unblemished olive skin. I hated my back, which was pale and freckled, so not only did I want her, I wanted what she had, too. One day we drove out to Muriwai Beach together, and when she pulled off her top to change into a wetsuit, I saw a tattoo curving around the side of her ribs and my heart stuttered. Okay, maybe it was somewhere lower than that. I couldn't help but objectify her just a little, although I berated Christian for doing the same.

The true confirmation that I had a crush on Alena came when she got a boyfriend and I immediately disliked him. It wasn't that he was a bad guy, in fact he mostly seemed like an eager puppy. He was blatantly not up to par, and I kinda felt sorry for him because I knew that Alena was surely going to come to her senses at some point soon.

I waited, and the months passed. Alena and I spent five hours in a car together on a ski trip, and for most of that time we ran through everyone in our agency, speculating about what each person would be like in bed. It turned me on. I was thinking about what Alena might be like in bed, and I wondered if she was thinking the same about me. That night, I drank too much because I still hadn't learned what having a casual drink was, and with the boldness of inebriation I decided to get into Alena's bunk bed in the room we were sharing. She didn't stop me. The feeling of her hot breath against the back of my neck gave me tingles down to my toes, and the feeling of her arms around me made me sad. I missed intimacy so much.

But still she was dating the Puppy. In fact, he'd moved into her flat. It wasn't her place any longer; it was theirs. I didn't go over for pasta anymore. Not until he was away, that is. But now, when I cuddled into her on the couch, she pulled back. Our physical relationship was no longer innocent, and she knew it.

Then she and the Puppy got a new flat of their own together, and I got worse at keeping comments about her boyfriend to myself. This sometimes made her mad and sometimes she agreed with what I said. That made me respect their relationship even less because I didn't think you should talk that way about the person you were dating—even though I was the one who prodded her into it. Sometimes we were great at being friends, sometimes I pushed it too far and sometimes she allowed too much. It depended on whether I was distracted with other women, and on how happy Alena was in each moment with her boyfriend.

Then it was the office Christmas party. I'd survived one year in my first real career job. I'd learned how to present to clients and so much about the art of copywriting. I'd fought with suits, I'd gone months straight without leaving work before it was dark, and I'd cried at the office because I didn't know how I was going to get through all the work and because I thought I was going to be fired. So when the Christmas party rolled around I let loose, fully submitting myself to the mayhem that unfolded in the car park of the agency.

It was getting to the point of the evening when the party was probably going to start winding down in an hour, when the sensible people had left and everyone else's wild dancing had descended into slurring, nonsense conversation. I was sitting on the concrete ground, leaning against the side of the building with Alena and chatting away, when I realised that her face was getting closer and closer to me. At first I wasn't sure if it was just the booze making me see things, but then I felt her lips on mine and we kissed. Ugh, it was amazing. But very quickly after that, Alena disappeared from the party.

I didn't let it get to me and joined the others who were dancing in the creative retail department under stark fluorescent lights. I was pretty happy with myself when I woke up in the morning. I put my fingers to my lips and tried to remember how kissing Alena had felt. The memory of a kiss is never enough, like an image you put through the photocopier twenty times until it's blurry and indistinct.

Back at work on Monday it seemed like Alena wanted to pretend our kiss hadn't happened, so I didn't make a big deal out of it. We'd kissed, but nothing else had changed. She was still with the Puppy. But slowly, over the weeks, we inched back into flirtation, to the point of our first fairly explicit text message exchange.

But this must have just been a slip, because then she got actual, real-life kittens with the Puppy.

That's when I realised that no matter how much we flirted and even if we kissed and had awesome chemistry, she was dating this fucking Puppy and she would rather date this guy who was not smart and not hot and not ambitious and all those other 'nots' than be with me in an official sense. And I decided that it was time for me to stop putting my hopes on this thing between us, that it would never become something emotionally rewarding. My friendship with her was great. But I needed to dial back the romance thing. I needed to move on, and, thankfully, there were other distractions.

I'd been staying away from Veronika ever since the weird night when I'd slept over at the place she was house-sitting. Perhaps it was this lack of attention that made Veronika call me up one night and say she was coming over to have sex with me. Not in so many words, but why else would she call me late on a Tuesday evening to see if I was home for a visit? She'd never visited me before, like we were friends or something. She always had an agenda, and tonight's was totally S-E-X. I knew it.

If I'd been the protagonist in a typical heterosexual romantic comedy, maybe I would have hung up, shrieked and jumped around in my bunny socks then rushed to shower, shave, spritz, slather and possibly curl my eyelashes—something I'd never done because those eyelash-curling machines looked scary in a kind of gynaecological way. Instead, I continued sitting on the ratty couch in our lounge with my flatmate James, drinking my bottle of Aquila sparkling wine and smoking rollie cigarettes.

It was a work night but, hey, I'd just turned 22 and hangovers didn't exist for me yet, not really, not in the head-pounding, vomit-inducing way they would in just a few years. So I sat there with James, drinking and drinking and calling the local student radio station to request the song 'Love Generation'. This was to annoy them because it wasn't hipster enough and also because James and I were obsessed with that song and really wanted them to play it. The only reason I can account for acting so blasé about Veronika wanting to sleep with me after all those months was that contrary streak in my personality, the one my mother used to despair about so often. I was not going to doll myself up (or sober myself up) just because she'd deigned to show me attention.

I went to the front door to let Veronika in when I heard her knock, led her to the gross couch and offered her Aquila in a mug because all our wine glasses had been broken at our last party. Then James suggested smoking weed, and I made the terrible decision to participate. By the time Veronika and I retired to my room, I was out of my mind. But I tried to shake myself out of it, because I knew Veronika would never give me an opportunity to have sex with her again if I turned her down now.

This is what I remember from the encounter:

The lights were off.

Veronika went down on me.

I faked an orgasm.

It was about the time she started moving down my body in a way that clearly signalled her intent to go down on me that I realised I'd really misplayed this. *Why did I not have a shower? Why did I not trim or shave down there? Why did I get so fucked up?* And then, 30 seconds or so into her going down on me, *Why did I let her do this?* I had a revelation that I didn't enjoy being on the receiving end of oral sex, not just from Veronika but from anyone. It was the position that left me the most vulnerable to all those bad thoughts flying in, because there was this physical detachment. Her head was all the way down there, my head was all the way up here ... there was nothing to do but lie there and try to keep myself in the moment. Maybe getting head is best enjoyed by people who don't get too in their head. That was not me.

I don't remember anything after that until the next morning when there was a knocking at the front door.

'That will be your boyfriend,' I said, shielding my eyes against the light coming in from the crack in my dusty, generations-old curtains.

I walked her down the hallway, and I could see the indistinct shape of the guy she was dating through the stained-glass door. He was one of the agency's clients, which would've no doubt been frowned upon. But Veronika didn't care about such arbitrary rules. She kissed me goodbye for one, two, three seconds, and then I hid behind the door when she opened it so I didn't have to face her boyfriend. He definitely would have seen the kiss through the glass. And I'm sure that was Veronika's intention.

After she left I couldn't help but feel like I'd really blown it with Veronika. Maybe if I had been fantastic in bed she would have continued to sleep with me or made things clearer about what this was between us. Or maybe I had simply served my purpose as a way for her to remind her boyfriend that she was in charge. Maybe none of those things. I didn't know what to think when it came to Veronika.

It was a Monday morning—about five months after Christian and I started at Ballingers—when Isabella wheeled into my life on an office chair.

We were having a special all-staff meeting in the kitchen to welcome a bunch of new people to the agency. The founder of Ballingers, a guy called David (never 'Dave') who exuded masculine power and seemed to enjoy making people cry, had purchased a boutique ad agency up the road, and all their staff were moving in with us. I was eager for new blood but also worried about my job. This other agency was known for its creative excellence, and Ballingers . . . not so much. If the aspiration was to remake this place from a money-making 'ideas factory' into an award-winning creative agency, the existing creatives like myself would be the first with our heads on the chopping block.

Standing at the front to address everyone was David as well as the founders of the other agency: two dudes in their mid to late fifties who looked like they'd much rather be drinking a chilled pinot gris at their beachside holiday homes. They said a few words that were meant to be motivating ('We're going to create great work!' and 'We're going to do things differently!') but really just struck more fear into all of us in the creative department.

'Right,' said the shorter and older of the two. He looked like someone's kindly grandpa, but I'd heard that he was the one who wanted to fire us all without a trial. 'Isabella is going to talk to you about some of our clients. Isabella?'

He looked around the room. 'Isabella?'

Everyone was silent, waiting. Then, from down the hallway came the sound of a repetitive tapping noise and plastic wheels rolling across the wooden floors. The room full of people waited as the noise got closer and closer.

And then Isabella appeared in the open doorway. She looked to be in her mid-thirties and was dressed all in black except for the gold chains that fell around her neck. Definitely real gold. She had a majestic mane of auburn hair that fell around her shoulders and set off flashing chestnut-coloured eyes. She conveyed the grace of a black-and-white film star, despite the fact that one knee was up on an office chair and the other foot—clad in an outrageously high-heeled shoe—was pushing her along.

She came to a halt and looked around the room with an expression I gauged as disgust. 'It is Too. Fucking. Early,' she said with a beguiling Italian accent.

There was a collective intake of breath, followed by a few nervous giggles and chatter. I looked at David to see his reaction. He was known throughout the industry to have a temper and, according to urban legend, once punched a hole in the wall at a recording studio when he wasn't happy with an edit. So for her to behave like this was very bold. His mouth twitched, but he stayed silent. Meanwhile, Isabella's bosses seemed completely unfazed, so I figured they must be used to this kind of behaviour. This must be Isabella.

I crossed my arms, impressed. And I didn't take my eyes off her for the whole time she spoke. She was terrifying and captivating at the same time.

A few weeks later it was the biggest advertising awards do in New Zealand. I always felt sorry for the minor New Zealand celebrities who accepted the hosting gig because drunk advertising people were truly the worst, and they were more ill-behaved than usual during these things because they were forced to sit still at a table for hours. During the breaks, dozens would squeeze onto the smoking balcony ten floors up, slopping booze around. I stayed close to the door during these times in case of a potential balcony collapse—surely the architects didn't consider the high ratio of smokers in the advertising industry when they designed the weight capacity.

After the ceremony, people poured down the road to the after-party and that's when things truly got loose, with women in beautiful dresses swigging straight out of champagne bottles and married men in booze-stained shirts who had long since lost their suit jackets trying to chat up age-inappropriate women from their agency. I was reclining in a booth, watching the madness, when I felt the cushion dip with the weight of someone sitting down. I turned and found myself face to face with Isabella, close enough that I could see every long eyelash. I froze.

Again I was struck by her classic beauty, poised and powerful. I didn't dare look away. She lit a cigarette, despite smoking indoors being illegal, and blew it just barely to the side of my head. She let the silence stretch out, not breaking eye contact.

Finally, she quirked her head and said, 'So. I hear you're gay.'

'Uh, yeah,' I replied, only just managing not to put a question mark on the end of it.

'That's cool,' she said, in a way that neither approved nor disapproved.

Isabella, I would come to know, often opened conversations with confrontation. During our friendship, when she'd ring me and I'd answer the phone, she usually skipped niceties and went straight to accusations, like 'Where the fuck are you?' or 'Why haven't you rung me?' before I even had the chance to say hello.

In the pause while I tried to figure out what to say next, Isabella said casually, 'I'm very open to these things.'

And I was left stunned once again.

I don't know who made the first move or how many minutes later it was. I don't know if we talked much first. But the next part of the story I remember, we were kissing. She was an aggressive kisser, which seemed to match her personality.

Then someone tipped over a glass of red wine, which ran to the edge of the table and spilled over, causing people to shriek and jump. Isabella yelled at whoever was nearby, giving them a death stare that would have made me wilt.

'They're on fucking cocaine,' she muttered.

'Oh,' I said with naivety, 'how can you tell?'

'Everyone is on fucking cocaine here!' she said in a way that seemed passionately angry for no good reason.

'Oh, right,' I said, looking around. I was just glad she wasn't angry at me. She seemed like someone you would not want to be angry at you.

We drank a lot more wine. My view of the room started looking like one of those time-lapse photos of stars in the sky, but still I agreed to move on to a bar down the road for a cocktail. Somewhere along the way we picked up two of Isabella's co-workers from her old agency, both young guys who—I could immediately tell—felt protective of her. Not this again.

'Stay away from Isabella,' one of them hissed at me after we ordered drinks.

'Come on, Isabella, let's get out of here,' the other one encouraged, putting emphasis on the 'Isabella' so I'd know I wasn't welcome.

'Oh, fuck off,' she said and laughed throatily. I loved her, and I hated them. Why did this keep happening to me? I'd never been considered a bad influence before. Not until I'd started living out loud.

After hovering for ages the guys finally realised they couldn't bully me or coerce her, and Isabella and I ended up alone, sitting on the stone steps outside the building. We talked nonsense and cackled at each other's jokes, and made out. It was Isabella who invited me home with her.

We reached her house in the posh suburb of Parnell and that's when my memory really collapsed in on itself, like my body did onto her bed. I don't remember much except for feeling the contrast between the plump softness of her skin and the silkiness of her high-thread-count sheets.

'I've never done this before,' she said as my hands slid under her top. 'Show me what to do.'

And that's when I stopped. I was so not in a state to be having sex with anyone, let alone being someone's lesbian sex guru. I'd learned that much from my recent encounter with Veronika.

'Let's just go to sleep,' I said. 'I am way too fucked up.' Or something like that, maybe. Maybe I just stopped and passed out.

A couple of hours later I woke up, dying to pee. Everything was unfamiliar and although I managed to find the bathroom, it took a long time of stumbling around in the dark, trying doors, before I found her bedroom again (there were only three rooms in the house—that's how pissed I still was).

In the morning we both woke up with killer hangovers, but Isabella made me breakfast and we sat in the sun on her back stoop and laughed about last night. She kissed me warmly on the cheek when I left, and I knew we were going to be friends.

Except our friendship was a little complicated.

'I'm not gay at all, but I fucking love kissing you,' Isabella said against my lips.

'Yeah, yeah,' I replied, pushing her back against the bathroom door of a bar downtown. She said this practically every time we made out, which we did all the time when we were drunk together. I got it. She was straight. She just loved kissing me. What was I going to do, not kiss a beautiful woman I was enthralled by?

Christian started banging on the other side of the door. 'Hey, are you two in there making out? Where the fuck did you go?' We'd left him in the bar alone for the past ten minutes.

He didn't completely approve of me carrying on with my female co-workers. Not because they were women or even because they were my workmates. He just thought I was going to get hurt, because they were pretty much straight or—as in Veronika's case—not straight, but seriously emotionally unavailable. But I thought I had a handle on it. Sure, it was a bit of an emotional mindfuck. It made me feel powerful to be the person these women 'went gay' for, and also without power because they were dictating the terms.

Isabella, at least, felt like an easier relationship to handle than what was going on with Veronika and Alena. With Isabella it was simple: we were friends who cared a lot about each other, and when we got really drunk we kissed. But I didn't want her the same way I wanted Veronika and Alena. I did want to bask in her attention, receive intimacy and experience being close to someone who held so much personal power. From the moment she'd wheeled into that staff meeting, not giving a fuck, I'd known I wanted a piece of what she had. And if I couldn't be that way myself just yet, I could be close to someone who had it. That was simple enough, right?

Isabella also kept me on my toes in a way that I liked. One day I was at her place, drinking red wine and sitting on the stoop overlooking her tiny back garden. She strolled over to the flower-bed that ran along the back fence with an exaggerated swagger.

'Do you like my flowers?' she said in her voice that became delightfully huskier the more cigarettes she smoked. She cupped a flower in her hand and cooed at it, making me laugh.

'Don't you like my fucking flowers?!' She turned suddenly, stabbing the cigarette in her other hand at me.

'Yes, yes, I like your fucking flowers!' I said, laughing more. She scowled and turned back to them, giving the petals a kiss. Then she chuckled and poured us more wine. She lit my cigarette. I think I smoked so much around Isabella because I loved the way she would lean in close and light my cigarette.

Volatility was something I hated in men. In men, it was frightening or annoying or something that I scoffed at—like when Christian had a temper tantrum at work and kicked the rubbish bin or threw something across the room. But I liked it in Isabella because you don't meet that many volatile women. We're taught to be pleasant and pliant. The patriarchal society we live in wears away our abrasive edges.

I'd watched many others falter at Isabella's verbal lobs, but I felt like I'd mastered how to handle her. I'd realised that her volatility was really just unpredictability and vulnerability, which are both underappreciated traits. However, interacting with Isabella really was a dance, and not everyone could improvise the right steps. Not everyone wanted to. But I did. It made me feel special to know how to manage her—to play along or to trade barbs or to submit. And in return she gave me something I desperately wanted, which was to be mothered. She often called me 'Mia piccola salsiccia'—'My little sausage'. She'd grab me around the head with both hands and give me smacking kisses on my cheek. She'd tell me when I looked nice and she'd berate me for the state of my eyebrows. 'They're like fucking bottle brushes,' she said disgustedly to me one time, licking the pad of her thumb and smoothing my brows with her spittle. I loved it. When I closed my eyes and thought about her, I was compelled to put my hand to my cheek and stroke it gently, thinking of what it felt like when she kissed me there. Both soft and also branding, possessive. I belonged to her now.

Surprisingly, it was Alena who got jealous when I started making out with Sasha, who'd just started work in our retail division.

'Who is she?' Alena said from the corner of my desk where she was perched. 'I don't know her.' I'd just told her how I'd hooked up with Sasha on the weekend.

'She works downstairs. She's a retail copywriter,' I said, surprised at the edge in her tone.

So, Alena was jealous of Sasha. Sasha, in turn, told me one day that she was slightly jealous of my relationship with

Isabella. Isabella wasn't jealous of anyone because that was beneath her, but Veronika seemed a little jealous of my close friendship with Alena. On top of being jealous of Sasha, Alena was also jealous of Isabella and had acted a bit weird when I'd hooked up with Veronika recently too. None of them actually wanted to date me.

'Show me a picture of this Sasha,' Alena said, so I opened up Facebook, which in early 2007 was a cool new toy.

'She's very pretty,' Alena conceded.

'Pretty' was not how I'd describe Sasha. More like 'bloody fucking hot'. I'd just come back from a weekend away at the beach with her and a few other girls from the agency, and the sight of her in a red bikini had nearly made my vagina burst into flames. I'd positioned myself on the beach at an angle that looked as though I couldn't possibly have been staring, then strained the width of my visual field to gawk at her from behind my sunglasses. Sasha had a perfect tan and somehow her skin seemed to glisten like she'd oiled herself up. Or maybe the appreciative tears in my eyes were creating that effect.

I felt a bit sorry for Sasha, stuck downstairs in the retail department. Not only was being a retail creative pretty shit—doing things like posters for the supermarket and TV ads for sports stores—but also in the Ballingers building they were segregated from everyone else. So I'd invited her out for lunch a couple of times, although I found it difficult to make the conversation flow naturally. She just didn't adhere to the usual social conventions of conversation and seemed oddly detached from feelings—it was like talking to someone through a pane of glass. Nevertheless, I was intrigued by her weirdness. Sasha was a writer who spoke like one too, with well-constructed sentences that had a tendency to surprise. She was very self-deprecating and her humour was dry as hell. So even though things didn't flow seamlessly between us, she was interesting to be around. Also, I wanted to sleep with her and that made it easy to overlook the many ways that we weren't exactly soulmates.

It's funny how sometimes you just know you're going to hook up with someone, even though the flirting is at such a low level it's impossible to verbalise how it's happening. And that was the case when we went away to the Kawhia Kai Festival. After spending the day in the sun eating hāngī, we all ended up at the local pub drinking pints. We were the only women in the joint and the youngest by 30 years. My kind of place. I'd read enough signals from Sasha over the day—we'd shared plastic cutlery while eating our hāngī, for example—that when she stood up to announce that she was going back to the campground cabins, I quickly jumped in to say I'd leave with her.

I knew the others wouldn't be far behind us, so when we got back to the one-room wooden cabin we got straight into Sasha's bunk. I had her top off when we heard loud female voices, and we barely had time to disengage before the door swung open.

If anyone noticed that we were in the same bunk bed or saw that Sasha was partially undressed and deduced what we'd been up to, no comment was made. Maybe it's different now that queer sexuality is more accepted and visible, but during my first years of being out, straight people really missed a whole lot of lesbianism going on right in front of them. Or maybe no one even considered that we'd hooked up because Sasha had a fiancé.

I don't believe Sasha was in the happiest relationship, which probably contributed to her willingness to cheat. Plus there was that weird emotional disconnectedness she had—maybe she just didn't care. In truth, I didn't spend time thinking about it. It was perhaps a few weeks after the Kawhia weekend when Sasha invited me over to the house she shared with her fiancé for drinks, just the three of us. I had no qualms about parading around playing the nice, non-threatening friend in front of him. I was on my sexual rumspringa, and I was also very much 'fuck heterosexuality' at that point. I truly could not muster one shit to give about innocent boyfriends.

Sasha's fiancé was nice but about as exciting as a tan-coloured moccasin. He was also completely oblivious to anything going on between Sasha and me, because at around midnight he left the two of us alone in the spa together and went to bed. I had some concern that the fiancé could see us from the upstairs window overlooking the spa, but Sasha told me not to worry so I sat on her lap, my back pressed to her chest. Her hands ran over my breasts, and I felt . . . nothing. WTF? I'd been salivating over her body just a week before, and now it just felt like pressing against a sack full of lumps. What was wrong with me?

We kept on for a while, kissing and fondling, but not a spark was struck. Having never been good at playing pretend and being extremely drunk (again), I decided to extricate myself.

'I'm gonna go . . .' I said.

'I'll drive you!' she replied.

'No, that's fine, I'll just get a taxi,' I said, confused by her enthusiasm to go out of her way.

'No, really, I'll drive you.'

'But you're drunk, right?'

Sasha reassured me that she was fine to drive, which I knew she wasn't because we'd had a ton of booze. But she was persistent and perhaps the most enthusiastic I'd seen her be about anything. Weird. It wasn't until we pulled up outside my house and she unbuckled her seatbelt that I finally clicked what was happening—Sasha was coming home to have *sex* with me. Ohhhhhh.

I wish I'd known then that if the circumstances weren't right in the moment, I didn't need to sleep with someone just because I'd been really, really wanting to sleep with them. And, yeah, maybe that time with Veronika had been my only chance, and maybe this moment with Sasha was my only chance, but if that was the case, if they only wanted to sleep with me in one moment and not the next day, was that someone I wanted to be sleeping with anyway? If I was unsure whether someone was attracted to me enough to want to sleep with me or just *drunk* enough to want to sleep with me, was that good for my emotional wellbeing? Obviously, no. Alas, I had no such surety of self. And maybe, just maybe, I thought that if we had sex and it turned me on, it would mean that my absolute lack of response in the spa had been an anomaly.

But first, in a continuation of great decisions, we decided to drink a whole lot more. I had not learned my lesson about drunk sex from my encounters with Veronika and Isabella.

There was one lesson I had learned, though: when we finally got to bed I stopped Sasha from going down on me. I didn't have the energy to pretend. Instead I turned her onto her back and ran my hand down her body. We started having sex, but after a while—which could have been ten minutes or less than one for all I remember—Sasha told me to stop. Did we stop that particular sexual act or the whole thing? Who knows.

The next thing I knew I was waking up early the next morning to find her gone. Was it a lack of forethought that saw me being so drunk each time I was in a position to sleep with someone? Or deep down was I hoping that if I was drunk enough I could have sex without getting too in my head? Whatever it was, it wasn't working. Being drunk—that drunk—never helped. Instead I found my body not responding the way I wanted it to, which added to my frustration.

A part of me had known since advertising school that being a creative copywriter wasn't quite the perfect fit. It was close, but after a year or so the small ways that it wasn't the right job for me began to feel bigger. I didn't like giving up my weekends to work on shitty soy-milk banners because some suit had sat on the brief for days, leaving only a few hours to come up with a concept and mock it up for presentation to the client. And while I loved socialising with everyone, I also found it emotionally draining to never be alone. Having a creative partner meant you did nearly everything together, and at first having a work husband was manageable. But the cracks had begun to show. I began making excuses to brainstorm concepts alone or to find a rare quiet place in the agency to write copy. Christian had a dominant personality and, although I considered myself pretty self-assured and confident too, it was easier to sit back and let him be the aggressive one in the partnership. But as a result of this I began to feel like I wasn't quite myself, and that wouldn't do. Not when learning to be myself had been the focus of my life for the past few years. But most of all, I didn't like working for someone else and not getting to make all the decisions. I wanted to be in control of my working day and my life, not busting my arse to make money for someone else while being paid $35,000 a year, no overtime.

One good thing came out of Ballingers' merger with Isabella's agency, something that made my working life more manageable. Christian and I had been getting pushed further and further off the creative brand briefs—TV commercials, radio ads, print ads and billboards—towards direct marketing. In the advertising creative food chain, a brand creative is at the top, direct is in the middle and retail creatives are typically considered the bottom of the barrel. So while Christian, who enjoyed the ideas part of our job, became more and more frustrated that we were being passed over for the good brand briefs, I was quite enjoying writing credit-card letters, mail packs for kids and website copy. After a few months, Christian quit. Being a strong character who demanded a lot and usually got it too, before he left Ballingers he convinced the owner and creative director of a smaller agency in town to hire him as an intermediate creative with a salary bump. Not bad, considering that most people weren't considered intermediates until they'd been in the business at least three years. Christian implored me to go with him, saying that we could be bigger fish in a smaller pond as opposed to being inconsequential tiddlers in the ocean of Ballingers. We could actually influence the direction of the agency and do proactive work that could win awards—the only way to advance to a high salary and the top agencies.

I said no. It was an agonising decision, but I just couldn't commit to starting at a new workplace when I wasn't certain I even wanted to be in advertising at all. It wouldn't be fair to Christian or to the new agency. I also hoped that flying solo—no longer being part of a creative team—might mean that I'd be put on more of the writing briefs I enjoyed. But, at the same time, having my other half taken away made me feel very vulnerable and anxious. Maybe it would show me up as the weaker half of our partnership? Christian was usually the one who came up with the concepts that sold. What if the agency paired me up with a replacement partner whom I didn't get along with? There were so many what-ifs, but staying at Ballingers—the devil I knew—seemed to be the smarter option.

And for a few months it was. I did get more writing briefs, which allowed me to hide away from the constant buzz of people going back and forth in our open-plan agency. And when I got creative briefs, I was paired with a freelancer called Bob, whom I liked. Meeting Bob would go on to change my life in less than two years. Because when I finally did quit creative advertising, I remembered Bob and how he got paid $100 an hour to do stuff that I reckoned I could also do. He was the reason I eventually figured out that if I became a freelance copywriter, I could focus on the kinds of writing jobs I enjoyed and was good at. And, most importantly, I could be in control.

But before that happened, I followed Christian to the other agency. My months without him at Ballingers had given me back some confidence in my abilities, and working on direct and writing jobs rather than big creative campaigns had helped me to work less and recharge my batteries. So when he begged me again to come and work with him, I gave in. And when I left Ballingers, I left behind all my tangled almost-affairs with those four mad women. Well, they weren't mad. But they were maddening.

The second and last time I kissed Alena was at one of my ubiquitous house parties—perhaps even the one celebrating my new job. We closed the door to my bedroom and fell back onto my bed together. Less than five seconds later, someone barged in. Bloody typical. This interruption was enough to break the spell.

That same night, I had my last kiss with Isabella. Less than an hour later, she left the party with a guy who she would go on to marry. I'd like to say I handled the situation gracefully, but instead I grabbed her arm as she was following him down the driveway and asked her what the hell she was doing. 'Just two hours ago you were having a go at him for being a dick to my flatmate! He's a fucking arsehole! And now what, you're going home with him?'

Isabella had shrugged me off, and I felt stung. It was supposed to be her and me against the world. It also didn't help that this guy was Veronika's new boyfriend's best friend. Now Isabella and Veronika could go on double dates together in their safe heteronormative relationships. It hurt.

The last time I kissed Veronika, I was asking for trouble. Her boyfriend was an ex-military guy who had left us alone in my backyard to go get his jacket at the tail end of yet another of my house parties. When I'd pulled her to me she sank into my arms in a way that made my heart thud. But like so many kisses that year, we were interrupted. Her boyfriend marched her away down the driveway. Watching a woman I'd been involved with walk away with a man on her arm was beginning to feel like a pattern.

And then there was Sasha. The last time I kissed her we'd been out to dinner and drinks after work on a Friday, and we were left standing inside the covered entrance to the restaurant once the others had left. I watched as she dug into her Prada bag, a present from her new boyfriend (she'd dumped the tan-moccasin fiancé), to find her phone. She called her boyfriend to come and pick her up. After she hung up, we looked at each other.

'Do you want to kiss?' I'd asked her, reading the mood.

'My boyfriend's coming.'

'I know.' I shrugged. 'Well, you can kiss me or not. It doesn't matter.'

Chapter 19
Exploring Family

**If we're going to find our way back to each other,
we have to understand and know empathy, because
empathy's the antidote to shame. If you put shame
in a Petri dish, it needs three things to grow
exponentially: secrecy, silence and judgment.**
— Brené Brown

I always dreaded the drive between the airport and my parents' house. It loomed in my mind as the hardest part to get through of any trip home, because when I was at the house at least I could escape to another room or go for a long walk. During the drive, though, it was just Dad and me. I think he was the one who instigated the awkwardness of those drives. I always came prepared with an arsenal of safe topics of conversation to run through, which I parcelled out throughout the hour-long drive. But, still, I usually ran out of things to say because he never seemed to pick up and run with any of my stories or respond with his own. From Tina Fey's book *Bossypants* I learned that the first rule of improvisation is 'Yes, and . . .' You never shut down what someone puts out there. Instead you have to take it, agree with it and add something of your own. Someone needed to teach my dad that.

When I told a story about doing something fun with a friend, he never asked who the friend was and how I met them. When I said I'd been away for the weekend, he never asked who I went with. Any story that involved some kind of emotion (perhaps something I found hard or something I loved or something I thought was interesting) fell flat. The things that got the most natural responses out of him were zany stories about working in the advertising industry, but even then he never asked too many questions. I think he was more afraid of straying into dangerous topics than I was.

That's why I was so surprised when, during one of those long drives between the house and the airport, nearly six years after I was outed to him and three years after I'd started dating Jess, Dad—in a hesitant, stumbling way—asked if I was seeing someone.

I responded carefully, not wanting to scare him off. 'Yes, I am. We've been dating for quite a while. Her name is Jess.'

The way he'd asked suggested that he already knew the answer. I wondered how he knew I was dating someone when, in the past, he and Mum had been so determined to avoid any knowledge of that side of my life, and I, in turn, hadn't spoken about my sexuality or my relationships for years. It had to have been my sister who'd said something, but I didn't think she would have volunteered that information. She didn't like to raise the topic of me with them. That meant either my dad or mum had to have asked her about it.

Dad made a sound of acknowledgement but he was quiet as he watched the road ahead. My mind raced with what to do next—how to take advantage of this small opening. I decided to push him slightly with something I didn't think he'd like.

'Actually, Jess's dad says he knows you a little from the industry. His name is Gary? I think maybe you've dealt with him once or twice.'

'Oh,' Dad said, and I could tell he was processing this information. I knew he wouldn't like that there was someone out there, in a related industry, who knew about his less-than-stellar response to having a gay daughter. What he said next surprised me. 'How is he with . . .' He struggled to find the right phrasing. '. . . all this?'

He could have put this a number of other ways, like 'Do you get along with him?' or even 'Does he accept you?' but what he did say betrayed his unease. 'All this' he said, as though my sexuality was some nebulous thing to be coped with. A situation.

This was my chance to get some of my own back.

'He's great. We get along really well. Jess and I were out at his place a few nights ago. I think he likes that I'm a bit of a smart-arse,' I said brightly.

I wanted to really rub it in that I was spending more time with someone else's parents than with my own, and I also wanted to imply that I could be myself with them, that I was free with them and they were free with me. Everything I didn't have with my own father.

I'm not sure if he got the point I was trying to make or if it hurt him the way I wanted it to. But after that, weirdly, the rest of the drive was easier than it had been in years. I hesitantly told him about Jess—just the basics, like where she was from and what she did and how we met. Not how we really met (online) because I felt like he'd pass some kind of judgement about that. And not how the first time we met in person I was wrestling a girl in an inflatable pool full of jelly.

Jess and I had been chatting online for nearly a year—just the occasional email back and forth on a friendship basis—when she'd mentioned she was moving to Auckland to start her postgraduate degree in fine arts.

'Cool!' I'd said, and invited her to a party I was throwing the weekend she arrived. The moment she saw me in my jelly-wrestling outfit, she totally fell for me.

Okay, so Jess tells a different story. In her interpretation, when she walked into our backyard that evening and I swaggered over to greet her, she took in my outfit with quiet surprise. I was wearing purple velvet platform boots, a $2-store cowboy hat and a white lace bodysuit over bright pink hot pants. I had a rollie cigarette in my hand that she would later see hanging from my lip, unlit, as I talked with others. My hair was matted with glitter-speckled gelatine from having my face ground into the slick plastic of the pit by my flatmate's overzealous German girlfriend.

Man, she'd thought, *Lilly is a lot rougher in person.*

Perhaps Jess's initial feelings about me were mixed, but by three in the morning we had created a bond that we both knew was going to be something special. Before she left we made a date for Monday.

'I'm freaking out!' I'd texted Emma, who told me freaking out was probably a good thing, in her usual wry and reassuring tone. It meant I actually liked Jess and saw a future.

My other friends were ecstatic about the news too.

'No more straight women!' one cheered.

'You deserve to be with someone who wants you back,' another told me in a scolding tone. She'd never approved of what she saw as Isabella and Alena leading me on.

Christian gave me a 'you've got a girlfriend' kit he'd made, which included things like a spare toothbrush and dental dams, of all things. I don't know how he even knew what those were.

I think Jess and I both knew pretty early on that we would be a big part of each other's lives for a long time. But at the beginning some things had been hard to adapt to. Having a girlfriend forced me to be more flexible, to try on a new form of vulnerability and to work through intimacy issues that I'd ignored for years. Even something like sleeping in a bed with someone else was strange at first. It also stung sometimes after I'd met Jess's accepting, open and emotionally invested family, because it forced me to look at the contrast between her family and mine. I would watch Jess's dad kiss her on the cheek when he said hello and pretend to be nonchalant when he leaned over to give me a kiss too, but inside I always felt a mixture of thrill and embarrassment. Sometimes he massaged her shoulders when she was sitting on the floor in front of him or grabbed the back of her neck when we were out walking in the forest behind his house. She would grimace and pretend not to like it. At least, I assumed there was no way she didn't actually like it, this spontaneous and loving affection. Jess's mum, meanwhile, called her at least twice a week, especially when she knew Jess had a piece of work due or some other life event, major or minor. Sometimes Jess would huff when she saw her mum's name pop up on her phone screen, and every time I would tell her to pick up. To appreciate having a mother who cared like that.

I felt lucky to have Jess's family in my life, a bonus to being in a relationship that I'd never thought about before. Even though there was the odd time, when her family were all laughing and talking over each other at the dinner table, that I would have to go away and collect myself, fighting the urge to cry.

At the end of our second year together, Jess and I travelled to her hometown—which happened to be the same place I was from—and we had Christmas at Jess's mum's house. It was strange to go back to my hometown for Christmas but not back to my own family. It felt good, though. It was the easiest Christmas I'd had for years, not having to spend it with my parents. Me being with them for Christmas seemed to be important to Mum and Dad, but I couldn't forget how quickly they had taken that away from me as a form of punishment. Now, the few times I'd spent Christmas with them since my coming out felt like an obligation.

A present from me to them, and one that I increasingly felt like I didn't want to give. So having Jess's family to spend Christmas with was ideal. I'd made up a vague excuse about who I was with to tell my parents, but they knew I was in town and judging from some of what my sister had passed on to me, were confused and a little hurt. Honestly, I could have come up with a complete lie to spare their feelings, but I think a part of me wanted them to know I was spending Christmas with someone else. I was in a new phase that was less 'desperate to be accepted again' and more 'I'm going to do what makes me happy and they can live with that as a consequence of their actions'.

And then, a year after that Christmas, I was in the car with my dad telling him about Jess. Somehow, that small-but-big conversation was enough to shake something free between us. It was almost as though me telling Dad about Jess's dad being totally cool gave him permission to try to be the same. Of course, it was nowhere near the same. And maybe that's not what it was. Maybe the change that happened after that conversation was driven by Dad not liking the idea that other parents were doing a better job than he was. Maybe he didn't want Jess's dad to look down on him.

Whatever the reason, the shift was pretty big. After that conversation, Dad would sometimes ask me how Jess was over the phone, and I could finally say 'we', which was a huge relief after all those years of the omitting 'I'.

Sometimes my mum would be on those phone calls. I knew Dad must have filled her in on me dating Jess, but she stayed silent in those moments. This wasn't a surprise. Mum's silence—

not just about my sexuality but about anything in my life that could somehow be related to it—was now the key feature of the distance between us. She was silent about it, and I had been silenced, until now. Now I could finally start filling in the blanks about the person I'd been dating for three years. Sometimes I did this carefully, colouring within the lines I could sense were there. Other times, when I was in a particular mood, I said more outrageous things, or used *that* word—'gay'—pretending it didn't ring in my ears every time I said it out loud in front of them. Strangely, acting as though things were fine seemed to push our relationship that way as well. It became almost normal to include Jess in my conversation topics. I'm not sure whether it felt normal for them too or if they made a conscious effort to ask how Jess was. But pretending that things were okay seemed to make them more okay.

But then, as the months went on, pretending made me feel . . . not okay. Being able to talk about Jess started causing me a huge feeling of bitterness. Why couldn't this have happened earlier? Asking about the life I had with Jess was really not that taxing after all, so why had it been such a big deal over the years?

When Margaret Atwood's *The Handmaid's Tale* was made into a beautiful but harrowing television series in 2017, I watched the show with my finger poised over the fast-forward button. I was reading an episode recap for *The Handmaid's Tale* by Laura Hudson on *Vulture* when this passage made me pause:

> Abusers are very good at that: at shrinking the size of your world, punishing you when you cross an invisible

line that is perpetually moving, until you are standing very still on a tiny patch of grass like a dog unwilling to cross an electric fence. It's amazing, too, how grateful you feel when they finally open the gate to take you for a walk, how even when they own you, even when you are still firmly on their leash, they can somehow make it feel like freedom.

That's what this period felt like. A growing realisation that the new freedom I felt was just an extension of the leash, one that there was no need to put me on in the first place.

Increasingly, I also began feeling like they were being let off too easily, getting to move forward in this way without ever having to address what they did. Ironically, being given the freedom to talk about my life made me think for the first time that it would be easier if I didn't talk to them at all. The roles had reversed, and now I was the one considering cutting them out of my life. The more they knew about Jess, the less I felt they deserved to know. And as the months then years passed, the more they thought they knew about Jess, and the more they talked about her with familiarity, the more ridiculous it seemed. They didn't know her—they'd never even met her.

Then Dad started dropping an occasional 'When we meet Jess . . .' into the conversation. Faced with this, I wasn't sure what to do. Did they actually mean it? When did they mean to meet Jess? Did they have some timeline in their heads? Were they ready now?

I forgot to ask myself two questions. The first being: do I

want them to meet Jess? The answer to the second question—does Jess want to meet them?—took me by surprise. The first time Jess told me she thought it was audacious of them to think they could ever meet her when they'd never acknowledged what they'd done, I was taken aback by her venom.

'Oh, right,' I said, leaning back against the windowsill of our sunny lounge and chewing on my bottom lip.

Jess was firm in her belief that they didn't deserve to be allowed to sweep this under the carpet by meeting her and pretending everything was normal. That made me rethink everything. I'd been so wrapped up in wondering when my parents would be ready to meet Jess, still treating them as though they were the ones with the power, that I'd forgotten we had a say in the matter.

I was forced to consider whether I actually wanted my parents to meet Jess, too. We'd been dating for over four years by then; I'd been out for more than seven. Maybe after all this time I didn't need them to meet her at all? Maybe that was just a ship that had sailed.

One weekend, everything that had been simmering under the surface came bubbling up. My parents were up in Auckland for the weekend, and my sister and I were going to take Mum to high tea at a fancy hotel in town for Mother's Day.

I'd barely slept and I'd had a stomach full of anxiety for hours when the time came for my parents to pick me up. The anxiety had been particularly bad this time, because Jess had told me the day before that she didn't want my parents to come into our house at all, even though she wouldn't be there.

'But they're coming by to pick me up, and Mum will want to come in to see the house,' I'd said, surprised.

'Lil. They are not coming into our house and snooping around our stuff. They can't behave the way they have for all these years and then just waltz into our house like everything's normal when they haven't even met me.'

'Maybe you could come to dinner on Saturday night?' I'd said hopefully, although I knew that my parents weren't ready for meeting Jess to become a reality.

'I told you, I'm not meeting them until your mother sits down and has a conversation with you and takes responsibility for all her shit!'

'Okay, okay,' I'd said, my stomach twisting. I knew that was never going to happen.

I understood where Jess was coming from—she'd been here before. Jess's last serious girlfriend had also had homophobic parents. Jess had assured her girlfriend that when they met her, everything would be fine. She'd been certain that if they met her they'd have a big mind shift. 'Parents love me,' she'd crowed.

Then they had met, and it had not been fine. At all. And Jess had been very, very shaken by the fact that their prejudice had been unbendable. So Jess believed that the same thing would happen if she met my parents. No matter what she did, she would never be enough. Until she'd had prior confirmation that my parents were ready to meet her with acceptance, she wouldn't put herself in a situation like that ever again.

And that was completely fair enough, but it put me in a really difficult position. Now I was not only trying to appease my parents, but also trying to satisfy Jess. I didn't know how to fix it. I was certain that my parents would be perfectly lovely to Jess when they met her, because that's good manners and they were big on manners (and appearances). And I thought there was about a 90 per cent chance that they would like her, and that it would stitch together a big wound between us. That's what well-meaning friends said to me all the time: if they just met Jess, they'd love her, she's so loveable. They'd also always said 'Your mum will come around' but I was sick of hearing that one after nearly a decade. They couldn't understand the extent of her stubbornness and fear. While I agreed that Mum would probably like Jess, I'd always strongly believed that she'd never be completely accepting. On top of that I didn't believe that Mum would ever try to fix things between us, because I had to believe this. I couldn't keep holding on to hope that one day Mum would sit me down or call me up and apologise. Even if she did, I thought, it was too late. There was no coming back from where we'd got ourselves to.

And so prior to this Mother's Day thing I'd tossed and turned for most of the night, furious that I was always expected to be the one to try to fix things. To be the brave one. I cried quiet tears of self-pity and frustration while Jess slept soundly next to me. The next morning, when I finally saw my parents' rental car pull up, Mum was already out of the car and about to climb the steps to our front door by the time I got outside to head her off. She was visibly disappointed that she didn't get to see our house as she loved interiors and nosing into the way other people lived. The way she felt was only a percentage of how it made me feel.

I wanted my mother to step through the front door and exclaim over how we'd made the small space work. I wanted her to run her eye over our wall of books framing the fireplace and think to herself that she was glad I'd found a partner who was as big a reader as I was. I wanted her to compare old pieces of knowledge she had about me and reframe them in the now, seeing how I'd grown into being an adult and exploring how Jess had influenced the way I chose to live. People want to share their homes because we want to share who we are. But, paradoxically, as Mum and Dad were finally seeking to know more about me, they were being restricted from doing so because of their past mistakes. Yes, they had done this to themselves and it was their punishment. But it punished me too. It hurt that, after years of wishing they would want to know who I was, I had to turn them away.

We had a perfectly pleasant high tea together, although my anxiety still simmered, as if my body knew that I hadn't yet got away from this visit unscathed. We still had a dinner planned for tonight. Dad volunteered to drop my sister and me back to our homes—Jen lived in Auckland now too—while Mum headed to the hotel to rest. There was an awkwardness in the air when dinner came up because my sister was bringing her boyfriend and I was bringing . . . not my girlfriend. I'd invited my old creative partner Christian to come with me instead, but I was starting to think that it had been the wrong decision. Taking him while Jess sat at home felt horrible, even though Jess had encouraged me to invite him for the emotional support. I liked to have an extra person around as often as possible when I was spending time with my family, to serve as a buffer.

For the first time, my parents also seemed to understand that this situation was a bit fucked up. We'd dropped my sister off and I was behind the wheel when Dad said, 'I'm sorry that Jess isn't coming to dinner.'

'That's okay,' I said, even though it wasn't.

'I mean, it would probably be okay if she came, but your mother . . .'

'Dad, it's fine.'

I gritted my teeth and focused on driving. Dad always told me I was driving too fast even if I was only a few kilometres over the speed limit.

'Your mother's coming around. She just needs to do it in her own time,' Dad said.

I rolled my eyes, and I was going to let it go but then I thought of all the bullshit excuses I'd silently listened to over the years.

It's hard on your mother. That was a constant refrain in the early years.

You don't understand the love a mother has for her child. That was one directly from Mum, and I could never comprehend it. If no other relationship structure could compare to the love a mother had for her child, how could she turn her back on me?

I feel like I've lost my little girl. Ooh, that one in particular— written in the letter she sent to my Auckland flat a year after I'd been outed to them—had made me so mad. When I was ten years old, I was hit by a car in front of Mum and my sister, and I'd nearly died. Apparently Mum had to be held back from trying to get in the car to murder the bleeding elderly driver, screaming 'You've killed my little girl.' With this in our history, it was really,

really hard to see how she could think of me coming out as losing her little girl when she knew how close she'd come to losing me for real.

Just give her time was simply the latest iteration of Dad trying to justify my mother's behaviour, and it made me mad that he was still so cowed by her. I'd always suspected that without her he would have come around to accepting me earlier.

I pulled over abruptly at the side of the road, and Dad looked startled.

'It's been nearly eight years, Dad. I'm sick of giving her time!' I exclaimed.

'I know . . .' he acknowledged, surprising me.

We fell silent, and I could hear the hot engine ticking.

'You know,' he began slowly, 'if we'd been an Auckland family, this would have been resolved years ago. But things are different in the South Island.'

I frowned. I mean, it's true that Auckland is the 'big city' of New Zealand, but this still sounded like a bullshit excuse.

'Just the other night we were out to dinner with Jack's parents and this other couple,' Dad said, 'and one of them was really horrible about their gay daughter. It was very uncomfortable.'

I was trying to figure out who this might have been and why he was telling me this when Dad continued. 'It made your mother and I feel sad for you. For the discrimination you'll face from people.'

What? I gripped the steering wheel and tried to process what to say through a surge of anger.

How did they think they were any different from this other

couple? They might not bad-mouth me to other people, but pretending that they'd never done anything wrong while treating me badly in private wasn't much better. I couldn't believe that their takeaway from that situation was: 'Poor Lil is going to face discrimination in her life.' Not: 'Oh, man, this is a horrible way for parents to treat their kid for being gay, and maybe we could have done better ourselves.'

How could I begin to explain all this to my dad when he obviously didn't get it? How could I begin to make him understand my life as a gay woman and how his reaction had impacted my life when we'd never had this kind of talk before? There was too much ground to cover.

I stared out the window with an unfocused gaze until I realised that all I could do was lay it out plainly.

'Dad. The only real and lasting discrimination I've ever faced for my sexuality has come from you guys. From my family.'

I could describe my dad's shock in physical terms, perhaps him squeezing the car seat like a stress ball or running his hand slowly down his mouth, stubble bristling under his fingers. Maybe he gasped or sputtered or simply froze. But I don't know what he did, because I couldn't look at him in that moment and couldn't hear anything past the blood beating in my ears. It was too bold a statement, the closest I had ever got to an accusation of his wrongdoing.

But, still, I could sense his shock in the charged atmosphere of the car interior, and I realised that he truly did not know this fact. The idea that he and Mum could be the ones who had hurt me the most just hadn't entered his mind—or, if it had, he had squashed it down so far it was unreachable.

Later, I would contemplate that this wasn't the first time Dad had shown he didn't understand the lasting effects of his actions or how much pain he and Mum had caused me. For now I just thought about how this comment had hurt him, and that I was pleased to have hurt him.

I decided to make the most of my advantage.

'I know Mum needs her time, Dad, but she also needs to be pushed,' I said. 'You can't keep protecting her.'

I gathered steam.

'Like, I actually have no idea what she really thinks about all this now. I've never even had a conversation with her since it all happened. I need to know where she stands. I need her to come to me and open the dialogue, because I'm tired of putting in all the effort and thinking everything went well but then hearing from Jenny later that Mum's thrown a tantrum after I've left because I've apparently slighted her in some way!'

'Yeah, yeah.' Dad had been nodding along. 'Okay, I'll try to talk to her sometime.'

And that's all he said. He'd just been baldly told that he'd discriminated against me, hurt me, but there was no apology. Not that I expected one. Sometimes I still hoped for one, but I'd never expected one.

I could sense that Dad was reeling from covering more ground in a few minutes than in the past seven or so years combined, so I started the car and pulled away from the kerb. I felt a surge of adrenaline—I'd finally got the chance to speak up, if only for a few seconds. But I didn't hold out much hope for Mum ever talking to me about what happened in the past or even about where she wanted our relationship to go. She was so scared, and I could see that fear in the cracks of our interactions, like looking down through a sewer grate and catching a glimpse of something rotten and heaving below.

'I'll see you at dinner, Dot,' Dad said as I dropped him off. He used my family nickname; we were professionals at pretending everything was normal immediately after an upset.

But this time, maintaining still waters didn't work. I was getting dressed for dinner a couple of hours later when my phone rang. My sister's name flashed up on the screen. When I answered I could hear wet breathing coming in short gasps.

'Jenny, what's wrong, are you okay?'

'Hi,' she managed, trying to control her crying. 'It's Dad, he just called me . . .' She trailed off into gulping sobs.

'Oh my god, what's happened?'

'Dad called me and he was crying. We have to cancel dinner.'

Dad crying? That was massive. 'Okay, what's happened?'

'I think he tried to talk to Mum about you and how she needed to try harder to sort things out, and she lost it at him,' Jenny said.

I'm not sure what I felt at this point, whether it was relief that no one had been hit by a car, resignation that this had turned out so predictably or sadness for Dad. I knew what it was like to be on the end of Mum's vitriol.

'What did she say to him?'

'I don't know. You know what she's like, she yelled at him and lost her shit and then she was crying and he was crying.'

This was classic Mum. Any time the idyllic surface of our family was pierced by some kind of conflict, all this other unrelated stuff came swirling up—the result of being a family that never addressed issues at the time.

I hadn't expected Dad to bring this up so soon, if ever, and a part of me was happy at this turn of events. It meant he wanted to make things better.

I reassured Jenny that it was okay, that Dad would be okay, that it didn't matter about dinner. I asked her if she'd be okay, too. She said yes, and we hung up. I put my face in my hands and groaned.

This family was so not okay. But the couple of times I'd suggested counselling, I'd been iced out. Why was I always the one managing the feelings of others? Trying to fix things?

After the dinner disaster, the idea of Mum ever talking to me about anything seemed ludicrous, and it was put away and forgotten. But something else had changed. There was an understanding that it was no longer going to fly for me to come to family dinners without Jess. It was almost a simple equation from there: they couldn't have family dinners without me and they wanted family dinners, therefore to have family dinners in the future, they needed to meet Jess.

Jess seemed to sense this too. A few months later, Mum and Dad were planning to visit Auckland and suggested meeting Jess and me for dinner. Just the four of us. And this time, we said yes.

It was a warm summer's evening when Jess and I got ready for dinner in our little house in Grey Lynn, the first home that was ever just ours. Once you'd climbed the five stone steps to the porch, opened the red front door and stepped inside, you came across a slim kitchen built in what was once a hallway. It was interrupted by a wall that separated our small portion of the villa from the much larger part at the rear, which was occupied by a woman in her late sixties who wore long beads and flowing skirts, and who I chose to believe was responsible for the mermaids carved into the totem pole in our front garden. Though it was tiny, we got the afternoon sun through our windows and we'd crammed the built-in bookshelf in the lounge with books—it fit all of our many books, what a luxury—their spines facing the wall because Jess said the colour of the covers would be too polluting for the small room.

As I put my make-up on in the en-suite bathroom, Jess used the full-length mirror in the bedroom. For someone who was decidedly low-maintenance, Jess was taking an incredibly long time to get dressed. Finally we were both ready, and I moved closer to Jess and reached out to stroke the hair at the back of her neck comfortingly.

'Don't touch my hair!' she shrieked, ducking away.

'Sorry, babes,' I said, laughing in surprise. 'Don't worry, this will be fine. They'll be polite to you.'

Jess muttered something that sounded a little like, 'Yeah, but they'll be judging me silently.'

I had to hold back the urge to chatter nervously in the car, but as we parked then got out and waited to cross the road to the restaurant I said it again: 'It's going to be fine.' I almost put my hand on Jess's back before remembering that she got twitchy when she was stressed in a public environment and touching her would've been the worst thing to do.

'Don't touch me when we're in there, okay,' she warned.

She was more nervous than I was, and I could see why. She didn't know what she was in for, whereas I knew exactly what to steel myself against. I'd prepped her about shaking hands as a greeting, given her key facts and areas of interest for each of my parents . . . there was nothing more I could do.

I led the way into the restaurant and spotted Mum and Dad at a table at the same time they saw us. They both stood a little too quickly with bright smiles, and I watched Mum's eyes flicker over Jess very briefly. My whole family were gawkers, but Mum was a particularly big one, and I knew she would have been dying with anticipation to see what Jess looked like. I don't believe I'd ever described to them what Jess looked like in the years they'd known about her. I mean, why would I? That was the last thing I'd tell them about her.

'Hi, Jess, it's really great to finally meet you,' stressed Dad.

That was his recognition of the situation. It came across as very natural, and I relaxed a little. All the times I'd imagined what the dynamic would be when Jess met my parents, I'd thought that Jess might end up liking my dad. He has a cheeky charm and quick wit that most people find appealing.

My mum greeted Jess with equal exuberance. Friends usually like Mum too when they meet her for the first time, particularly if she's on her own turf. She's a warm and considerate host, always feeding people, always offering things they need or might want. But Jess wouldn't like my mother, I thought. No way. She knew too much.

Everything went well with the handshaking and we settled into our seats with those fluffy statements that groups make. 'This is a nice place.' 'The lighting is lovely.' 'The gnocchi is supposed to be amazing.' The moment directly after these sentiments is always a dangerous time; if you don't segue into real conversation fast enough there is a deeply awkward pause.

Thankfully, we sailed right past that and, would you believe, the conversation flowed for the rest of the night. And it was mostly because of Jess. I've never met anyone so good at talking to any kind of person. Jess's skill was grounded in being able to balance both the telling of interesting anecdotes and facts— full of her own personal insight—with an equally impressive listening ability that enabled her to get very quickly to the stories people most want to tell about themselves.

I could see that Mum and Dad liked her immediately. Dad's face was receptive, and he laughed and said 'Really?' in a way that I knew meant he was impressed. Mum was harder to read because she's so good at presenting an engaged front while the cogs are whirring endlessly in her brain, assessing, comparing.

But then, around the time we were finishing up our main courses, when we'd each had a couple of glasses of wine and I could see a rosy flush coming over Mum's face, I noticed her beginning to lean more into the conversation, to interject and start telling stories about me from when I was young, in a conspiratorial tone. Perhaps she even touched Jess's arm when she started a story. 'Oh, Jess, Lilly was such a stubborn kid' is something she might've said. She always seemed strangely proud of my stubbornness.

'She's just as stubborn now, in all honesty,' maybe Jess said back. And it was a moment like that when I was made certain that Mum had been won over. I could see it in the way they turned to each other and began to gossip about me, just like parents are supposed to do with their child's partner. It all felt so . . . normal. And that's what made it incredible. Surely every parent must hope to bond with their child's partner, to get that feeling of relief as they assess that yes, she picked a good one, I don't have to be worried, I can be happy for her. I don't want to assume that's what they thought, but I could see the tension draining away from my parents. And Jess, wonderful Jess. She'd shown not one ounce of nervousness since the moment she'd walked in the room, an ability she had that I would be reminded of again and again every year into the future we'd share together. And even though I knew I'd need to reassure her—when we got in the car and again when we got home and again the next day, telling her yes, they really did like her, that she'd said everything right, that she'd impressed them—I never doubted her. I truly believed that she would make them like her in the space of an evening.

As I sat at that dinner, watching the person I loved chat and laugh with the people who'd raised me and given me such a good beginning to my life—and yes, who I also loved—I realised that none of this mattered. It didn't actually matter if we all walked away from this evening and then my parents never wanted to meet her again, or they decided they weren't okay with me or her or us. That was of no consequence, because the relationship that did matter to me was mine and Jess's. The person whose opinion of me I cared about was Jess's. I was no longer the nineteen-year-old who used to cry sometimes and think, *I want my mum back.*

Nearly a decade before, I'd made the decision to come out because I knew that if I didn't do it on my own terms it would happen on someone else's. It would have leaked out of me—in my interactions, in the way I responded to things, in my relationships with people. I simply could not keep it inside. And I didn't want to. I couldn't live as a version of myself that was false, because it would have torn me to pieces.

When control of my coming out was taken away from me that night in my parents' home, the way they didn't accept my sexuality and how they chose to express that was devastating. But I wouldn't change what happened. Maybe if I hadn't had a rough time I wouldn't have become so passionate about being a visible part of the queer community and helping others within it. I wouldn't have met some of my best friends. And I really don't think I would've had the same strength and self-assurance that I have today.

Every experience I've had that was to do with my decision to live out loud, despite the times I was discouraged from doing so, has shaped me into the person I am now. And I love that person, which is why I wouldn't change one thing about how it went down, for fear of losing her.

Things will never be completely okay with my parents and me, I know that. There will be new challenges ahead as we try to negotiate the impact of years passed. But I have gained a new empathy for them. I've started thinking about things like how they went into being parents with nothing but their hopes that they would do a good job, and how they made mistakes they never could have predicted. Maybe they think about those mistakes. Maybe they won't understand those mistakes until they too are older. Or maybe they will never understand exactly how and where they went wrong.

Here is where I think I'm supposed to say that I've forgiven them. But life's not that simple and feelings certainly aren't. I think my feelings towards my parents are something I will be actively managing for the rest of my life. I want to forgive them but, for now, holding on to that feeling of not forgiving them is like keeping a little bit of strength tucked away, just in case. Just in case there is a time when things go backwards again.

In the years since I came out, as things have slowly warmed between us, my parents have had to relearn who their daughter is. On that night they found out about my sexuality, time froze. Then the static picture they had of me degraded under the effects of fear and hurt, and all the other feelings that have come about. For many years we communicated little, and only about superficial things. As I've relaxed around them, one painful millimetre at a time, my humour has come back and my ability to be silly around them. There are times when I make a joke and my dad laughs with surprise in his eyes. Maybe he'd forgotten about my sense of humour. I can see he delights in parts of our relationship that have been missing for so long. My parents haven't seen all aspects of my sense of humour yet. They don't know what my friends are like or the shape of my passions, but they are learning, particularly my dad. He is adding to the picture of who I am in his head. That can be a slow and arduous journey. I know, because I traversed a similar one to find out who I was many years ago. And I am so thankful that I found the strength to forge through all those feelings and fears and experiences and mistakes to find the most honest version of myself I could be. A version of myself that I now have the privilege of living every day.

After dinner we gathered on the footpath outside the restaurant. Jess and my parents shared a hug goodbye, and there was a palpable warmth between everyone. Mum returned my hug, patting me on the back affectionately. In that moment the past eight years were forgotten and, caught up in the feeling, I wanted to say 'love you' to them as Jess and I turned to go, but I considered it for too long and then the moment passed, leaving me blinking away unexpected tears. Jess and I crossed the road and got in our car. We both took a deep breath and before I turned the key in the ignition she reached over and laced her fingers through mine.

I looked over at her and smiled.

'We made it,' I said.

And then we went back home to the life we'd built together.

Acknowledgements

I want to acknowledge Rainbow Youth, who not only do amazing work supporting queer, gender-diverse and intersex youth in Aotearoa, but also—through having me along to tell my coming-out story as part of their high-school education programme—lit the spark for me to write this book. Please look them up if you need support, or if you would like to donate.

Thank you to Meli, the first person I shared this story with, and whose enthusiastic cheerleading has made me smile time and time again. Your lesbian sensei loves you.

Thank you to Heather Hogan, a goddamn queer superhero, who gave this fangirl one of the greatest experiences of my life when she agreed to beta-read my draft, and whose thoughtful and unduly kind comments brought me to tears many times. This book wouldn't be half as good without your input, but more importantly you made me believe that this story could make a difference.

To my publisher, Michelle, who made my dream come true

and who believed in the importance of this story from the get-go. To Megan, for the beautiful cover. And to my editor, Claire, who is a scary, scary woman with her attention to detail, and made my book so much better because of it.

And finally, to Bethy, who has always believed that anything I care about is important and has supported me unflinchingly. You are my favourite person, my inspiration, and I hope I've made you proud.